SOWETO, MY LOVE

SOWETO, MY LOVE

Molapatene Collins Ramusi
and Ruth S. Turner

HENRY HOLT AND COMPANY
New York

Copyright © 1989 by Molapatene Collins Ramusi
All rights reserved, including the right to reproduce this
book or portions thereof in any form.
Published by Henry Holt and Company, Inc.,
115 West 18th Street, New York, New York 10011.
Published in Canada by Fitzhenry & Whiteside Limited,
195 Allstate Parkway, Markham, Ontario L3R 4T8.

Library of Congress Cataloging-in-Publication Data
Ramusi, Molapatene Collins.
Soweto, my love / by Molapatene Collins Ramusi. — 1st ed.
   p.   cm.
ISBN 0-8050-0263-4
1. Ramusi, Molapatene Collins. 2. Civil rights workers—South
Africa—Biography. 3. Anti-apartheid movements—South
Africa. 4. Tlokwa (African people)—Biography. I. Title.
DT779.955.R36A3   1988
968.06'092'4—dc19
[B]   88-12262
                                                            CIP

Henry Holt books are available at special discounts
for bulk purchases for sales promotions, premiums,
fund-raising, or educational use. Special editions
or book excerpts can also be created to specification.

    For details, contact:

    Special Sales Director
    Henry Holt and Company, Inc.
    115 West 18th Street
    New York, New York 10011

First Edition

Designed by Katy Riegel
Printed in the United States of America
10 9 8 7 6 5 4 3 2 1

This book is dedicated to the children of Soweto, victims of the Soweto massacre of 1976; to General Whirlwind—my son, Selaelo Ramusi; and to all the heroes who marched and sang their Song of Freedom against unyielding tyranny, laying down their lives to water the tree of freedom in their fatherland, South Africa.

Also, it is dedicated to my beloved wife, Thabo Mary Jane Morare Ma Selaelo Ramusi, who watched, waited, and served others with love—always patient, gentle, and compassionate, as a wife, a mother, a nurse, and a community leader—and who now lies buried beneath the soil.

This book is dedicated further to all the women and children who support their men in the struggle to be free, and who in their own way also march and sing the Song of Freedom.

Contents

Prologue ... 1

PART ONE
The Early Years

1 Clan and Tribe ... 5
2 Family ... 15
3 Khurukhutšhu ... 24
4 Missionary School ... 29
5 Pretoria ... 39
6 Lemana ... 54
7 New Development ... 69
8 City of Gold ... 86

PART TWO
The Turbulent Years

9 Profession of Angels ... 97
10 Defiance ... 110
11 My Jewel ... 117
12 Giant Rising Up ... 128

CONTENTS

13 Mthembu   135
14 America: A Taste of Freedom   146

PART THREE
The Revolutionary Years

15 Back Home   169
16 Warrior in the Court   175
17 Our Guests   182
18 Deception   192
19 Viva Frelimo   212
20 Crucial Turning Point   218
21 General Whirlwind   230
22 *Siya Yinyova*   241
    Epilogue   254

Acknowledgments   259

Soweto, my love

Prologue

You are about to read my life story—the story of a man who was once a herdboy in Molemole, and of my people, the Batlokwa tribe, and of those whose children are the courageous children of Soweto, many of whom died in the Soweto massacre of June 16, 1976, and of many others detained by police without trial, without bail, snatched from our streets, our schools, and homes, unseen again by parents or lawyers, children as young as ten years of age. You will learn of my early childhood memories, of the history of my tribe and its first encounter with the white man, and of the conflict with the missionaries, who attempted to Christianize and westernize my people and myself.

This is the story of some of South Africa's people and the pathos, pain, and cultural differences that separate them with shocking, tragic, and sometimes humorous results. My story moves from herdboy to social worker, anthropologist to freedom fighter and practicing attorney, with time out for eight years of exile in America.

My destiny is intertwined with my country's as I am propelled by an unshakable faith in the eventual emergence of South Africa as a free and democratic multiracial society governed by representatives of all its people.

This is not quite a memoir in the literary tradition. In *Soweto, My Love*, words have sprung to my pen as thoughts have come to mind. I tried to capture the cries of others—their aches, agonies, pains, tears, their hope and courage—as I sought out my own. Memory has undoubtedly played tricks, especially in the recounting of my early years; yet, paradoxically, these are the most clear to me. In the political chapters I have concealed much for security reasons; my son, for example, served in the underground before he was killed. It has been a long, long night seven times cursed but not sealed. I have seen the coming of the dawn, and the rising of the sun. I have heard the singing of the whirlwind.

I have told things that my tribe has not shared with the outside world before—things unwritten and unspoken beyond inner circles. I can only hope that my people will try to understand my reason for revealing old secrets.

As my pen writes the last words of this book, the blood of my people continues to flow as they struggle to be free. South Africa is at war, thousands are jailed without trial, and the tanks, the cannons, the guns, and the troops occupy the black townships. White men, some with Bibles in hand, preach brotherly love and tell us to turn the other cheek, even now, after we have endured centuries of oppression. And these who counsel us have already taken away our land and our wealth, and, earlier, they sold our brothers and sisters into slavery. We have pleaded with the officials of the South African government to stop the insanity of apartheid. We have pleaded in vain. Now the pot has boiled over; the caldron has poured out its contents over all of South Africa; the revolution is here!

The world stands by and watches the unmerciful massacre of our people. I wonder, do they stand by and watch because we are black and the oppressive regime is white? If the reverse were true, would they still stand by and watch? We have pleaded with the world, especially with those who call themselves Christian and freedom-loving nations, to help us; yet the Western nations continue to support the regime despite modest economic sanctions. Is it that our gold and diamonds, our country's wealth, are more valued than our lives? Than our unarmed schoolchildren mowed down in Soweto?

Help us before it is too late, or watch South Africa turn red with the blood of its people—as those who fight to keep racism, privilege, and apartheid as a way of life are opposed by those who seek to destroy apartheid forever.

PART ONE

The Early Years

1

Clan and Tribe

The only certain facts about my birth are that I was born in the village of Ranhlokana in winter, in the land of the Batlokwa people of Molemole, during the reign of Chief Ntwamala Puledi Masenyane Machaka, of the northern Transvaal, South Africa, the point where the Tropic of Capricorn cuts across at 30 degrees longitude, two miles west of the international highway that winds like a ribbon from Cape Town to Cairo, 240 miles north of Johannesburg, and 100 south of Zimbabwe, where, unlike our people, black men breathe free of colonial rule.

Ranhlokana was one of the many villages that came under the jurisdiction of Chief Machaka, who lived more than one hundred years and ruled wisely. My father, Mothibi, was the headman of Ranhlokana, a tiny community of a little over thirty inhabitants at the time of my birth. To the south of Ranhlokana were many other villages, including the royal village of Mphakane-a-bo-Sekgala, the royal kraal of the Batlokwa people of Molemole, where the reigning king lived.

No record of births, marriages, or deaths was kept in our tribe. Birthdays are not particularly remembered among us, but when they are recalled it is in terms of disasters, like years of famine, locusts, droughts, wars, and of the traditional *Bodika*, where boys become men, and *Bjale*, where girls become women.

In my clan, shortly before a boy reached puberty, he was taken to the ancestral school, *Komana*, to be initiated into the deepest secrets of the clan. Only certain clans observed this custom. Mine, the Babirwa clan, was one of them. The objectives of this school were, among others, to introduce me to the spirits of my ancestors—the Living Dead, who are believed to continue living beneath the soil.

When I was about twelve years of age, I was taken by Petša Ramusi, my father's brother, to be initiated and enrolled in the school. For thirty days I went through the ritual and the music of the ancestors: drums of Kubjana-Ramokgadifela, the owner of the school; the whistling *ditlaatšane* blowing their muted great-bone trumpets; fires and sacred formulas everywhere night and day—while the men made incisions in the skin of the students' cheeks to mark them permanently as members of our various clans and worthy to walk in the footsteps of our ancestors.

These thirty days were not only an initiation ritual but also an intensive instruction in the mysteries of our clan. Since we had no written language, all learning was transmitted by word of mouth. Beliefs and philosophies were transmitted through singing, chanting, and the talking drums. I was taught respect, honor, praise, veneration, and worship of my ancestors. I have not forgotten the commandments of my ancestors. I must never forget.

In the first stage of communication with my ancestors, I learned the royal hierarchy of ancestral spirits, their praises, and how to speak with them. I could interact with my family and join in the world of the spirits of my clan. After I had gone through the Komana school, at about fourteen years of age, my uncle took me to the Bodika school at Mokutu, where I was prepared for marriage and the role of adult life and manhood.

In my tribe a boy could not become a man until he had gone through the Bodika, or circumcision school. Any boy who did not go through this school remained forever a nonman, a *leshoboro* (uncircumcised) or perpetual child, according to tribal tradition and culture. He would be banned from the *Kgoro* meetings, where men discussed important tribal affairs, and rudely expelled from important tribal events and social gatherings.

Bodika was a hard school, tougher than Sparta. The first three nights we practiced Bodika rituals and songs *(re bata letswai)*, while the elders introduced us to the rites of passage. The Bodikana initiates lived naked through the cold winter months, our bodies and faces painted with white lime, in which we had to bathe at three o'clock every bitter morning. This is a disguise, a sort of uniform, which prevents individual recognition. Our circumcised penises were elevated in a kind of cradle, or ring, made of grass, to isolate and protect them from infection.

The surgeons who performed the operations were extremely careful and able. At my own circumcision I was bewildered, and mesmerized by it all. Overcome by bleeding, I felt dizzy and passed out; I thought for sure I was going to die. My first day was spent sitting naked under thorn trees. Thereafter, I was shepherded into Moloto to join the rest of the initiates. A reign of terror went on for three months: fingers were regularly crushed between hard sticks *(dipudi)*; backs were lashed with long switches and buttocks cut by them. Another test was in the eating of deliberately hardened food, and in the denial of water. Survival was a matter of skill. We had to sleep naked in roofless enclosures made of stalks, reeds, poles, and grass in constructions called *dikgote* (sleeping sheds). All that prevented us from freezing to death was a fire in the middle of the enclosure.

Every morning we were aroused to sing and chant the Bodika hymn *"Tlou Wetzee,"* which was followed by instruction in wisdom and life by our elders. We chanted day and night while we underwent the tests of manhood. By midnight we fell exhausted on the cold ground to sleep a few hours before being aroused at dawn each day to undergo more rituals and to learn the chants, taboos, and values that related to actions of past rulers and heroes.

We emerged as strong as fattened bullocks, thanks to the hardened sorghum porridge, the locusts, grasshoppers, and small birds which we killed secretly while hunting and hid in our mouths and buttocks until we could roast them in the fire at night while the ritual singing and dancing were going on.

When girls matured and began to menstruate, they were isolated and kept away from the males. I was told that my sister was a *Kgopa,* meaning she had matured into womanhood and was bleeding vaginally for the first time in her life. I was not permitted to see her or to speak to her during that period. She was kept in a separate hut by the old women of my village. This isolation lasted for a week. I heard strange noises and drumming at night in the hut in which she was being initiated.

Bjale was a school for girls. A girl could not become a woman without going through it. All my sisters went to Bjale. I do not know what was done to them. The women never tell, and I dared not ask. At the end of three months initiation, they returned to their homes as women ready for marriage and full participation in tribal affairs.

The village was built on a rocky hill covered by creeping trees. It consisted of cattle kraals and six compounds, made up of huts in which the extended families dwelled. The huts were of different sizes, but all were round, built of earthen bricks, and roofed with grass, sorghum, or millet stalks. At the back of each compound were small huts in which peanuts, beans, sorghum, and millet were stored whenever the harvest was good.

In the center of the village was the compound of my father, where he lived with my mother, Motswetla; his second wife, Ngwakwana, and their children. When I was small it was not easy for me to know which of my father's two wives was my real mother, because his second wife loved and cared for me as if I were her own child.

Of the six huts, two served as living room and kitchen and four as bedrooms. In front of each compound stood a big kraal for cattle, goats, sheep, and donkeys. To the south and to the north lay four other compounds belonging to fellow villagers, including Khaola Mohlopi, my father's righthand man, the tall ever-trotting elephant buck of Mabjanene, who ran as fast

CLAN AND TRIBE

as a Molemole deer; and Mathumo, the traditional doctor, an expert in midwifery, a gentle soul who knew how to save the lives of those afflicted by the maladies that baffled the medical science of the time. The "lightning men," traditional doctors who killed by lightning, feared and respected him, and dared not harm him.

It was an established custom for boys and men to sit at the fireside in the cattle kraals when evening came and listen as the elders told heroic tales of bravery and manhood. One evening at the fireplace during the Kgoro, after my father's death, when the moon was shining and the stars were glittering in the firmament, Khaola told me that I was born during the *Marema* Bodika session. He was kneeling at the fire, fanning up the smoke from the burning green marijuana leaves through his long reed pipe. Suddenly, he struggled to his feet, turned, and spoke to me in the poetic manner of my people, who seem to sing when they speak.

"Do you know who you are and when you were born?" he asked.

I hunkered down on my haunches, my back pressed against the rough bark of a thorn tree. The fire in the clearing flared and fell, and the red embers hissed and moaned like women sorrowing.

In the flare of the flames, the face of the men loomed, their eyes glowing embers, shadows deepening the hollows of their temples and cheeks. Khaola rose. His arms waved toward the glowing coals of the fire, and his chest heaved.

> *You are Mafa-a-Molapatene,*
> *Kotoleleele-a-bo-Matšhipi,*
> *The long leg that marches to Senaka,*
> *To the territory of the iron-smelting tribes.*
> *Do not play a fool at Mabjanene,*
> *The son of Maubene feeds on bravery*
> *The blue-eyed Mmirwa—Motua.*

He praised my name; then Khaola sat down to rest his old bones, and Mathumo, the doctor, added more wood to the fire. The smoke, glowing with flying red sparks, squeezed tears from our eyes. Mathumo looked at me and said, "Mothibi-a-Ramathathe was a big black man, industrious and good, a man we still affectionately remember as if it were yesterday when he lived; with his big heart, he was generous and hospitable to strangers, friend or foe. That is the man from whose loins you sprang—Mothibi-a-Ramathathe, your father."

I looked at Mathumo with awe as he unfolded the past of my father, and realized that I was in the midst of the sages of my tribe. My admiration for both old men began to grow as they revealed knowledge of the glorious history of my parents, their parents, and ancestors long departed.

Khaola, the ever-trotting elephant buck, smoked his green leaves; blowing and splashing water, he tapped me on my shoulder, then began to speak the praises of my father. Khaola trotted up and down while he chanted the praises, waving and shaking his fist in the air as if addressing a mighty crowd, although we were only a few at the cattle kraal.

From the huts nearby, women and girls, who heard Khaola praise Mothibi the Good, started to chant and ululate until the whole village was vibrating with the praises for my father and his ancestors.

It moved me to think of my father as if he had never gone, and as I recalled his face I asked Mathumo, "But, when was my father born? Who was his father?"

Mathumo looked at me with a compassionate gaze and said, "Your father was of the age-group of *Maphaswa-Manaila, Kgomo tša mmala wa botse*—Maphaswa-Manaila, the black and white gracefully moving cattle," meaning that my father was of the age-group of Maphaswa.

Khaola now began the praises of Maphaswa, the age-group of my father. "Your father, Mothibi, went to the Bodika before Mathumo and after me. He became a man of men."

Then, after a puff of green leaves, Mathumo rose and looked up at the full moon, blowing smoke from his mouth and nostrils and splashing water; looking straight at the moon with his eyes fixed, as though in a trance, he chanted: "Moraba-a-Mantedi, Kwetlepa, Ngwana-a-bo-Mapulene!" He was chanting the praise name of my grandfather, Moraba. The two old men unraveled heroic tales. As the aroma of the roasting antelope wafted through the cattle kraal, more men and boys joined us at the evening fire, where the feasting soon began.

Khaola added: "Moraba Ramusi was a very wealthy man before the arrival in this territory of the white men from unknown lands." He told us that, like many Africans, Moraba owned thousands of cattle, sheep, goats, and donkeys. The land on which the Batlokwa tribe lived stretched from Polokwane to Vendaland, some seventy miles from south to north, and sixty from east to west.

Khaola scratched in the earth. When he looked up slowly, his eyes were piercing. "One day up from the south a horde of white men came advancing on the tribal land like locusts, devouring the food, and driving out the cattle." Khaola shook a fist in the air. His voice trembled with anger. "Moraba-a-Mantedi Ramusi and the other men of the tribe took arms against the invading whites and fought like men. The battles were bloody." He explained that the tribesmen used *assagais* and spears and were overpowered by the white men's cannons and guns. They tried to protect the women and children by retreating to Molemole. Moraba and a handful of warriors held the invaders for many weeks, until the women and children were safe at Molemole. In the end, Moraba and the last bastion of the defending warriors moved, herding their long-horned cattle, goats, sheep, and donkeys numbering in the thousands to Molemole. They were forced onto a patch of land too small for so many cattle, an arid area of four square miles, which was not sufficient to accommodate even the sheep and goats. The stock began to die, like the people, who were crowded inside huts without grass for their roofs.

Moraba watched the cattle die for want of water and grass, Khaola told us. He watched the people wither as the babies died of hunger. Moraba became poor like the green leaves that withered and died as the land dried up and became a desert. Moraba grieved for his people. His heart stopped beating, and they buried him at Sethithone, Khaola said.

On this night I learned what my great-grandfather, Moshweu-a-ka-rema-ka-Ripahanya—the mighty warrior who chopped his enemies to pieces at war—had done during the war against the Zulus under Mzilikazi.

Now Mathumo began the praises of my mother's ancestors, Matsapola.

> Motswetla, daughter of Moraka Matsapola-a-Mathokgadi-palelo, and his wife, Mokgadi-a-Matsie, the hyena of Mankala-a-Bokone, which sleeps with—

He stopped when the women approached with sorghum porridge in wooden dishes and calabashes. The graceful, swaying figures with hand-carved wooden vessels on their heads knelt in the moonlight before the men to show their respect, offered warm water for the men to wash their hands, and served the porridge. One of these figures of the night, bringing food to the fireplace, was my mother, Motswetla-a-Rasekgothoma, daughter of Moraka Matsapola.

Mother had a disarming and infectious smile. She was a big, tall, and graceful mother of seven children, loving and caring to the end of her days. When my people praised her name, they always said: "The hyena of Mankala-a-Bokone; hyena that sleeps with a carcass in a kraal and still desires some more meat," meaning she is a brave person. Mother was born in exile, in Vendaland, where her people fled from the invading Boers, who attacked them for their land.

"The white nosy strangers invaded our land. Our fathers defended the land." Thousands died. The strangers killed men, women, and children for their land and cattle. Our people retreated north to the land of the Venda and continued to fight. "We lost everything," she told me, "our land, our cattle, our sheep, our goats; our homes, our rivers, our mountains. The white settlers had taken our land for themselves." Mother said, "They packed us onto a small piece of land that they called Matoks Native Reserve because they could not pronounce the word *Botlokwa*."

Judging from the year my mother attended the Maphaswa

Bjale school for girls at Molemole, 1905, she was born around 1885.

My father died when I was too young to know him well. I cannot recall the month or year when Mother and I accompanied him to Elim Hospital, but there is one thing I shall always remember: his big arms and eyes, a handsome man lying on his back and breathing hard, the black and beautiful body of my father when he was dying, lying in his cart pulled by two black donkeys trotting along the dusty road to the land of Ngungunyane, taking him to Elim Hospital for treatment, and later to Bochum Hospital, where he died. Somewhere on the grounds of Bochum Hospital is the grave of the man from whom I sprang—a grave we are unable to find. Only precious memories remain to us of my father, Mothibi-a-Ramathathe.

My tribe was like family to me, especially Khaola. Khaola Mohlopi, a tall and strong man who towered like a colossus at Ranhlokana village from the days of my birth until I was in my last days of high school at Lemana Training College. He had a marvelous head, with kinky white hair which was never allowed to grow long, and a proud bone structure—his face looked as though it were carved of rock, with a stubborn chin and downcast red eyes. He was powerfully built, with long arms and hands. He called himself by many names for many reasons: To his father and mother he had always been Ngwako Mohlopi, but he called himself the mighty man of Maphorokwe. Maphorokwe was the village of his birth, which lay about a mile to the east of Ranhlokana village. He also called himself the mighty elephant of Mabjanene. Mabjanene was where the remains of his father and mother lay—his ancestral home, where his king used to dwell for years and years. He would say, "I am Kimbel, Dabula-Masait, Scombish," meaning that he was Kimberley, after returning from the Kimberley diamond mine, where he had worked. It took him six months to cover the 600 miles on foot one way. While in the diamond mine at Kimberley city, he worked underground, hence his names Kimbel and Dabula-Masait, which were his way of saying he blasted the earth in its bowels at Kimberley city. I have never understood why he called himself Scombish.

The greatest love of his life was the smoking of what he called "the green leaves of Mabjanene." He and his fellow smokers dug a shallow hole and filled it with marijuana leaves, placing a long reed in that hole to puff the smoke as the leaves began to burn. Khaola would fill his mouth with cold water and draw the marijuana smoke with the reed while the water gurgled in his huge mouth.

His second love was fighting, and the man of Maphorokwe could fight like a lion. He once challenged the mission station of Khurukhutšhu to a fight—the whole Christian community. It is not known what would have happened to him if his brother, Setiriti, had not arrived in time, before the elephant of Mabjanene commenced his battle against the children of Israel and Abraham, as he called the Khurukhutšhu Christians. When the Christians saw the two terrifying brothers standing before them, they prayed to their Christ and scattered like fleeing rats. This was during the difficult times of the civil war between Mfumo and Mohlekhu—the war in which Khaola successfully defended the kingdom of his young king, Kgarahara Edward Machaka, who became the monarch of Molemole soon after my birth.

Khaola was a man who could hate as strongly as he could love. Of all the things Khaola hated most, at the top of the list was the Christian church, its school, and Western culture. He maintained that the Western way of life was a challenge to the culture of his fathers, that white schools and churches were the agents of destabilization and corruption. He swore that he would go down to his grave fighting against these Western menaces. He did not have one good word for the Christian people of Khurukhutšhu. He referred to them constantly as *Mafamolebe*, meaning they were a good-for-nothing bunch of crooks who were corrupted from top to bottom. He also called the Christians and the educated people of his community *Mafaufau*, meaning they were the unreliable, the untrustworthy, and the useless members of Molemole—no better than human excrement.

2
Family

Mother had given birth to ten children prior to the birth of my eldest sister, Tipe: none had survived before her. Mother feared that Tipe would be lost soon after birth like the others, but she survived, as did the rest of us who followed. After Tipe, meaning "dipping tank," came Moraba, Mokgadi, Nkwatlapi, myself, Moratwa, and Matsapola.

I asked my mother why my sister was named Tipe, and Mother explained. "That name has nothing to do with the first dipping tank that was sunk at about the same year of her birth: we named her Dipping Tank because I lost some ten children soon after their birth before her. It was feared that she was also born to go down the dipping tank after her birth but she survived, and thereafter all of you children survived."

Tipe, a tall, pretty woman of few words, was old enough to be my mother when I was born. She was always soft-spoken—the only time I heard her speak aloud was when she would sing and dance at the women's traditional tribal dances. What a singer and what a dancer! She was also a tribal beautician and potter.

When she became a Kgopa Tipe took an additional name, Puledi. She was named after King Ntwamala Puledi Masenyane Machaka, who was the reigning monarch at Molemole. After Kgopa our people praised her name:

Puledi Masenyane.
King, stretch your arms.

SOWETO, MY LOVE

> *King, stretch your arms so that you may*
> *Enfold your nation up to the great Mohwadi River.*

Tipe helped my mother bring us up and keep us all alive after my father's death. She was able to give us food from her own home, and she kept us warmly clothed whenever she could. Like my mother, Tipe lost ten children soon after their births. The only one to survive was Mahlare, whose name means "leaves." And, like his dear mother, Mahlare was expected to perish like leaves of trees, which wither and die. But he survived. He grew into a big man and is still teaching in the Kgarahara High School to this day.

When my sister got married, she was given a third name, Mamoloko Machaka. This name was given to her because she married a relative, a cousin, after having been jilted by her father's sister's son—cousin Motlatšo Isaiah Maphala, who married a girl from Johannesburg. He left my sister no other choice than to marry a prince, Matome-a-Ramantšana Machaka. When my people praise his name they say:

> *Matome-a-Ramantšana Rathobja,*
> *Matome-a-Machaka Maimela*

He was a gentleman, a man of great dignity and presence. He walked gently wherever he went and exhibited great wisdom in his judgments in the royal courts.

In all, there were seven of us children. I had three brothers and three sisters. I was the fifth child.

My father had been a wealthy and well-respected man by tribal standards. He owned many cattle, sheep, goats, and donkeys. When he died he left us very well off, even though the white people had left the tribe only a small grazing area—not enough for all our animals.

The family sent for my father's younger brother, Petša Ramusi. Uncle Petša left the Crown Mines, where he worked as a cook, to come back to the tribal land to manage my father's extensive wealth and to inherit his wives. It is a custom amongst my people that whenever a man dies leaving wives, the surviving brother is expected and obliged to inherit them as his own, and to father children for them if they happen to be of childbearing age. Thus, Uncle Petša inherited my mother and my father's second wife to continue bearing children for my father. In addition to inheriting my father's wives, Uncle Petša inherited my father's wealth.

Uncle Petša was non-Christian, and he liked to live the life of a fun-loving big spender. He would walk into the home of a woman who brewed sorghum beer for sale and stop the sale by instructing her to serve all the beer to the patrons with a promise of a beast—sheep, or goat, or even a donkey—as payment. He might barter my father's livestock, which was then "his" property, for old trousers, jackets, or household items. I was a herdboy of this flock. Village people would come to demand that I give them one piece of livestock or another for the trivial things for which my Uncle Petša had bartered. My mother, my brothers, sisters, and I were helpless to object because not only were we young and frustrated but we were also Uncle Petša's wards. My mother bore him two children, Manthibi Moratwa, a girl, and Matsapola, a boy, while my father's second wife, Ngwakwana, bore him two boys, Sam Mamabolo and Mabala Cleopas; later came Sedupane, a girl, and Mantebele, a boy and the youngest member of the family. All six were considered to be my father's children and not half brothers and sisters.

Things that stand clearly in my mind are my father's sheep, goats, and donkeys and the big kraal that housed them, together with the long-horned cattle grazing leisurely along the meadows of Piti beside Maseloma Mountain.

My brother Nkwatlapi and I were the shepherds of the flock. I remember vividly the tender touches of the kids nestling against me and tickling the palms of my hands while I fed them grass and leaves. The kids were the first gentle little friends I ever had in the village of Ranhlokana, my father's village. They seemed to understand me as I talked to them. They knew my voice as I gently stroked their backs. They seemed to understand my need for friendship in this lonesome and quiet village where few people lived. They would bleat as if they were saying: "Here is our friend coming to feed us and give us water to quench our thirst."

As herdboys, we brought firewood from the veld when we returned with the stock in the evenings. We would milk the cattle while other boys made the fire at the Kgoro—fireplace for the male members of the community. A different boy took his turn making the fire every morning and evening, and woe unto the boy who would come back from the veld without firewood: he would be prevented from sitting at the Kgoro, disgraced and expelled. Made to sit with the females and little children in the hut.

Khaola was usually the first to greet us as we returned from the veld. Mostly he scolded and chided us about this or that: "Why did you boys allow the goats and sheep to wander into my fields today? I warned you many times not to let your animals eat my crops. I know what you need on your backs. Lashes! Hard and cutting to teach you to be responsible members of your community. You must remember that a herdboy is never to take his eyes from his flock."

Khaola monopolized the discussions with his thunderous voice. He never wanted to repeat anything he said, except when he had used a vulgar word or phrase against the Christians of Khurukhutšhu. I laughed with excitement when Khaola told us what he did during the war against the Christians of Molemole during the clash between Mfumo and Mohlekhu.

Khaola's voice boomed. "My brother, Setiriti Mohlopi, stood by my side as the two of us faced the men and women of the Christian faith numbering about fifty at Mangata Mission Station." He paused to add emphasis to his words and to observe our reaction. I was thrilled and delighted to hear the mighty man of Maphorokwe, tell us how the Christians were turned into cowards by their newly acquired religion.

"Have you ever visited your Aunt Malekanyane Maphala's home?" Khaola asked, looking me right in my face and shaking his white hair and heavy head in a knowing disbelief.

FAMILY

"Never," I quickly assured him.

"Have you ever seen your mother entering your Aunt Malekanyane's house?" he asked, touching my shoulder. I was slow to answer him, and he shook me hard to emphasize that he was addressing me.

"Never!" I replied.

Khaola continued: "Have you ever seen any of your brothers or sisters going into your Aunt Malekanyane's home?"

"No, sir!" I said, walking away from his red and penetrating eyes. I was never quite sure whether the quiver of excitement running through my insides was fear or love and admiration for Khaola—that loud, bossy, fearless warrior, the powerful, fast-trotting elephant buck. I knew only that I wanted to grow up to be powerful like Khaola.

I shivered with excitement whenever I joined the men and boys who were the great hunters of Ranhlokana. The other herdboys and I were daily testing our hunting skills while herding the flocks in the veld. Uncle Petša had a variety of hunting dogs with which I learned to hunt. Robby was one that could tackle and overpower the most vicious of the game; Sibby, another, was the fastest, and so quick and nimble that he could jump and turn in midair then pounce on his prey.

The other herdboys and I often hunted rabbits, dithakadu—anteaters, springboks, meerkats, kangaroos, wild boars, and soars. The kangaroos, wild pigs, and dithakadu, we hunted by night. The other animals tried to escape by hiding in their holes as they saw and heard the barking dogs and the herdboys running after them. We would then dig down deep until we captured them. I especially liked hunting the dinoko—a type of porcupine that defends itself with raised quills as it fights.

Among the beautiful game birds I watched and hunted were the thekane, mokowe, and dithaha. The owl and bat were nocturnal animals we hunted during the day as they were sleeping. Some people in my tribe used to eat owls, but my young friends and I killed them for pleasure. When we trapped doves and small mammals, we roasted them over the fire while hunting. The bigger game we carried home with us at the end of the day.

While I was still young and learning from older herdboys and men, all manner of wild game was plentiful in the valleys, dens, and mountains of Ranhlokana. Big game—including lions, tigers, zebras, hippopotamuses, leopards, cheetahs, elephants, and rhinoceroses—were common. Where we recognized the spoor of a dangerous animal, we would shout an alarm, *"Sebata-Kgomo,"* to alert the community to be on the lookout for a marauding animal.

One time some shepherds had spotted the spoor of a lion and raised the alarm. We took out our spears and joined the hunt, knowing that our quarry was most probably a deposed and desperate older male lion, too slow to hunt game. Such solitary animals become dangerous if they move close to villages in search of food.

I joined the group led by Khaola to follow the spoor on nearby Ranhlokana Mountain. We moved from bushes to tall grass, checking the spoor, until the trail led to the edge of the Mononono River.

I suddenly felt uncomfortable as we moved under a large overhanging rock. I looked up directly into the eyes of the lion. My warning scream alerted Khaola just as the lion leapt toward him. Within seconds the lion was on Khaola's back, forcing him to his knees. The fallen Khaola was at the mercy of the big cat. I threw my spear, which momentarily distracted the lion. Khaola jerked the lion by his mane, grabbed the spear, and rammed it into the lion's side. The mighty man of Maphorokwe held the big cat with both hands, choking and shaking it like a rag, while I offered loud prayer to our ancestors for the safety of Khaola.

The lion and Khaola were bleeding freely. I was afraid the lion was going to kill Khaola, but as the hunters and I made distracting noises, the lion pulled itself away from Khaola and disappeared into the bush, leaving a trail of blood behind. We attended the bleeding Khaola. As we did so, Khaola told us to go after the lion; it would be more dangerous than ever.

Khaola was accompanied home. The hunt continued. It went on for three days. At first the injured lion was easy to follow because it was bleeding, but after two days the blood was less noticeable and the trail became more difficult to follow.

On the third day, Tau Motau, a brave young Mmirwa warrior, wandered off from the group on his own. When we spotted him, Motau and the lion were rolling on the ground. Motau was stabbing the lion desperately, and the lion was mauling him mercilessly, each one fighting for survival, both covered in blood. I watched in horror as the lion used its remaining strength to embed its claws in Motau's trachea before collapsing dead on top of the dying warrior.

One day I was herding my father's stock on Mamokhwibidu Mountain when I saw a lion and a lioness making love on a flat rock. The male lion was patting the female's back with his front left paw; I thought they were playing. He changed and patted the female with his right paw. It was only after some time that I realized the lion was caressing, enticing, and stimulating the lioness, getting her sexually aroused. I saw the lioness elevate her behind and open her hind legs to receive the penis, while the male slowly mounted the lioness. Then suddenly it was all over, and I saw the male bouncing on his back, kicking and jerking his legs up in ecstasy, and roaring so as to inform the world that he had great joy. The female rolled on her back, following suit. That was the first time I ever witnessed lions making love, and I realized when I later witnessed lovemaking amongst other animals that the lion was the most romantic lover of them all.

I enjoyed watching animals make love, tend their young, and forage for food. Sometimes, though, it was frightening. Perhaps the most frightening moment was my encounter with a python. Of all the reptiles, the biggest and the most vicious is the python, killing its prey (animals and men) by strangulation. I saw a python grab one of the goats I was herding and crush its bones slowly but surely until the goat was dead. It smeared the goat with saliva until it was well lubricated; then the snake began swallowing the goat, head and horns first. I bided my time, knowing not to intervene until after the python had swallowed the head and horns, rendering itself defenseless. Then I took my sharpened spear and killed it. Opening the snake's belly, I removed the dead goat, skinned it, and carried it home. It was eaten at the Kgoro that night.

Khaola was there to welcome me, praising and scolding as always. "Why did you allow the goat to stray where the python could get it? You did well not to let the python have the victory and to know when to intervene without getting killed."

I thought I saw a slight smile on Khaola's face when he looked at me that night, but it was quickly gone as he roared, "You have to know your enemies and strike them at the right moment or they will destroy you. You have to be watchful; you have to beware." But to Khaola, our biggest, most vicious enemy was neither the lion nor the python, but the Christians. Warning us of them, Khaola said, "When the white men came here, they first sent their 'men of the book' with a Bible in their hands. I warned Chief Machaka, the headmen, and the tribe about these missionaries. They gave us their Bible book and now they have our land. There stands their damned church building. Where is our land now? Where? Gone!" Khaola cursed and spat.

Once Khaola woke up in the dead of night and started to sing a strange song from the top of Ranhlokana Mountain, where he lived. He sang his strange refrain for many hours until dawn:

> *Oh people of the book!*
> *Come to common terms*
> *As between us and you;*
> *That we worship*
> *None but God!*

The more he sang, the louder he sang. He sang this song to all the people of Molemole, pouring out like the powerful mokowe bird, using the only weapon he could to defend the culture of our fathers, the song of ridicule and chastisement.

Day and night his voice echoed from distant places and from

the mountaintop. The people of Molemole began to sing Khaola's song. In the end, however, it was not the Christians who came to terms with us but my mother, my sisters, and I who were forced to come to terms with them in order to survive. My three brothers—Moraba, Nkwatlapi, and Matsapola—never came to terms with the Christians. They continued with the religion of their forefathers, the worship of their ancestors. I, and later my mother and two sisters, were baptized in the church of the Son of Man. At baptism, the Christians discarded our African names and assigned new names to us as if we were things unnamed at birth.

3

Khurukhutšhu

Half a mile from Ranhlokana village stood the Lutheran Mission Station of Mangata, renamed Khurukhutšhu after Krutzenburg, the town in Germany from which the Lutheran missionaries came.

Aunt Malekanyane towered above the other women of both my village and the Mangata Mission Station, where she stayed. She frequently visited us and helped my mother to bring us up after our father's death. We all loved her, so I could never understand why we didn't visit her at her home.

Aunt Malekanyane was brought up as a non-Christian by her father, my grandfather, Moraba Ramusi. Her husband, Nicodemus Maphala, was converted to Christianity after marrying her, and she too became a Christian. My father; his younger brother, Petša Ramusi; as well as my grandparents, remained non-Christians.

There seemed to exist a rift between the people of Ranhlokana and the Christians of Khurukhutšhu, brought about by the fact that the Christians of Khurukhutšhu refused to visit anyone at Ranhlokana village because they considered us "heathens." They appeared to despise us and viewed us as inferior, unclean, "untouchables" not worthy of their visits, respect, or consideration. It was always "heathen" this and "heathen" that.

There were constant clashes between the Christians of Khurukhutšhu and the non-Christians of Ranhlokana. The Lutherans threatened that all who did not belong to their church would be engulfed in a lake of fire and burn perpetually in hell. Their threats and other charges offended and angered the non-Christians. Problems arose between the people where none had existed before. Families became splintered by an anger that spilled over into the tribe and tore at tribal institutions. Turmoil resulted. Khaola vowed never to forgive the Christians of Khurukhutšhu for stealing our land and destroying our people.

The church stood on a huge slab of rock. Mangata village itself was built on a small mountain of many rocks. In the rocks were hollow caves—deep caves, which looked black inside. Lizards and other reptiles lived on these rocks, where creeping trees grew and mountain birds chirped and twittered. We had to be careful not to be seen by Christians when we played, because the buttocks and feet of heathen children were not supposed to touch the Christians' rocks of Khurukhutšhu. But we jumped and trotted from rock to rock to our hearts' delight and hid in caves when Christian parents approached.

One day the Khurukhutšhu Lutheran Church was struck and destroyed by lightning. A few non-Christian men of Mangata laughed and took credit for having burned it with fire and fury. Others alleged that it was destroyed by the wrath of our ancestors and God.

Even as a small boy, I felt the intense humiliation that hit me whenever I entered a Christian home. If I asked for water to drink, I could not be served from a glass or cup. They would look for a broken piece of calabash or broken earthen pot from which the heathens were served. If I touched their glass or cup accidentally, it would have to be washed immediately to remove the trace of a heathen's lip and hand.

The Christians of Khurukhutšhu used to complain that the "heathens" of Ranhlokana had a nasty odor. In spite of their dislike of our alleged odor, the Christian girls of Khurukhutšhu gazed with interest at the "heathen" boys of Ranhlokana, while the "heathen" boys looked down upon the Christian girls because they did not go through traditional Kgopa and Bjale schools and thus fell outside the category of the fully accepted belles of Molemole. Even if they were pretty, we pretended not to see. At times they crawled from the mission station to play moonlight games at Ranhlokana. Then we would touch the breasts of these "book girls" of Khurukhutšhu, behind dark trees. But after that, the "book girls" of Khurukhutšhu became our friends. They would even make a little love with the "heathen" boys behind closed doors.

We soon began to visit the Christian homes and even drink tea and coffee in enamel cups. The girls would quickly wash the cups with boiling water so that their mothers would not detect the "heathen" smell on the Christian cups.

Not only did the mission station have attractive uninitiated girls but it had a variety of foods I had never seen at Ranhlokana: jam, cakes, bread, buns, sugar, tea, and candy. They also had teapots, cups, saucers, spoons, forks, and knives. The bread was nice to eat, particularly with a little jam on it. Fat cakes were nicer when fried with lots and lots of sugar. Tea and coffee were served only to Christians. I must have been fifteen years of age when I tasted tea and coffee for the first time. In those days, tea and coffee and bread were considered absolute luxuries by the people of Khurukhutšhu, and bread spread with jam was considered the greatest of Christian delicacies.

I first tasted bread on a Christmas morning. Aunt Malekanyane had invited me for Christmas. I rose and washed thoroughly before sunrise and went to visit her. As I crossed the Piti stream, I heard a bell toll and looked toward the east to see the glowing sun rising. It was more beautiful than the rainbow in summer. As I walked toward Khurukhutšhu, I thought happily of the bread, jam, sugar, and coffee that I would be given on Christmas for the first time in my life.

As I approached Khurukhutšhu, I heard the beautiful voices of the "book people" singing:

Hallelujah! Hallelujah!
Dumela Hallelujah!

KHURUKHUTŠHU

Hallelujah, we greet you;
Hallelujah!

This was the first Christian hymn I had ever heard. I walked gently, slowly, and listened to the singing inside the Lutheran church. They began to sing another beautiful and melodious hymn:

How blest are the poor;
The Kingdom of Heaven is theirs.
How blest are the sorrowful;
They shall find consolation.
How blest are those of a gentle spirit;
They shall have the earth for their possession . . .

As I continued walking to Aunt Malekanyane's house, my thoughts were heavy with the music and the words I had heard from the church. The music spoke of poverty and sorrow, consolation and gentleness of spirit, hunger and thirst, and mercy. I had known them all.

I sat outside my aunt's house until she arrived from the church service. She was very excited to see me and took me inside and gave me bread smeared with jam to eat. As I was eating, she gave me tea with lots of sugar in a blue china cup on top of a saucer and gave me lots and lots of cakes and candy.

From that day, I began to develop a different opinion of the Christians and their religion. Up to that time, I had only experienced rejection in Christian homes. Now I could see that not all Christians shunned us.

As more of our people became Christians, more of our culture suffered. Our institutions and traditions were denounced by the Lutheran church. They dismissed those who partook of traditional African home-brewed beer. We were perplexed when they refused to accept into their faith men who had more than one wife, while at the same time they accepted their wives and children. Our tribal music and dances were condemned as pagan activity, but the Christians themselves danced breast to breast, glued one to the other! We wondered what on earth they were doing, particularly those who were not husband and wife. Such dancing was considered obscene by the people of Molemole.

One day I arrived at the royal house of Machaka at Mphakane and found the queen mother, Makhurumetša Machaka, and other members of the royal family, including King Kgarahara Machaka himself, pouring libations to their ancestors in the royal courtyard. The queen mother was kneeling on the floor, holding a calabash in her hands, sipping water from it. She spoke to those who lie beneath the soil—the Living Dead—and yet she was a member of the Roman Catholic church. She began to speak to her ancestors, pleading with them to help her granddaughter, who had been married for many years without conceiving a child.

4

Missionary School

One day my cousin Anna Mokgokong, the daughter of our local Lutheran minister and a teacher at Khurukhutšhu, visited our home and asked whether I would not like to attend school. I told her that at fourteen I was too old to go to school with small boys and girls, and besides, my Uncle Petša Ramusi had said I had a responsibility as a herdboy of my father's stock. Uncle Petša opposed Christians, Western culture, and education and was supported by Khaola and others who wanted nothing to do with the missionaries. But after a time I agreed to go and try. Fortunately for me, Uncle Petša was no longer there. One morning when we woke up, we discovered he had disappeared with his youngest wife, bag and baggage—gone to a faraway land to practice as a witch doctor. Because I was still a herdboy at this stage, my brother Nkwatlapi and I decided to devise some means to enable us to both attend to the flock and go to school. While one looked after the livestock, the other would go to school and vice versa.

I arrived at Khurukhutšhu Mission School on a Monday morning following our Sunday meeting. I knocked at the door and watched Anna Mokgokong coming to the entrance; she welcomed me to her classroom. Within minutes Anna taught me the alphabet. The vowels and consonants captivated my interest. Saying them was like music to my ears. I could clearly see that if I mastered them I would not have difficulty constructing sentences and even reading.

Anna formed the foundation of my education, instilling

within me a love of learning before sending me on to Phillipos Mokhufi, the handsome man from Vendaland. He was a cheerful teacher with a beautiful, musical voice, always smiling, full of love in his heart—love even for the "heathen" boys and the poor. He taught me well.

Anna Mokgokong and Mokhufi promoted me to grade two within seven days. In another four weeks Mokhufi saw me through to the third grade, and at the end of the first year of my elementary school I was already in grade four. The principal of the school, Nelson Mabitsela, and Mokhufi encouraged me in my studies. Of course in those days the teachers did not spare the rod, but I was never whipped because I always did my work and knew what I would get if I started to play the fool. My age may have made it a little difficult for the teachers to whip me, since they knew I was already a man from Komana and Bodika initiation schools.

The school building was a dilapidated village church house, furnished only with the humblest and barest educational equipment, but the teachers were dedicated. It was Mokhufi, especially, who made it possible for me to do eight years' course work in only four.

My mother and sisters as well as my eldest brother, Moraba, did not know I was progressing well because they had never been to the white man's school. My family tilled the land for a living, and my mother obtained schoolbooks and clothes for me in exchange for maize, beans, peanuts, eggs, millet, and sorghum. But there were many things I wanted which my mother could not afford.

Once, a classmate's brother bought him a pair of tennis shoes that were too small for him but fit me perfectly. He offered to sell them to me for fifty cents, but my mother told me she had no money. I needed some sort of shoes in order to participate in the competitions for school choirs to be held at Pietersburg. I begged and begged until my mother began to sob. I cried for the whole night to impress upon her the depth of my desire for the shoes. All she could do was allow me, the following morning, to ride a fast-trotting donkey from our kraal to Ramalapa village to try to arrange for my classmate to give me

MISSIONARY SCHOOL

the shoes in exchange for a promise from my mother of a few gallon tins of beans after the harvesttime. I rode the donkey to Ramalapa, but they would not give me the shoes. At least my mother had convinced me that she cared.

When I had to drop out of the school choir for lack of shoes, and could not participate in the music competitions at Pietersburg town, I did not blame my mother. I realized that our poverty was beyond her control. Many times I came back from school and found nothing to eat. Nothing! But that did not discourage me from going on with my studies. I walked barefoot until the end of my elementary schooling.

The school concerts that were held from time to time did much to fill me with the joy of learning and of being at school. But poetry was the subject that uplifted my spirit, inspired me, and consoled me the most. Whenever I was asked to recite a poem I was happy. I could recite Wordsworth's "Daffodils" by heart from beginning to end. Longfellow's "Village Blacksmith" was another favorite poem.

It was while I was attending elementary school that I was baptized as a member of the Lutheran church. They discarded my three given names—Mafa Molapatene Kotoleleele—and renamed me Collins William Ramusi. As they baptized me and threw away my names, given me by my tribe and family, something indescribable happened inside me. Deep within me there was a stirring when my names were discarded. Memories of my father absorbed me.

Although I was a baptized Christian, I continued to join my mother and sisters whenever they prayed and talked to the spirits of our forefathers. On days when I was not herding the flock, or when I came from herding the flock at night, I sneaked out of Ranhlokana to visit my friend and classmate, Victor Majutle, who lived with the principal of the school, and my teacher, Mokhufi. Neither had wives, and Victor, with my assistance, showed appreciation for his free room and board by cleaning and cooking. Victor and I became best friends, and we spent a lot of time at the house he shared, studying together.

White children received compulsory education, up to a certain age, paid for by the state, while there was no compulsory, free education for black children in South Africa. We had to pay school fees and sports fees and buy books and uniforms. It was a constant struggle to stay in school. The eggs, maize, sorghum, and beans that bought my slates and exercise books could not buy the required khaki shirts, trousers, and jackets. For the first two years I managed somehow with the help of my mother and older sisters Tipe and Mokgadi. In the third year, however, when I was due to take the seventh-grade examinations, poverty compelled me to drop out of school. My dreams were shattered. I was frustrated beyond measure, and had nowhere to turn for help.

I made up my mind to go to Pietersburg, a town thirty-five miles from home, in search of work. I left at midnight without telling my mother or sisters. I walked until sunset of the following day, when I could walk no farther. Bone tired, I crept into a hole under a small, bushy thorn tree, wrapped myself in a tattered blanket I had taken from my mother's hut, and fell asleep.

The sun was bright and clear when I crept out of the hole like a kangaroo, and saw the town of Pietersburg sprawled before me. I looked back toward the north, but I could not see the deep blue mountains of Molemole, where my people lived.

Suddenly, I caught sight of a police car traveling along the main road. Fear gripped me. I did not have a pass. It was a crime for a black person to go from one place to another without a pass, particularly when traveling to urban areas. Our people were commonly jailed, and some had died for breaking this unjust law. I ran like an animal avoiding a predator. I dropped to my hands and knees. Quietly, as quickly as possible, I crept toward the town. My knees, ankles, and elbows began to ache. Exhaustion gripped my muscles and bones. I could crawl no farther. I fell flat on my stomach and called out the name of my long-departed father and begged him to save my life.

Just then I heard voices on the right side of the main road. I summoned my last ounce of strength and courage and crawled in the direction from which the voices had come. I thought there might be a house there. I was hungry, breathless, and thirsty. Two days and nights had passed without a morsel of food or a drop of water passing down my throat. About 500 yards from the main road I found a cattle kraal filled with fat and hornless cattle. Near the kraal was a massive house that could only have belonged to a white man. I crawled into the kraal and found a thick pole; I stood up, leaned against it, and slept through the night in a vertical trance. I had left my tattered blanket outside the kraal to protect it from the ticks and the cow dung.

That night I dreamed of my mother and father. In my dream, my mother stood before me and wept as my father looked at the cattle and shook his head. I was still trying to speak to my father when a man shook me and said, "Who are you?"

"I am Molapatene."

"Where are you from?"

"From Molemole."

"Why do you sleep in a cattle kraal?"

"I am sorry. I am lost. I am thirsty. I am tired. It is cold. Water, water, please!"

I drank buckets of water before my thirst was quenched, then I helped Moloto milk his employer's cows. Moloto gave me whey to drink. Later he gave me food.

That morning I was hired as a house, garden, and dairy boy for fifty cents a month by a white bricklayer from Annadale, where the poorest of Pietersburg whites lived. I was shown a dilapidated shack some 300 yards away from my employer's house. It was only four feet high, four feet long, and three feet wide. Here I would sleep. This was my house!

The roof of my shack was made of sacks, cardboard, and hessian bags. It had neither a door nor windows. At that time I was five feet six inches tall, so I slept with the greater part of my body outside the shack. The floor was made of dirt. There was no furniture in my "house," only dust and the dirt floor on which to lay my bones.

My employer was an Afrikaner, a poor white, descendant

of settlers from Holland, who worked all over the northern Transvaal, building houses and dams, coming home only on weekends. He was a tall, knock-kneed man. His face was as hard as granite, with bloodshot eyes. I never knew his name, or the name of his wife, and they never knew mine. I called them "Baas" and "Missis," which is how black workers are supposed to refer to their employers in South Africa. They called me "Jim," "*Hei,*" "Boy," "*Auta,*" "*Pikinini,*" "Jan," "*Jy,*" "*Jong,*" "Piet," "*Klonkie,*" "*Ka,*" "Willem," "*Kaffertjie*"—all degrading names that meant nothing but hurt to me.

They had one child, a nineteen-year-old daughter named Sannie. She was a big-busted, plump, round-faced high school student who somehow reminded me of the mean Christian girls at Khurukhutšhu. She was madly in love with a train driver who blew loud toots on his whistle whenever the train passed the house on its way northward to Zimbabwe.

One day I had just finished milking my employer's cow when he summoned me to his living room. I found him sitting on a bench behind the door. He was a poor man, and the only furniture in the house consisted of two benches, one black coal stove, and a dilapidated iron double bedstead. His daughter slept on the floor, just as we did at Ranhlokana.

He sat with his legs stretched out, with the palms of his hands resting on his knock-knees and his walking stick beside him. The moment he saw me he shouted, "Bring me warm water in a washbasin, boy!" Then he added: "*En, kaffer, maak gou!*" meaning, "Kaffir, be quick!"

I said, "Ja, my baas." I fetched the water and brought it to him. I placed the basin in front of him and started to walk away. He called me back. He poked his walking stick hard against my chest, like one does to a donkey when it is urged to pull. I staggered backward. Fear and anger gripped me. Sweat broke out all over my body.

He pointed his stick at his heavy, muddy-booted feet.

"Undo them!"

"Baas?" I looked at him thinking that I did not understand.

"Take them off my feet, kaffir!" He snarled like a dog at me.

I bent down to unlace the boots that looked like gray bricks.

MISSIONARY SCHOOL

I struggled to undo the laces, caked with what seemed like the mud of weeks. With a sick, dizzy feeling, I managed to undo the left boot. The right boot proved harder. When both boots were finally loosened, a stench emerged from them that was worse than the stench of human excrement. The boots and the socks were glued together with dirt. I tried in vain to separate them. Finally, boots and socks came off together, and the whole place stank like a dead donkey. I closed my nose with my fingers, but the man poked my fingers away with his stick.

"Wash my feet! *Was hulle!*" he screamed at me in his mother tongue.

The cold, mean manner of his command hurt me at the very center of my being, the very core of my manhood. Trembling with fear and disgust, I knelt there in front of the man with one of his bare, filthy, pallid feet, unable to bring myself to lift it up and put it in the basin, appealing to him, without saying a word, not to humiliate me that way.

He poked at my face with his stick. "Hurry up! What are you waiting for, kaffir? Who do you think you are?" He sneered at me.

Suddenly I realized who I was! I was a proud black man of Ranhlokana.

I dropped his stinking foot like a sack of corn, went straight out to my shack, picked up my treasured, tattered blanket, and climbed over the barbed-wire fence, which tore a hole in my shorts and cut my buttocks as I left. I walked determinedly down the road toward the unknown, the tear in my shorts flapping and my buttocks bleeding. Inwardly, I was bleeding, too, from all the humiliation and hopelessness. But God is not dead, I told myself.

It was dark, windy, and cold. I wrapped myself in the blanket, and shouted aloud to myself while walking down the road:

> *I am who I am.*
> *No stinking feet can tread me down.*
> *The seed of Moshweu,*
> *Moraba, and Mothibi!*

But when, after walking for some distance, I saw the red lights of a police van coming toward me, I remembered the proverb of my people: Once a bulldog crosses a rivulet, it is a puppy. I ran into the bushes beside the road and hid. The van passed several times while I crouched petrified in the bushes. I was in the suburb of white men, where blacks were victimized and terrorized for no crime or reason. I could be arrested for loitering or for not having a pass.

Suddenly a car screeched to a stop a few yards from my hiding place. My heart jumped. Torches flashed. I realized that the police were combing the woods for black men who might be there without passes. It occurred to me that my ex-employer may have reported me to them for one offense or another. I climbed up into a marula tree and sat as quietly as a dove among the branches until the police went away. They must have been there for an hour, searching for their prey. I fell asleep. When I awoke, the sun was already up and shining on the green trees, grass, and multicolored wildflowers. The air was fresh and sweet smelling.

Carrying the tattered blanket that was my only possession, I started walking toward the black township of old Pietersburg, the residential area for blacks who worked in Pietersburg town.

I arrived in the black township and wandered around until I saw a man and some boys milking cows in a kraal. I went over and helped with the milking uninvited. I needed the comfort of being near someone who would treat me like a human being. The man admired my ability and offered me accommodations and food if I would stay in that home, milk the cows, and take them to the grazing pastures daily. I agreed and remained there for a week.

That was my first experience of life in a black township. Stark discoveries imprinted themselves on my mind. The whole family lived in one room, where the only bed was separated from the rest of the room by a thin cotton curtain. A man and his hefty wife slept restlessly on a dilapidated iron bed while the children lay sleepless and watched the two entangled figures rolling and tossing on the bed. Some nights between their grunts and gasping cries of pleasure I could not sleep.

Twelve children were packed into that one-room house. Some slept under their parents' bed, while others slept under the table. Others rolled and tugged in one blanket, shared by boys and girls together. On the seventh day I could not take it anymore. That last night I kept on hearing my mother's voice calling, "Come back home! Come back! Come, come, your mother cries, Mafa, come home, child."

The next morning after milking the cows, I took them to graze as usual, then went to the area where people from Molemole camped ox wagons whenever they came to town. I searched for people from home who might be going to Molemole. I found the headman, Mokadikwa, whom I knew well. He was a senior member of the royal lineage of Maimela and was accompanied by his daughter, Mangwakwana. She looked at me and shook her head. She asked me whether I did not wish to go back and return to school, then offered me a free ride. She spoke to me with the conviction and strength of character of a mother of people. "Lift up your head and wipe your tears even from the inside of your heart that cries for life. Square your shoulders and look your adversaries in the eye. You are not a dog, my child. Have courage and strength. Who can tell? Perhaps Molemole can survive through children like you. Who knows? Soldiers of truth. Lift up your head, my son! Your place is not here. Arise and walk! Move toward the skies! Fly! Go! Go to your gallant mother! She will continue to feed, clothe, and shelter you. Your mother loves and cares for you."

Mangwakwana stood up and looked toward Molemole—toward the north. She clasped her hands and closed her eyes; while tears streamed down her cheeks she said, "I am a mother and have given birth; I know the pains of childbirth and motherhood. I know how your mother must feel." She wiped her tears and asked me to fetch my possessions.

The night I arrived home, I promised my mother that I would never again run away to work for poor whites who made me wash their stinking feet. As I made the promise, that horrible strench came back to my nostrils. Mother gave me cold water to wash it away.

The next morning she took me to our local elementary school at Manthata village, the same school that I had left for lack of funds, to continue my studies in grade seven. Nelson Mabitsela, the class teacher, was the principal of the school. A good and kind man, he smiled with obvious joy when my mother brought me to his class. He told me that somehow he had known that I would come back. I continued with my education and completed the elementary school when I was about nineteen years of age. But then I reached a second dead end.

The lure of boarding school taunted me night and day. I wanted to learn the things in books. I was curious and hungry to learn more and wanted to help my people. Maybe there was something in the books that could help me bring the water to the land, to turn our desert green, to bring food to the starving people, to keep our babies from dying, our women from growing old too soon, and our men from dying of heart failure. But there were no funds for me to enter the boarding school, and no one able to help me. The eggs and produce which my mother had used to educate me at the elementary school could not meet the cost of a boarding school. And in those days there were no local tribal high schools. The South African government did not encourage "kaffirs" to become educated. Instead they preferred them to remain providers of their comforts, doing the whites' dirty, unpleasant work as house servants or heavy laborers.

After pouring libations and praying for a solution to my problem, I finally gave up and decided to go to Pretoria to seek work, like other young men of Ranhlokana. But the pass laws in South Africa decreed that to do so I must have a special traveling pass. I made an application for one. It was refused. However, I obtained a visitor's traveling pass to see an old friend of my father, Paul Sono, who had worked for many years at the South African Royal Mint. I was on my way to the seat of the oppressor's regime.

5
Pretoria

When I arrived in Pretoria, Paul Sono found a job for me at the Royal Mint, but because I had come to the city as a visitor, I was not allowed to take it. Legally or illegally, I had to have a job. I had to raise money to go back to school. Without a permit I couldn't work for a company. I was advised to seek employment with a private family who might not report me to the authorities. I looked for work and found myself in a section of Pretoria city where the poorest of the white community lived. It was called Vuil Skoen, meaning "dirty shoe," an area so depressed that the whites who lived in it were considered dirty even when they were clean. I was employed by a tall, muscular, athletic Afrikaner whose name I never knew for certain. I concluded it was Cloete, because once a visitor asked me, *"Waar is baas Cloete?"*

Baas Cloete hired me at a salary of thirty cents a month, the pay for domestic servants in Vuil Skoen, Pretoria, in 1944, for working in the homes of white people as kitchen boys or girls and garden boys.

My sleeping room was a corrugated-iron shed that reminded me of storage rooms at Molemole. It was a hole without a door or window, just like the one I had lived in at Annadale, except this one was made completely of corrugated-iron sheets. It was about seven feet long, by six feet wide, and five feet high. When the weather was hot, my room was hotter, like the inside of an oven. When the weather was cool, especially at night, my room was colder than a fridge.

Mrs. Cloete, the poor Afrikaner's wife, seemed old and in very poor health. Sannie Cloete, their only child, came galloping like a mare into the house each day from high school. Robust, athletic, big busted, with thick thighs and legs, she walked like a man. There was a look on her face whenever our eyes met that I could not comprehend.

Mrs. Cloete seemed more kindly disposed toward me than her husband and daughter. She made me believe that she felt motherly toward me by always calling me "my kind," "my child." She called me "my child" so often that I began to boast to other black domestic workers that my Missis was the best employer in Pretoria even if she paid me only thirty cents a month, because she never called me "kaffir" or "infidel." Her husband always embarrassed me by calling me "kaffir." I resented it deeply.

Sannie puzzled me. From time to time she would look at me and flush red and laugh. I wondered if I looked funny to her. It never occurred to me that she might be attracted to me until one day she brought me sweets and cakes to eat. Sometimes she would stop by my "hole" and talk to me.

One Sunday she wore a white velvet blouse, which I openly admired, never having seen white velvet before. I did not know the difference between a blouse and a shirt, having come from a village where such finery was not worn. I even suggested I would like to have a shirt like that one day. Sannie giggled and said, "Maybe I will sell it to you." She swished her skirt and galloped off.

I went into the kitchen to get on with my chores. When I was through with my cleaning for the day, I went to visit my relatives and friends at the Industrial Steel and Iron Corporation (ISCOR) hostel. I boasted to them about my employer's wife and daughter treating me kindly and not using racial insults.

The next day I was sitting in my hole and whistling to myself when Sannie entered, wearing the white velvet blouse.

"Do you still like this blouse?" she asked.

"Oh yes, Nonnie, Miss!"

"Have you ever touched velvet before?"
"No, Nonnie!"
"You want to touch it?"

She moved toward me, her breasts rising like small mountains beneath the white velvet. I moved back into the farthest corner of my hole. A smile rippled at the corner of her mouth. Suddenly she pulled her blouse off over her head, threw it at me, and said, "Take it, my *dingetjie*—baby!"

This was the first time I had ever seen white breasts. My mouth dropped open, and I stared at the pink nipples.

"Oh, Nonnie! What are you doing, Nonnie?"

I was afraid. White people hang black men who touch their women. I envisioned myself being dragged from my hole to be hung by the neck until I was dead.

She thrust the blouse into my hands and said, "Take it, it's yours."

"Oh, no, Nonnie!"

"You must take it. I want you to have it!"

"But how will I explain having your blouse to the Missis and Baas? They will say I stole it and put me in jail," I stammered.

"You can tell them I sold it to you."

"But, Nonnie, I only make thirty cents a month. How could I buy such a fine blouse?"

"You can have it for seventy-five cents . . . and a few special favors."

We heard footsteps. Someone was coming. Suddenly she grabbed it from my trembling hands, slipped it on, brushed against me, and ran away. Later that night she brought it back to me to keep for good.

The next day my cousins Malema and Makgoba visited me for the first time in Vuil Skoen. Since I was the Cloetes' kitchen boy, I served them tea with my Missis's kitchenware. When I told them I was hired for thirty cents a month, they looked at each other and in unison said, "Poor white trash exploiting our people! Shame! Shame!"

I assured them that my Missis was really treating me well. While I was still boasting about my wonderful Missis of Vuil

Skoen, I saw her peering suspiciously through the doorway. I was frozen with fear. Mrs. Cloete stood there transfixed, fuming and breathless. Her mouth opened, and she screamed like a cow about to be slaughtered. *"Gaan uit, kaffers*—Get out of here, niggers!"

As my cousins jumped like frightened rabbits, I stood petrified and trembling. She swore at me with every vulgar word that her Afrikaans language could express. She insulted not only me but also my mother and father, and my race and all black people on earth, with words I cannot put on paper.

Mrs. Cloete looked much uglier when she used foul phrases. Anger made her appear older and more miserable, more sickly than usual. I went behind my iron shed and stood still as she waddled toward her kitchen door. I covered my mouth with the palm of my hand, as I laughed aloud at Mrs. Cloete. I laughed at her ugly face, at her inability to breathe when she was swearing, at the way she thrashed her arms and legs like a fat bug whose body is too heavy for its appendages. The more I thought about this, the more I laughed, till Mrs. Cloete finally heard me.

"Kom hierso!"

I pretended not to hear.

"Kom, jong!—Come you!" she said.

I tried to speak, but I couldn't stop laughing. I laughed until my lungs and ribs began to ache! Slowly I moved toward the kitchen and Mrs. Cloete. She stood there, at the door, breathless, angry, and in tears. The nearer I came, the more she cried and threatened. Then she jumped at me in an attempt to hit me, but she missed and fell. Her dress flew up over her head. She wore neither panties nor petticoat; there was nothing to cover her colorless body as she lay prostrate at the bottom of the steps. I covered my eyes with both hands. By the time I opened them, Mrs. Cloete had pulled down her khaki dress and was walking into the house. She told me to follow her, which I did.

"Who told you that you could use a white man's plates?" she asked me.

I did not reply. I began to sweat.

"Who told you that you, kaffir, could use a white man's spoon? Who told you that a kaffir could ever become a white person? Who told you?" she demanded.

"Missis!" That was all I could say. I felt like a wretched little dog with its tail between its legs. I wished that the earth would open up and swallow my black body so that Mrs. Cloete could not jump on me any longer.

I began to realize then that the trouble was caused not only by the presence of black people on the Cloete premises without permits but the fact that three blacks also had used the white woman's spoons, knives, forks, cups, sugar, sugar bowls, teaspoons, and teapot. This was considered taboo by white South Africans. As far as Mrs. Cloete was concerned, I had done the most hideous thing by using her cutlery and dishes and sugar to feed my relatives. She yelled at me until she was hoarse. "*Blaadie donner se kaffers!*—Bloody damned kaffirs," she repeated several times.

She was still trying to get her breath when Sannie came prancing home. I wondered whether Mrs. Cloete had seen me showing the blouse to my cousins in my hole and whether she was going to confront me about it, when I saw Sannie approaching and remembered her pink nipples.

I greeted Sannie. "*Hallo, Nooientjie!*—Miss!" I heard myself saying "Nooientjie—Miss" in an affectionate sort of way, which frightened me, because for the first time I was horrified by the discovery that a white man's daughter was behaving like the beautiful belles of Molemole when they fall in love with boys.

Just then Mr. Cloete arrived. Mrs. Cloete began to cry. Was she crying because I had used her utensils? Or because I had seen her naked body? Or because I had her daughter's blouse and she had called me her "little bitty baby—*dingetjie*"?

In any event, I was dismissed for using the white people's sugar and utensils. So it was that I lost my first job in Pretoria after two weeks. I picked up my torn blanket from the iron shed, and on my way out to the street I looked into the kitchen window of the Cloete house and saw Sannie shedding tears. I walked out onto Church Street. Suddenly, I was gripped by an intense fear of being shot at, and I began to run in the direction of the ISCOR compound, where my cousins lived and worked as migrant laborers. They were at the compound when I arrived. That night I was told that the shirt I was so fond of was a girl's blouse. I never put it on my body again, but I kept on wondering why Sannie Cloete had given it to me.

My brother Nkwatlapi was working in Pretoria. He helped me find another job, this time in Pretoria West, which was better than Vuil Skoen. I was employed as kitchen boy in the home of another Afrikaner, who worked in the General Post Office—one of those lower-middle-class South African whites who could afford a kitchen boy and a washerwoman, both black, and cheap. He was viewed as rich by his neighbors because he owned a radio. In those days, only the rich had radios, and this employer's was the first radio I had ever seen or heard.

His name was Meyer. It was difficult to believe that he was an Afrikaner because he was such a gentleman, always quiet and peaceful, with a pleasant manner, even to black people. Mrs. Meyer was an Afrikaner housewife about fifty-five years of age, shapely and beautiful. Unlike her husband, she never smiled except when she was addressing her bulldog, which she seemed to prefer over her husband. I never saw her caress or kiss her husband, but she would kiss and caress the poor dog as if it were a man. She didn't like female dogs or female cats. She loved dark things: dark glasses, dresses, shoes, gloves, hats, dogs, cats. Her furniture and her radio were all black—like her servants.

Mr. Meyer employed me for seventy-five cents a month to clean the house and do the gardening, but Mrs. Meyer made it very clear that an important part of my job was to feed, wash, comb, and please her bulldog in every way. The other dogs and cats I merely had to feed and wash.

Both the Meyers and Mrs. Meyer's mother, who lived with

them, were pious members of the Dutch Reformed Church of South Africa and went to church every Sunday. I was already a baptized and confirmed member of the Lutheran church. My knowledge of the Afrikaans language was good, and I noted that a church service was broadcast daily on the radio at 11:00 A.M. This was my scheduled time to clean the huge sitting room, where the radio was and where Mrs. Meyer and her mother joined in the broadcast service.

At first I couldn't imagine why Mrs. Meyer insisted on my cleaning the room just when the church service was in progress. I found out only on the day I lost my job. They wanted to kill two birds with one stone—enjoy the service and make sure they received their full seventy-five cents' worth of work from me.

Mrs. Meyer and her mother would sit on the couch with their legs stretched out in front of them. I was expected to clean the rug around their legs and under the couch, so I devised my own special way of doing it. Like the people in the Lutheran church, Mrs. Meyer and her mother both closed their eyes during prayer. I waited until the radio announced "Let us pray," and as soon as their eyes were closed, I knelt down and cleaned under the couch. In this manner I hoped to escape the danger of cleaning under the women's white thighs in a country where black men went to jail for touching white bodies, even accidentally, in a Christian church or home.

One day Mrs. Meyer called me back to the sitting room after the morning radio service. She knelt down, put her hand under the couch, and touched the floor with her delicate white fingers and painted nails. She then exhibited some little bits of dust on her fingers and looked at me as if I were ugly death. Frowning, she said, *"Kyk! Kyk hier!*—Look! Look here!" and abused me for not having cleaned under the couch. I said that I had, and that she had not seen me doing it because she and her mother had both closed their eyes. Her mother said that neither she nor her daughter ever closed their eyes, even in prayer, when it came to watching black people work, because blacks were cheats and thieves.

It was not true that I hadn't cleaned the rug under the couch, yet I had committed another sin. I had chased the bulldog out of the sitting room during the service, and Mrs. Meyer had pointed at me furiously, warning me not to treat her beloved dog like that. Now, suddenly, I felt like challenging Mrs. Meyer, and I confronted her like a man from the Bodika school. I had witnessed a strange spectacle earlier that day. I had already cleaned the bedroom and was not expected to go back again when I remembered I had taken the mat out for airing and forgotten to return it. I decided to return it before proceeding to clean the other rooms. I quietly opened the bedroom door and saw Mrs. Meyer kneeling on the floor and Bulldog playing on top of her. I gasped at the sight, and she very rudely told me not to enter her bedroom without knocking.

Through the huge sitting room window, I could see the imposing building of the Dutch Reformed church on the other side of the street, with a cock made of steel on the dome and the cross on top. I looked at Mrs. Meyer. She was still stroking her bulldog as if he meant more to her than anything else in the world. I looked at her mother, who appeared to be uneasy about something. I no longer felt afraid of them. I said, "Old Missis! Does your church over there welcome black members of the Lutheran church to their Sunday services?" She looked away without answering.

I wanted to say what was on my mind about what I had witnessed earlier, but I held back. Instead I asked, "Why do you have dogs in your bedroom or even in your sitting room?"

"What? What?" She looked at her daughter. "Is he mad?" she asked.

Now I asked Mrs. Meyer, "Missis, do bulldogs, or any other dogs, understand the radio church services?"

Mrs. Meyer said, "Kaffir, Bulldog is my dog, you hear? I don't care what you do to the other dogs and cats, but you must never insult Bulldog either during the radio service or at any other time." She called me insulting names. "Bulldog is my—" Her mother broke in, "And no kaffirs are allowed to attend radio church services in white homes, you hear?"

"Yes, Old Missis."

As they went on telling me what kaffirs might not do to dogs, cats, church services, and Christ, a bout of laughter seized me, and I laughed as I had never laughed before—not even at Mrs. Cloete when her dress covered her head.

There were many unanswered questions in my mind as I left that mad, white home. Why was I told to clean the sitting room at the hour of the radio church service if kaffirs were not permitted to attend such services in a white home? What kind of Christianity did those two women believe in—a Christianity for whites and dogs only? These were the questions that troubled me as I walked to the ISCOR hostel to tell my brother Nkwatlapi, and my cousins, Malema and Makgoba, of how I had lost my second job in Pretoria.

That night the three of us slept on cold slabs, like the slabs dead men lie on in mortuaries. Before I slept, I knelt down, and I spoke to God:

> *Oh God of our fathers,*
> *Deliver me and our people*
> *From the white people.*
> *Oh God!*
> *Give me peace, God.*
> *Give me sleep, God!*

My cousins both worked in the section of the ISCOR foundry where the furnaces roared twenty-four hours a day. One day Malema accidentally fell into a furnace and burned to death. We took his body to Molemole, where he was buried with his father and mother and our Living Dead.

After working at two restaurants in Pretoria and being dismissed for trifling reasons without being paid, I found a job at a small fruit shop in the city. The shop was owned by a Mr. Bernard, a kind Afrikaner who was also a schoolteacher. He had a wife who looked like a deformed man, and a tall skinny son with wobbly knees, weak, long legs, and squinty eyes. He looked much younger than myself and seemed to me a very small boy. His name was Piet.

Piet called me "boy" or *"kaffertjie*—little nigger." I complained to him and warned him to stop, but he continued. One day he said, "What can you do to stop me calling you kaffertjie?"

"I can thrash you, Boertjie," I shouted.

"What?"

"Beat you up, little farmer!" I insulted him.

"Who—me?"

"You!"

"You can't beat me up, you little kaffir. Your mother's—" He swore at my mother, insulting her and her private parts. My left uppercut landed on his jaw. Within seconds of the insult to my mother, Piet was flat on his back, helpless and bleeding. I had never before seen a white bleed; I observed with satisfaction that they have the same red blood that blacks have. Nor had I seen a white boy running away from the fist of a black man. Years later I would see many white fighters knocked down by black fists during boxing tournaments in neighboring Lesotho and Swaziland, when these two countries became free from colonial domination.

Luckily Piet's mother and father were not present when I flattened him at the fruit shop. The two of us were alone. He got up and staggered away like an overloaded bicycle, drunk with dizziness. I panicked. All I had to eat was an orange and a mango, but I left, and I never went back to that fruit shop.

In all the months I worked for one white employer after another, I was never paid. I received my pay only when I obtained my first "big-time" employment as a worker with the Pretoria municipality.

I found a job as a cleaner in the Proes Street Men's Hostel. My salary was about two dollars a week. It was a most depressing environment. Thousands of black men were packed into that dreary building, many of them respectable family men whose wives and children were barred from joining them by the pass laws of the white South African government. These laws would not allow a woman to enter the hostel, even as a visitor to see her lawfully wedded husband.

Men had to peer out through windows to admire the beautiful black women who bore their children. I saw pretty women standing like unwanted objects near the gloomy gate of the hostel, waiting for their men to pass in or out. The men came from many ethnic groups in South Africa. They were subjected to degrading conditions from which whites, persons of mixed race, and Asians were exempt.

White people argued and argued amongst themselves about whether black people should be allowed to live or work in cities and towns. They ultimately agreed, in their all-white parliament, that Africans could come to the city only if they were coming to sell their labor to whites as temporary sojourners. The women and children were not allowed. Some women desperate for their family life used to risk arrest and humiliation by wearing men's clothes and slipping into the hostel to sleep with their husbands. If detected, they would be tried as criminals for violation of the pass laws.

Scrubbing floors in the rooms in which these men lived, removing garbage cans, cleaning toilets, and brewing beer, as if I were an old woman at Molemole, was a demoralizing job. "Why should I brew the stinking beer?" I asked myself. "Was this the life I was meant to live? Scrubbing floors, emptying garbage cans, and living in a men's hostel like an unwanted man? A reject? No!" I was dying to go back to school. I applied to many offices for scholarships, but I did not obtain a single reply, not even to acknowledge the receipt of my applications. In one office I was told by a school inspector that the South African government had no money to throw away on scholarships to blacks.

On weekends I took my tattered blanket, covered my head with it, folded it around my thin body, and lay on the lawn thinking about my fate. Tears came into my eyes, and I wept thinking of Molemole, my mother, Annadale, school, my teachers, and the classmates who had gone on to high school.

SOWETO, MY LOVE

I cursed poverty, cursed my fate, and cursed everything that stood in the way of my obtaining a higher education.

I was in Pretoria when thousands of my people were dying in the Second World War in defense of the white world and a freedom we had not known since the white man came to our land. I lost many of my relatives in that war: my mother's sister's son, Mokgashi, was among those who were killed at Tobruk. My father's youngest brother came back alive from the battles where the Nazis and racists were humbled by the children of the black cradle, who could not be brushed aside.

In spite of the eighth-grade certificate I had obtained at Manthata School, I was not then able to read a newspaper very well. I listened to those who could read well discussing the latest news from the war zones, and I learned a great deal about the brave deeds of our people in that war.

I was still scrubbing hostel floors, removing garbage, brewing beer, and watering lawns, when a miracle happened. It was a Sunday morning in September 1944. I had just watched one lean, sickly looking white policeman drag three black men from their hostel room to a waiting police van in Proes Street. The van was packed with men who were the cream of our race, taking them to captivity like the ancient slaves for minor and even nonexistent offenses.

I lay on the grass outside the hostel, wrapped in my old blanket, and wept silently. Suddenly, there was a gentle tug on my shoulder. I looked up and saw a man, smiling and black, about five feet six inches tall, with soft kinky hair and brown eyes. His teeth were very white, his nose high bridged, like Caucasian noses. He looked like a member of our clan, the Babirwa. Something told me that he was the Messenger of the Babirwa clan, the bearer of good news from the Living Dead, from the world where our ancestors had gone. He gazed at me smiling and said, "I am your brother, son of your father's brother. I am Molatelo, Mmancha's father. You are the blood of our clan. Arise! Cry no more!"

I looked at him and informed him, "I don't remember your face at all."

"You were only a small child when I saw you last. Your father and mother brought me up. They taught me love. They cared for me and even helped me to marry a wife. They were like my father and mother. When I became a man, the mining agents recruited me to go and work in the mines. I left Molemole and used my hands to help build up the huge Industrial Steel and Iron Corporation foundry. I came from there, where I worked for more than thirty years for no good reward. The white man is heartless and cruel to us blacks in this country."

I asked him when he was last in Molemole and how they were at home. He said, "The tribe starves, the women starve, the children starve. The rivers are dry, the grass is gone. The blood of Tsherane lives in pain. Hunger and thirst are everywhere. Disease, distress, and misery are written on every face. Mabjanene has become a dusty piece of land where the green grass no longer grows."

He said he had met the teachers who taught me at Molemole. That was why he had come. "They told me everything about you, my brother, about your classmates, your schoolwork, your final examination results. Your teachers are concerned; they are worried about your future. They appealed to me to help you, to pay for your education through boarding school." He put his hands gently on my shoulders, looked with compassion into my face, and said, "I have come, Motau, I have come, Mmirwa, I heard the voice of our Living Dead say, 'Son of Selaelo, your brother cries for help. Go!' and I have come to you, my brother. Wipe away your tears, fear no more. An orphan who does not die awaits riches, as our people say. Now, show me your room—the room in which you sleep in this hostel. Come."

I led him to the room where I lived with eleven other men and threw myself down on the dilapidated iron bed. He sat on the end of it. The room was poorly ventilated, crowded, and depressing. The bed had no sheets, mattress, or pillow. I had only the tattered blanket from my mother's hut in Molemole.

I wanted to ask him why black people were so deprived.

Why our people did not have land, water, money, homes, or even the bare necessities of life. But I did not have the courage. And I thought that perhaps only God Himself could answer these questions. I asked my brother only, "How long do you think we must suffer, brother?"

He replied with another question. "To which boarding school would you like to go, my brother?"

"To Lemana High School." I had no doubt about it.

"Then make your application for admission to Lemana. Write to them. Tell them that Molatelo Manyathe Piet Ramusi will pay all the fees for food, sleeping room, books, sports, health, and any other fees they may want."

It was eleven in the evening at the railway station. The train pulled off to Johannesburg, taking Molatelo, my guardian angel, and Mosehlaphala Maitša, my brother-in-law, with it. I started trotting back to the hostel, about two miles away, to sleep. I sang quietly to myself as I ran, when suddenly a torchlight flashed in my face. The light flickered again and again, and a fat-bellied Afrikaner policeman shouted and warned me not to move.

"Pass, kaffir!"

"My pass is at the hostel!"

"I say, night pass, kaffir!"

"Please, please, my baas, I forgot my pass at the Proes Street Men's Hostel. I am working there. I work. Please, my baas, please forgive me. Baas, I work. I am not a loafer. I—"

"Shut up your mouth, kaffir. Jump into the van! Quick. Jump in. *Maak gou!*—Quick!"

My pleas and broken Afrikaans, mixed with some broken English, did not save me.

It's a frightening thing to go to jail in South Africa. Within seconds I heard the police van doors slam closed, and I knew I was in there. This was Pretoria, the home of police atrocities and vans packed with black men. One black man was beaten by a police baton, his head was bleeding, he groaned in pain. No one paid any attention to him.

After driving around the city for three more hours, packing

the van with more alleged pass law offenders, we were brought to the Pretoria Central Police Station and put in a cell built for about ten people. There were over one hundred of us packed in there. We simply stood as if in a trance and tried to sleep, body pressing against body—young men, old men, men in tattered clothes, and men in dress suits all locked up like pigs standing together. One old man fell down, and fellow prisoners trampled his body. I felt sorry for him. I tried to lift him up. There was no space.

"All right, kill me!" he cried.

The bleeding man had been asking for air during the unforgettable torturous trip. Now he lay dying at our feet. "The pass law—the greatest enemy of the black man," he moaned.

It was my tenth arrest for violation of pass laws. That morning I appeared before a magistrate.

"Ten shillings fine!" said the lean and small-headed white magistrate. "Take him away, Mr. Interpreter, and tell him that if he comes before this court for a similar offense I shall have no hesitation in sending him back to his tribal home! Does he understand?" Now I was pushed down to the basement of the courthouse to pay my fine; then I ran out of the building like a scared rabbit.

Three more arrests and convictions under the pass law followed before I bid good-bye to Pretoria and returned to Ranhlokana, the village of my father.

I smiled as I went to the station. I smiled again as I purchased my train ticket to Pietersburg. I smiled as I boarded the train to go to the land of Tshaka Maimela, Botlokwa, Molemole, the land of Kgwadu, Matlalaohle, and Puledi Masenyane. My home!

I looked through the window of the slow-moving train at the Proes Street Men's Hostel and felt happy that I was leaving to find a new world ahead. I said to myself, Son of Mothibi, you are on your own from this moment on. I heard the steam engine gathering momentum, and I knew I was going north to my home, Molemole!

6

Lemana

In the homeward-bound train, I mused about the acceptance letter I had received from Lemana High School in response to my application. I was excited. My dreams were going to be realized. I was going to be educated at last!

At home with my mother, sisters, and brother Matsapola for four memorable days before the opening of school for the new semester, I tried to find out from students already enrolled at Lemana what was required of me concerning luggage, blankets, clothes, toiletries, and so forth. They gave me valuable advice and information concerning the mode of travel from Ranhlokana to Bandolierkop Railway Station. I was informed that Mr. Kadi had a comfortable and fast-moving donkey cart that conveyed students from Ranhlokana to the train station to catch the train for Louis Trichardt.

I ascended Ranhlokana Mountain and sat on my favorite spot under the mphaha tree to think. I was deeply concerned and anxious about my future. How was a despised tribal boy like me to manage to overcome these chains that bound and prevented me from looking at myself as a fully developed human being? I looked toward Mphakane-a-bo-Sekgala Mountain, the mountain of our people's rulers, where our royal ancestors were laid to rest, and asked myself, Were these Christians and whites not born of women like myself? Do they not consist of genes as I do? Were they not conceived in the same manner? There were other questions which I refrained from asking.

I shall always remember the days I spent with my family at

Ranhlokana village before proceeding to Lemana in January 1945. I realized who I was: Mafa Molapatene Kotoleleele, Matšhipi's brother, a man walking tall and proud in the village of my father, on the soil of Puledi Masenyane.

Amongst my people, leaving home is considered a serious business. Prayers and libations are offered to the ancestors and to the Almighty to make the journey safe. On the morning I was to leave home for Lemana, my mother summoned my family members together to speak to the spirits of our ancestors, to urge them to open my way and watch over me. Listening, I realized how deeply concerned my people were for my welfare and the welfare of my clan and of the whole nation. I was touched.

Meanwhile, Mahwai Kadi had harnessed his two donkeys to his brand-new donkey cart to take me to the railway station at Bandolierkop, to catch the train from Johannesburg on its way to Lemana. But something had happened outside the cattle kraal. There stood the cart without any donkeys!

Up came Khaola, the ever-trotting elephant buck. "Mafefo! Mafefo!" He pounded his giant bare foot on the ground, looked angrily over at Khurukhutšhu, and said, "I let the donkeys go! I released them! No donkey cart shall go to the train of Mafaufau, Mafamolebe! Mothibi's child shall not go to the school that was cursed by our ancestors!

> *O, you of the Babirwa clan!*
> *And o Mothibi!*
> *O, you spirits of the ancestors!*
> *Stop this abomination!*
> *Stop this rape of our traditions and culture!*

His old voice and his old body were trembling. He leapt at me as if he would strangle me rather than let me go to what he called the "White man missionary school of witches." Furious, he walked away.

I quickly fetched the two donkeys, harnessed them, and amid the trills from my mother, sisters, aunts, and the belles of Molemole, I left my mother's home and went to the land of

Ngungunyane and Ramapulana. The ululating continued until I disappeared from the village. The trotting donkeys dragged the cart for some miles, leaving dust and dilemmas, Khaola and the village of Molemole behind.

The donkeys pulled and dragged until they reached the Tropic of Capricorn Bridge across the Mononono River. On both sides of the road were sweet-smelling flowers. What a delight this was to my nostrils, which were still full of the stench of dead animals, the carcasses of the cattle that had died of malnutrition at Molemole. The mokowe bird screeched and shrilled; the sparrows twittered in the bushes beside the road. And goats with bells on their necks bleated happily on the lands of the white Mafomolela farmer, who had thousands of fattened beasts while we, the black owners of the land, had none upon which to feed our offspring. The white farms blossomed with fruit trees—peaches, oranges, guavas, mangoes, papaws, figs—beautiful and ripe, and swarming with honeybees. The grass grew on farmlands that once belonged to Molemole. Slowly the donkeys began to ascend the steepest of the hills between Molemole and Bandolierkop, Serore, the hill that has tired out many a strong horse, mule, ox, or donkey.

Looking back toward Molemole, I saw dust, bareness, desolation, and a few pitiful figures moving about in a pantomime of living.

The donkeys' strength began to give in, and they pulled to the right of the road, toward the luxuriant green grass that grew fresh and tall on the white farmer's land. They nosed under the fence to nibble at this banquet until they gathered some strength. Then, slowly, with great coaxing from Mahwai Kadi and me, they grudgingly left their feast and managed to arrive at Bandolierkop before the train.

"There! There it is! *Ntsho Makgala*," Kadi said, and pointed to the approaching black train. It came into the station hissing and puffing like an awkward giant carrying hundreds of men from the mines and labor camps crammed into the third-class coaches reserved for the black people of South Africa. I was one among the many black students going to Lemana and

Tshakhuma schools for further education—one among many young men and women who had left their homes in search of knowledge and the chance to rise and take their places in a new South Africa.

The train pulled out of the station toward the north, toward Zimbabwe and Messina, and I sat down next to a passenger from the Vaal Reef Gold Mine. He started to cough, and to spit up reddish sputum. He said that five members of his family had died of diseases contracted from digging gold from under the earth at the Vaal Reef Mine. He and his brother were on their way to Vendaland, their home, to die and be buried in the kraal of their father's fathers. I recalled the rage and despair I felt in Pretoria.

The man spoke as if addressing a crowd of Venda men and women, saying praises of his name and of his clan. "I am Sibasa. I am the bird, the bird that sits on the tree. The wind blows and blows, but the bird never falls," said the agitated Sibasa, who now looked like a man fending off despair in the face of death.

"*Ndau*," I said, as the Venda traditionally say when they greet, clapping my hands gently to show respect. He continued, as if I had said nothing. He told me that policemen had arrested him several times in many cities in an attempt to chase him away. They chained him like a mad bull, loaded him on the train to dump him at Louis Trichardt to die. They told him that the cities belong to white people only. They said that their pass laws did not permit him to work there. Sibasa had come to the cities to work for his family, to feed his wife and children, to clothe them. They told him that he did not have such a right in their cities. Four of his children had died of starvation before he had decided to go to look for work in the city of gold, Johannesburg.

He wiped sweat from his face with both hands. I asked him how he got to Johannesburg without a pass.

"The wisest animal is man," he said. "I walked three hundred fifty miles from Tshibase to Johannesburg. Me! Thirty days on the road. Sleeping in holes. Me! I walked until my feet were swollen and bleeding. Three times I collapsed and slept like death. Then I got up and walked. I am Tshibase. The wind blows and blows, but the bird never falls," he repeated, to emphasize his powers, his strength, manhood and courage—his dignity, which had been all but stripped from him. He looked up, clenched his fists, lifted his right foot, stamped hard on the floor of the moving train, and said, "I am Ramapulana, Sibasa, the rain king of lightning and thunder that crackles in the clouds. The rain bird that sits on a thin branch but never falls. *Nyamiyabo!*" He cursed the white man.

Not yet hardened as Sibasa and many others were, by the black man's plight in South Africa, the students sang their songs until the train arrived at Louis Trichardt station.

The bus to Lemana roared and hissed as it commenced the final journey that took me to my future. We were greeted by shouts. "*Mesela!*—Bushytails!" shouted some old students to remind the new students that they were not yet initiated. "Mesela!" We were bullied and ragged as part of the process. But that did not worry me at that time because I knew that it would not be easy for anyone to tackle me with bare hands. I could box, and I was already a man of the regiment of Matladi from the Mokutu Bodika school. So I took my seat at the rear of the bus and watched every move of those engaged in the bullying. No one approached me.

The bus ascended higher and higher along the meandering road to the hilltop, till we stopped right at the boys' hostel. "Bushytails, bushytails! Freshers, freshers!" shouted the old students from all over the hostel grounds as we got off the bus, looking for our respective dormitories.

Lemana was built by missionaries of the Swiss Mission Society, and named after Lake Leman, one of the most beautiful lakes in that country. The school sprawled over a hilly area covered with luscious, subtropical vegetation—mimosas, jacarandas, gum trees, and pines stretched for miles. To the north of the boys' hostel stood the administrative offices, library, bookstore, clinic, assembly hall, and the training college for teachers. Beyond the training college lay the Douglas Laing Smit High School, an imposing white structure where I was to spend five long years of intensive studies.

Close to the boys' hostel lay the main garden. It looked like the biblical Garden of Eden: papaws, guavas, oranges, avocado pears, bananas, figs, sugarcane were all over the garden, with magnolias, roses, carnations, kikuyu grass, and a host of other plants and trees. South of this garden was the girls' hostel, Motsana; the home of the future educated mothers of Africa. Motsana was surrounded by green pine trees and fragrant flowers.

Homes of white teachers surrounded the garden on the east, west, and south, and on the northwest tip lay the black teachers' quarters. The white homes looked like palaces to us. The black quarters were dilapidated shanties. Lemana was an eminent institution, with a strong Swiss tradition of independence and tolerance, but it failed to house its black staff members decently. In the classrooms, however, black and white teachers mingled in the cause of knowledge and humanity.

For a full fortnight it was "Mesela! Mesela!—Bushytails! Bushytails!" all over the school premises. Cold water would be poured on a freshman's bed, while others were beaten up, deprived of their food, spat upon, whipped, made to sing nonsensical songs or to stand on one foot for long periods of time. After two weeks, the "tails" were cut. I discovered that I was left alone because it was rumored that I came from Pretoria and not from Molemole. Boys from big cities were considered too dangerous to be touched. But two weeks later, Moses Mbowe, a tall, knock-kneed, big-eyed student teacher attempted to bully me.

"Stand up, you bushytail!" He croaked like a frog and leaped at me, ignoring my warning. "Mesela! I say. Mesela! Mesela!" Grabbing me by the collar of my shirt, he tried to drag me out of the study room.

I nailed him against the wall. Blood flew everywhere before he realized he was lying prostrate on the floor. A senior student, Eduardo Mondlane, intervened to save the vanquished boy.

Mozambique, barely a hundred miles from Lemana, lay to the east of Kruger National Park. Mondlane came from Mozambique; he was the son of a Shangaan chief from the district of Gaza in southern Mozambique. Like me, he was the first of his family to get an education. Strongly built, with thick lips and nose, he was tall and dark. He towered above his fellow students like a Colossus and spoke with a slight stammer at times. Deeply religious, Mondlane had a sense of selflessness that was nothing less than saintly. While other students played soccer, Mondlane prayed and spoke to his God. He was to become my friend, but little did I suspect then that he was to liberate the children of Gaza and Ngungunyane from five hundred years of Portuguese colonial domination and found the modern People's Republic of Mozambique.

We lived in four dormitories: Aggrey, Khama, Booker T. Washington, and Khoja. We slept on mattresses stuffed with green grass on hard iron beds. H. E. Ntsanwisi, the house master of the boys' hostels, was a small-bodied, white-haired, bespectacled, strict but kind man, from Mohlaba's tribe. He filled the roles of both father and mother to all boys who were placed under his care. Ntsanwisi would often lecture us in the dining hall after meals. "You are the leaders of the future," he would say. "Tomorrow's leaders. Wake up! Look and see! The white man does not want to see you in schools. He wants you to stay illiterate and backwards. He wants you to dig his ditches, and clean his toilets, and become a source of cheap labor for his mines, his farms, and his factories." Sometimes Ntsanwisi would stop, remove his glasses, open his eyes wide, and gaze at the students for a few minutes as if he were in extreme mental pain. He often ended his speech by saying, "Those who have ears will hear. You are our hope for the future. Africa awaits your leadership. Africa beckons you. You must become the generation that excels."

Soon after my arrival at Lemana I visited Njankajaka, the local chief. Seated under a mango tree, he told me of when the missionaries first came and asked for a place to sleep in the bush. He said, "We were still listening to them speak, when we realized our land was gone. They said they had come to Christianize and westernize our tribe. There are still Bibles in every corner of my tribe. Hymnbooks and brandy everywhere! And tears and wine and gin! But no real Christianity! My land is gone! Day in and day out I sit in this shade that is no longer cool and ponder." He paused.

I asked him, "How many of them came to ask for a place to sleep in the bush before they took your land?"

"They were three," the chief said. They brought a bottle of brandy the next day and gave it to him as ruler of the land. He thanked them for the tribute they paid to him. "Little did I think that they might interpret the tribute as the sale price for my land. Now they say our land is theirs, my village is theirs, my rivers and mountains are theirs. Police stations all over my land, and starvation, thirst, dirt, lice, bugs, and death are all they have brought to my land. But, one day they will get what they never dreamed of."

I was taught for the first time by white teachers: French, German, Jewish, English, and Afrikaner. I remember how uneasy I was when P. W. Nutt walked in to our English class. "White teachers teaching blacks?" I said to Edward Sono, another first-year student in my class. Sono came from Johannesburg, and was to become my lifelong friend. "What?" Sono laughed. "You will see."

P. W. Nutt was the new principal of the high school. He taught us English grammar. Within a few minutes, I no longer saw Mr. Nutt as a white man but only as a teacher. When he taught, he smiled, and when he smiled, he was charming, especially when he would say,

> *A thing of beauty is a joy forever:*
> *Its loveliness increases; it will never*
> *Pass into nothingness,*

as he entered our classroom to start his lecture.

O. Mahangi, a black man, taught us English literature. In his class I met my first Waterloo. My English left a lot to be desired. When I tried to read *Robinson Crusoe* aloud in class, I stumbled over the words. Other students read aloud correctly, but not I. Sono read fluently and with apparent comprehension. I realized that I had to make an effort to teach myself to read. My future was in jeopardy. I remembered the sayings of my people back home, who always reminded each other that "the word *impossible* is written only in the minds of fools." I dare not fail, I told myself.

One day I went to the forest, where I followed a narrow trail through the woods below the high school until I found a sweet-smelling mango tree. I climbed from one branch to the next until I found a comfortable place to sit. I opened my book, *The Sorrows of Satan,* given to me by a cousin, and began to read it aloud. The more I read, the less I understood. Then I started all over again with the aid of a dictionary, and read louder and louder until the whole forest was vibrating with my voice. I did this every day for four full months, until one evening in a debating society meeting I rose from the back of the hall and heard myself say: "Mr. Chairman, Secretary, ladies and gentlemen . . ." Faces turned toward me in disbelief, while I cleared my throat to continue. "I move that the church choir be abolished in this school," I said to a shocked and puzzled audience that had never before heard my voice in public debates. For the first time, I spoke English before an audience.

"I second the motion," said Mondlane, who was well respected for his dedication to the Swiss Mission church.

After an hour's debate, the powerful Lemana church choir was in danger of being done away with. It took six college teachers to convince the audience that Mondlane and I were mischievous debaters, and that the motion would be a very dangerous precedent if it could be carried out, even in a mere debating society meeting. The motion was lost, but I was elected president of the Lemana Debating Society. I occupied that office for most of my high school days and served as the president of the Students' Christian Association, the Lemana Athletic Association, and the Blue Cross Association—a temperance organization.

The most onerous position of them all was that of head prefect of Lemana students. It was a position of responsibility over all the boarding students in matters pertaining to discipline and order. All suggestions and complaints were brought to my notice. I began to develop a sense of responsibility, to realize the wisdom of forgiving the wrongs committed by fellow students. I grew and matured with my peers.

Soon after I arrived at Lemana, a cow died from unknown causes. The Reverend A. A. Jacques ordered the kitchen staff to cook the carcass in the huge pots of the school's kitchen for the students' supper. We entered the dining hall as usual for our evening meal, said grace, and sat down. Suddenly plates of food went flying through windows and others were smashed against tables. The students refused to eat the meat of a cow that had died from unknown causes, or any meat that had not been slaughtered on the hoof. I was amazed at this outburst of anger and violence, because when it began I was already eating the meat. I did not know that it was wrong to eat the meat from such an animal, because at Ranhlokana it was unheard of to throw away meat simply because the beast died from unknown causes.

Students marched and sang in a demonstration to protest the suspect meat. This was my first taste of a demonstration. I saw that the white men were scared and concerned. Mr. Nutt entered the dining hall through a window in order to identify with the students. The Reverend Mr. Jacques ran out of the assembly hall looking scared to death when a student shouted, *"Moer hom!"* which was an Afrikaans way of saying, "Attack him!" I was surprised to see black students defying white teachers in the school. The demonstration ended with the expulsion of all the senior students who were alleged by school authorities to have been the ringleaders. The missionaries never again tried to feed the students meat from such carcasses.

I remember some of my teachers at Lemana and their spouses and relatives. The Swiss teachers formed a fascinating group. Dr. Samuel Jacques was a colorful scientist, scholarly and religious. Polished, big-eared, and bright-eyed, he taught mathematics and science with difficulty because of his lack of proficiency in the English language. His wife was a charming lady and a musician, also from Switzerland. She refused to be corrupted by any South African racism and was the first woman to invite me into a white home at Lemana. She taught me to play a few notes on her piano and also served me tea and cakes. She even invited me for dinner.

At that time I had been reading Dr. Kwegyir Aggrey's *Philosophy on Cooperation Between Black and White Peoples*. "You can play a tune of sorts on the white keys, and you can play a tune of sorts on the black keys, but for harmony you must use both black and white." That message came to me loudly and clearly as I was learning to play the black and white notes on the keyboard. As I listened to the chords, I also thought of my future and the future of my generation in South Africa. While I was still at the keyboard, Dr. Jacques entered the house with his lovely five-year-old daughter, smiled, and greeted me.

"Well, well, you certainly mix your notes on the keyboard very well."

"*Merci, merci!*" I said, imitating Mrs. Jacques. I was beginning to think that a South Africa of united people, black and white, could indeed be possible, a people living together without any regard to race, color, religion, or creed.

Mr. H. G. Mercutt was the second principal of our high school after Mr. Nutt left; he was a scholar educated at Oxford University in the humanities and theology. He was also my English teacher. He and his wife one day invited our whole final-year matriculation class to their home for chamber music. By this time, my perspective was changing because of cultural contact with white teachers and families. I slowly sipped tea and listened to the cellos, trumpets, string basses, saxophones, and drums and said to myself, What a wonderful world! But most teachers kept a safe distance from those they taught. I was always conscious of the fact that in Lemana whites were a separate entity.

Fryer was my Afrikaans teacher. He was reported to have fought in the Second World War. He was a heavyset white man who giggled without end, particularly when he was poking fun at blacks and the English. He often proudly announced to us in class that he was a Boer who liked neither the English nor the blacks: *"Die rooi nekke en kaffers."* I often wondered why he and other whites like him bothered to teach blacks in English-speaking institutions.

He was big and strong, and walked with a limp because he had a peg leg. It was pathetic to see him struggling to climb steps. He was provocative at times, calling blacks "kaffirs," and I asked him why.

"Because I am not an Englishman. Only the English like to call you people Africans or natives, or Bantu. We Boers call you kaffirs." Then he walked to the blackboard and wrote the word *Voortrekker* and asked us to write a composition on it. He did this almost every week. "Do not forget to state that the Boers, my people, are a good and God-fearing people, a chosen people, the Voortrekkers who came to South Africa and treated the kaffirs kindly," he said to a hushed class of shocked students.

"Keep quiet, Martha and Collins! Write down what I am saying. And do not forget to say that Boers who traveled from the cape to Rhodesia deserve a monument to celebrate their achievement in finding a home for themselves in a rich South Africa, where today they rule supreme." They got their monument.

The whole class often went to the principal's office to complain about Fryer. Soon we learned from reliable sources that he was a member of the ruling all-white National Party of South Africa, and of a secret society of Boers known as the Broederbond. Both organizations were well known for their strong antiblack activities in the country.

The principal, the Reverend A. A. Jacques, spoke many languages fluently: Tsonga, Sotho, Afrikaans, English, French, and German. He was the author of many Tsonga books and the composer of many musical pieces. He belonged to that old school of missionaries who were strict, patriarchal, and dogmatic. He was the founder of many institutions of worship and education among the children of Ngungunyane—the Tsonga. I admired him deeply.

I was the president of the Christian Students' Association when the Reverend Mr. Jacques fell seriously ill. He was removed to the home of his sister, Mrs. Demitrius, who lived three miles from Lemana. I was already aware of his greatness when I went to see him in the last moments of his life.

It was not easy for me to visit in a white home. Black people are not expected to visit white people, and I felt uncomfortable going against custom.

There he lay, big and long, with a white sheet over his body. The imposing missionary, now prostrate and sick, reminded me, at that moment, of my father, who many years before lay sick and dying only three miles northeast of where I was standing, gazing at the dying Reverend Mr. Jacques. I saw him breathe and blink in the same manner I had seen sick people do at Molemole. He tried to speak to me, but his voice was too weak. He shook his head and smiled gently in a manner a father does at Molemole, blessing his wards before he dies.

Eduardo Mondlane saw him the day before, and the Reverend Mr. Jacques talked to him for a long time and commanded him to free Mozambique!

The Reverend Mr. Jacques was later flown to Switzerland, his home, where he was buried in the land of his fathers. His widow and three children remained to carry on with his good work amongst the children of Ngungunyane. He was succeeded as principal by Malan, an Afrikaner.

Shakespearean dramas captured my imagination in my second year of high school. The first play I acted in was *Julius Caesar*. The Reverend Mr. Jacques was already gone at the time of this performance, but his widow was there. She was sitting in the assembly hall when Sono ascended the platform as Brutus and exclaimed, "Hear me for my cause . . . If any one of you here would like to know why Brutus rose against Caesar, to you I say—"

And the audience roared: "None, Brutus, none!"

Sono continued. "Then none have I offended . . . Here comes his body, mourned by Mark Antony."

Then I entered the assembly hall through the side door, carrying a bench wrapped in a black blanket, in the way the people of Molemole wrapped coffins with hides for burials.

"I come to bury Caesar, not to praise him," I said, and Mrs. A. A. Jacques applauded me. Tears began to roll down my cheeks. "The noble Brutus has told you Caesar was ambitious. . . . But yesterday the word of Caesar might have stood against the world; now lies he there, and none to do him reverence. . . . It is good that you do not know that you are his heirs."

The audience roared again: "The will, we shall hear the will, Caesar's will. Read it, Antony."

"Shall I descend? Will you give me leave?" I said.

"Descend! Come down! The will! Read it!" the audience commanded.

"Before I read the will, let me show you the body of he who made the will."

At this point I noticed some members of the audience openly and unashamedly crying. And I said, "And now you perceive—"

Curtis Nkondo, who had been planted in the audience, rose from the back of the hall and said, "O piteous spectacle!"

"O noble Caesar!" cried Maboko, from the audience.

"O most bloody sight!" Rasengane cried out, while more members of the audience screamed.

Mahlabe and Mahlare shouted in the center of the hall simultaneously. "We shall avenge your death."

"Plunder, kill, burn. . . . Let not a traitor live," cried out Mtshetwene, Maboko, Nkondo, and Rasengane from the back, front, and sides of the hall.

At the play's end, Mrs. Jacques ascended the stage. She said to me, "Come home. Come to my house tomorrow with the members of the cast so that I may take your measurements and make costumes for your next performance of *Julius Caesar*." Mrs. Jacques, the widow of the late Reverend Mr. Jacques, was determined to promote goodwill between all races in a land torn by white supremacy.

"I wish the Reverend Mr. Jacques had been here with us this evening to witness your play," she said. "He would have been proud of you, your acting, your language, your English. It was beautiful. I am so happy. Perhaps you can stage the play again to raise funds for the erection of a church here at Lemana, a church in which all races can meet and worship and know God," she said.

"Yes, a mighty church in the memory of the Reverend Mr. Jacques," I said.

7

New Development

In the school library I opened the *Johannesburg Star*, an evening newspaper, and read about the massive mine strike. The Native Representative Council Chamber was reverberating with the news, and a call was made everywhere to boycott, strike, disobey civilly, and refuse to cooperate with the government of General Smuts so that national freedom could be achieved. Selope-Thema called for a protest against the government for breach of faith toward Africans, while Smuts stated that he was not unduly concerned, accusing the leaders of agitating and the strikers of having no legitimate grievances.

Newspapers carried stories of the growth of a squatter camp. It was reported that 25,000 Africans who had no houses in Johannesburg had simply built themselves a shantytown near Pimville and Albertynsville under the leadership of E. Khumalo. It was built on a bare, windswept, open space in the winter of 1946, immediately after the Second World War. In a forced eviction the shacks were destroyed, leaving the inhabitants exposed to the cold and the rain. A tornado swept away mothers, children, and grandmothers—babies screamed day and night while the storm raged.

The mine strike and growing unrest among other workers unnerved whites, who took steps to ensure not only their economic status but supremacy in all areas of life. The miners complained of poor wages and unhealthy working and living conditions. The Native Representative Council Chamber called on people everywhere to refuse to cooperate with the government of General Smuts. Smuts ordered out his military force. But the men gathered courage and revolted to break the shackles that bound them in the mining industry, even in the face of an army that shot them. Smuts's government was ousted in the elections, and the Nationalists came to power in 1948.

In spite of the good missionaries' endeavors at Lemana, several months after the performance of *Julius Caesar,* Fryer walked into our classroom and wrote an unfamiliar word on the blackboard: *apartheid,* a codified plan devised by the Afrikaners to separate one ethnic group from another in South Africa. "Apartheid," he said, "is a new word. It was coined last week by our leader, the Reverend Dr. D. F. Malan, the leader of our National Party of South Africa and the great pastor of the Dutch Reformed Church of South Africa. *Hoor julle?*—Do you hear?" he asked.

"That word sounds like some kind of hatred," blurted Curtis Nkondo from the back of the class.

"Apartheid was revealed to the Boers, the descendants of the illustrious Voortrekkers, last week in their national convention in Pretoria," Fryer said boldly. He erased the word from the blackboard and wrote it again in capital letters: "APARTHEID." Then he moved about six feet away from the board, stood looking at the word, and smiled proudly. "Apartheid," he said, "means kaffirs one side, coolies one side, Boersmans one side, whites one side. Do you understand? Dr. Malan says apartheid means the separation of races in South Africa in every material respect. Do I make myself clear, Martha and Collins? Apartheid means blacks one side, Asians one side, mixed race one side, and whites one side as of *now!*"

"Do your Boers and your Dr. Malan mean that the white people are to leave this country, and go back to Europe, leaving us Africans our land, South Africa?" I asked him.

"The white man goes nowhere," he said. "The white man is here to stay. The kaffirs must leave the cities, towns, and other white areas. They must return to their tribal areas to develop there. The white man must reside alone in the cities and towns, and on white farms. The white man is the boss. Don't forget that! The Asians and mixed race cannot live in the cities either. The white man will find a place for them. The cities and towns belong to the Europeans. Do you understand?" he frowned.

"Who will work for the white man if you chase away blacks from the cities, towns, and white farms?" I asked.

"Blacks will only be allowed to remain in cities and towns as migratory and temporary sojourners, yes, only as temporary visitors to come and sell their labor to the whites, and as soon as they are no longer required, they must return to their tribal homes in the reservations," Fryer said to the amazed class of black students.

"Where will the blacks live who work in the cities and towns for your people?" I asked mischievously.

The class burst out laughing, as the limping teacher tried to draw the new map of South Africa, showing where each racial group would live. Fryer was obviously upset by this. He told us blacks would live in areas twenty to thirty miles outside the white cities and travel by buses, trains, bicycles, and taxis to and from work. Black men would live separately from women and children in hostels erected for those who worked in the cities. "The men will go once a year to their tribal homes to see their wives, and to renew their permits to seek work in the cities or towns—if the whites still want them back," he said.

"But why are you doing all this? Why?" I asked.

"Our national survival is threatened. Multiracialism cannot be tolerated by the ruling National party under Dr. Malan. That is why! The government of Smuts fell. Thank God! Apartheid is the policy that we initiated this year, 1948, with the change of government. On September 15, 1948, Dr. H. F. Verwoerd said in Parliament: 'The ideal of total apartheid gives one something to aim at. We have said so clearly. Malan said so. Strydom said so, I have said it repeatedly, and I say it again, that the policy of apartheid constantly moves in the direction of ever-increasing separation. The ideal must be total separation in every sphere.' "

Every day Fryer tried to rationalize the policy of apartheid embarked upon by the new South African government. Finally, he asked me what I thought of it. I remember my answer, almost word for word: "Apartheid emphasizes the power of evil over good, inhumanity over humanity, death over life, despair over hope, irresponsibility over responsibility, hypocrisy over sincerity, immaturity over maturity, and selfishness over unselfishness."

Not all the teachers agreed with the new policy. Dr. Hershovitz, who was said to be Jewish, was my arithmetic teacher. He was short and hefty, and spoke English with a heavy accent. He had a theory about what he called the madness of the Boer political party, which ruled South Africa after the Second World War. According to him, the Boers were influenced by the Nazi party of Germany.

Among my black teachers at Lemana was J. L. Rammala, a tall, suave, scholarly man who spoke English as if it were his mother tongue, read and wrote Latin fluently, and was equally at home with mathematics, science, and history. Of all my teachers, J.L. was most responsible for the beginnings of my political awareness. He led me through the myriad paths of South African politics and its ramifications. "My boy, look here," he said. "Apartheid is segregation gone completely mad. Whom God would destroy He first sends mad. Let it be so with the Boers."

The same week I first heard the word *apartheid*, I took the chair as president of the debating society and presided over a debate on whether apartheid is better than integration in South Africa. In a brief statement from the chair I made my position clear and issued a warning to the new generation of boys and girls to unite with all fellow South Africans to live as brothers, or perish as fools.

The debate was attended by students, black and white teachers, nurses, missionaries, people from Elim and neighboring villages. The assembly hall was full to capacity. Fryer sat in the audience making gestures and faces, shaking his head to indicate displeasure as one speaker after another condemned apartheid. At last, Eduardo Mondlane rose and took the floor amid deafening cheers. The man from Gazaland, the land of Ngungunyane, cleared his throat and walked up to the platform. He looked at me and said: "Mr. Chairman, ladies and gentlemen. I come from Mozambique. I come from the land where for five hundred years the Portuguese have brutalized our people. I thought it might be different here in South Africa."

He wiped his forehead with his handkerchief and continued. He called for a society where the majority would be motivated by a strong sense of justice, while the minority could feel secure. He argued: "The salvation of the whites does not lie in the preservation of white privilege but in equal sharing with their fellow men. For I know of no system that guarantees white national suicide better than the policy of apartheid as applied by this government of South Africa, the government of Dr. D. F. Malan."

He paused, and as soon as the applause died down, he went on. "South Africa, it is becoming clear to me, needs to embark on a new course of action if the perilous path of racial confrontation is to be avoided." Looking upward, he called on the past rulers of Africa—Gaza, Ngungunyane, Tšhaka, Dingane, Moshoeshoe, Sekhukhune, Khama, Moroka, Sobhuza, and Kgwadu—to deliver the Africans from apartheid. Then he sat down, while the black audience rose to its feet in hysterical applause. The whites sat silent.

Somewhere in the back of the room someone started singing the African national anthem, *"Nkosi Sikelel' i-Afrika"* (God Bless Africa). I saw Fryer storm out of the hall. By then, another song was in the air:

> *The enemy of the black man is the pass!*
> *The enemy of the black man is the pass!*
> *The enemy of the black man is the pass!*
> *Come back, Africa!*
> *What have we done, we Africans?*
> *Let passes be abolished!*

SOWETO, MY LOVE

> *Let our freedom come!*
> *Come back, Africa!*

The song was heard everywhere in the assembly, throughout the institution, and outside in the dark along the road. The students sang like soldiers on the march, until the voices faded as they returned to their dormitories.

A new generation infested with discontent and desire for political action was born. A new black nationalism was vigorously speaking out, attacking the African National Congress (ANC) as compromisers of the black cause. As I lay awake that night on my hard iron bed, Mondlane tiptoed over to me, and we left the dormitory to talk.

"Tell me something. Are your parents, brothers and sisters truly illiterate people?" he asked.

"Why?" I asked.

He explained that his father, mother, brothers, and sisters had never been educated in any white man's school and were scorned. Even his father, who was their chief, was called a "heathen," and Mondlane felt ashamed of them. "I never wanted anyone to know that I came from a despised home, despised mother and father, sisters and brothers. But from this night on, I will never again be afraid of who I am. I am what I am. So are my family. They are what they are. They are the pride of my life. Now I will live at peace with myself. I felt I must tell you this before I sleep because it was only when you mentioned from the chair in the debate that you were proud of your illiterate mother, father, sisters, and brothers, that I felt a new awakening and rebirth within me. I then realized who I was. I still cannot explain what happened within me, but I know I am free now from the chains of fear that have bound me ever since the Christians made me believe that I was a worthless, despicable heathen," Mondlane said.

I, too, felt a moment of self-realization, of perfect peace with myself. I saw myself as I looked at Mondlane. Part of me was big, strong, black, and proud, as I was at Molemole in the presence of my peers, dancing, singing, playing, hunting,

NEW DEVELOPMENT

and developing into a man and a valued member of my tribe. I saw the daughters of Molemole standing before me, and bubbling with life and desire, and I shook my head in disbelief when I saw my other self: a scared, miserable, wretched, despised heathen, unable even to take my respectful place in the presence of Christian students. The moonlight continued to shine on the face of Mondlane. For the first time I realized that the Christians of Khurukhutšhu had dwarfed my image, and reduced me and my people to "heathen kaffirs."

I heard a fox howl in the valley below and the flap of wings as an owl flew out of a tree nearby. Mondlane coughed and spoke words which I could not at that time understand—*"Shikwembu shi no matimba,"* which was a Tsonga way of saying "God is omnipotent."

Since apartheid, strict pass laws had gone into effect, and changes were taking place all over South Africa. No African was permitted to enter urban areas and remain for more than seventy-two hours without a pass. All Africans were barred from towns except those born in urban areas or those who had worked for the same employer for ten years or more or who had lived in the area for at least fifteen years. Children under the age of sixteen needed a permit to live with their fathers in urban areas. If they entered without a permit, their parents could be arrested, and fined, and the children deported to the tribal reserves. Blacks could not work without a pass. They first had to go to the native commissioner to apply for a pass permitting them to travel to the urban area to seek work. If the commissioner refused to grant them the pass to seek work, they could not go. If they went anyway, they could be arrested and deported. Even those who merely wished to visit had to have a pass which stated how long they could stay. If you overstayed you could go to jail. If you lost your pass or failed to have it with you at all times, you could be arrested. Not only had the white man taken our land and our wealth but now he was controlling our movements in the land.

We would soon see our hope for change in our more promising students. Mondlane, for example, was expected to become a great religious leader. His utter honesty and unselfish devotion to duty, his careful and conscientious work, his tireless quest of truth and justice, his complete lack of any kind of treachery, his piousness, his brilliance—all combined to make him a fine, fearless, and outstanding student with a potential in world leadership. His qualities were the envy of those of us who acknowledged his intellectual superiority. As I look back, I cannot recollect him offering a single harsh or unkind criticism of anybody. He made allowances for frailty in others which he did not tolerate in himself. He had a clear vision for a free Mozambique, but circumstances at home made it clear we had a long distance to travel in South Africa.

The only letter I received from my mother while I was at Lemana came a day after my talk with Mondlane. She had dictated it to my former teacher, Mabitsela, because she could not write. In the letter, she asked me to tell her where a place called Bethal was located in South Africa, "where they say white farmers make our children to eat human excrement, feces." The language and handwriting were clear, but the contents of the letter puzzled me. It continued, "A farmer from Bethal was here at Molemole to steal my sister's son, Matlela. Matlela is gone. He was taken into slavery. His mother and I cry. Day and night. Write quick and tell me where Bethal is."

Mahlangu was a student teacher from Bethal, some two hundred miles southeast of Molemole, where white farmers had large farms on which they cultivated potatoes, peanuts, beans, and corn. I immediately went to ask him what he knew.

"It is true," he said. "The white farmers do enslave black workers in Bethal. It began long before I was born. Long before my father was born. They steal them from all over the country, even from Swaziland."

"My cousin is there," I said.

He told me if my cousin was there he must be in extreme danger if he was lucky enough to still be alive. Mahlangu said they were given garbage to eat, and occasionally a little por-

NEW DEVELOPMENT

ridge, but never enough. They slept on dirt or rough cement floors, with tattered sack to cover them. At 3:00 A.M., they were awakened and taken to work in the fields. Each man was given a row on which to work—planting or harvesting or hoeing, bending their backs for hours. Any man who tried to straighten up as he worked his row was whipped on his back. Any slave who dropped from exhaustion or hunger was whipped until he got up. They were made to work from dawn until after sunset. If, while they toiled, they appealed for mercy, water, or rest, they got whipped. "I grew up in slavery myself, like my father. My father died in slavery during Hitler's war. We buried him on the farm where I grew up. We wrapped his body in sacks and buried it," he said, almost without emotion.

"But don't the slaves ever escape?" I asked.

Mahlangu said many had tried, but the farmers always caught them and brought them back. Many were flogged to death; some were lynched from trees by their feet or their necks. Some were killed by pouring boiling water into their mouths. The corpses were used to fertilize the fields, like cattle manure. "There is no peace in my soul. Because of this, I cannot sleep. I have nightmares. I see hanging corpses all over this room, including the corpse of my father," Mahlangu said.

That evening I promised my mother in a letter that I would never rest until I had found Matlela. For twenty-one years I searched high and low, until I found him on a rich potato farm at Bethal, Transvaal, where he had been enslaved all those years. I carried him away and watched my mother smile with joy as she beheld her sister's son alighting from my car. His own mother was already gone to the world where the Everlasting Presences have gone to lie with other ancestors beneath the soil.

School vacations were twice a year. The months of June and July were our winter vacation, and November and December, our summer vacation. I spent them with my mother and sisters at Molemole. They looked at me with pride as I returned to the village for these long visits. They never had the slightest idea of what I was studying, yet they encouraged me to continue.

When it was time to return to Lemana after the vacations, they provided me with the little they had—corn porridge and wild vegetables. In the summer months, I would sometimes be given green peanuts and beans for the road. I was always touched by their gesture. Sugarcane and small watermelons were at times added to my provision basket. What remained of the provisions was shared with my roommates in the dormitory. I had learned from our saying "Children of one man share a grasshopper's head!" For the children of Kgwadu and Maimela, where I grew up, this was their way of saying: "Share the little that you have with others because, among other things, food is considered the dirt of teeth." We would sit in our dormitory on our return from vacation and eat all kinds of foods from many homes as more students arrived to share what each had brought.

Each month while I was at Lemana, I succeeded in getting a ride to the Bandolierkop train station, thirty miles west of Lemana, to meet my youngest sister, Manthibi Moratwa, who walked twenty miles to meet me. Sometimes she arrived before me, and I would find her sitting under a tree, tired from the long walk. My mother could not afford to give me pocket money to purchase food, and she and my sisters wanted me to stay at school. So, once every month, my sister came to bring me the additional food that I needed.

Four miles from Lemana was a farm, Sweetwaters, owned by a wealthy white dairy farmer named Heuning. He sent milk to the Bandolierkop station daily. Heuning, tall and robust, had the Boer arrogance of a true slave owner, which may be surprising when one considers that he lived near a mission station. He hated the English language and liked to be addressed in either Afrikaans or Tsonga, the local African language. I would go to his farm and beg him for a ride to Bandolierkop. "I am asking for a ride in the dairy truck for Saturday." He

NEW DEVELOPMENT

would walk away and ignore me. Suddenly, he would stop and shout, "All right."

One day my mother sent me twenty-five cents through Maupi Makgamatha, a friend and fellow student from Molemole. "Your mother said I should give you this money to buy what you need." Maupi smilingly placed a brand-new twenty-five-cent piece in my hand.

"Poor Mother, she must have sold everything she owned to raise so much money," I told him. That was the first and last pocket money my mother ever sent me in five years at Lemana. I opened a savings account with it and kept it in the bank until I got married. A rare gift I shall always remember to the end of my days.

It was hard to live and study at Lemana without pocket money. Even with what my sister brought me, food was not always sufficient. Those who had pocket money supplemented their scanty diet with local food purchases, but very often I left the dining hall still desperately hungry. Occasionally a friend would help me out by giving me what he had. So it went, until one day when Molatelo Ramusi, my guardian angel, sent me a small box camera. Students wanted to be photographed, and they paid me to do it. I used the money to provide myself with food. I even managed to purchase shirts and other things I needed. I no longer needed my sister to walk long miles to Bandolierkop to bring me food. I could even buy for my sweetheart, Maphala.

I bought wood for myself to make furniture, which I wanted to take to my mother's hut. But I found I was not permitted to use the school's workshop. Only student teachers had that privilege. I wanted the furniture desperately, so I crept into the workshop in the dead of night, every night, until I was caught and severely reprimanded. But my punishment—to make four chairs and a table out of mahogany wood—was served with smiles all over my face. Months later I smiled even more when I was permitted to take the furniture home, including the pieces I had made in the night. I felt good when Christians of Khurukhutšhu came and saw the furniture in my mother's hut. My sister Manthibi Moratwa smiled, and my sister Mokgadi giggled, while Mother silently watched with deep joy. I beamed and was setting the table to serve some of my fellow students, who had come to visit me at home, when Khaola entered the hut. He looked at me and looked at my sisters. He gazed at the cups, saucers, teaspoons, sugar, teapot, and bread on the mahogany table and shook his big, woolly white-haired head and said, "Mafefo! Mafefo! Even you, Mafa Molapatene? Even you, the seed of the Babirwa clan, you son of Mothibi, have you joined the cursed seed, the nothing-of-nothings who eat behind closed doors?"

Then Khaola, fuming with rage, rushed at the laid table and overturned it, smashing cups, saucers, teapot, and all the chinaware. Before he left the hut, he looked at the puzzled guests and said, "Now even the seed of Mothibi-a-Ramathathe is finished. Mafaufau! These Mafamolebe have corrupted the youth of Molemole. Tsherane's land is dead! Molemole must weep in pain for the lost sons and daughters of Maimela." As he bent his towering body to get out of the hut, he said, "Cry, Molemole! Cry!"

He stood outside our kitchen hut and cursed all the Christians of Khurukhutšhu and their Lutheran church, until his eyes became red like fire. He only stopped cursing when his aged voice began to fail. He spat on the ground, pounded the floor, spat again, and pointed a finger at the Khurukhutšhu Mission Station with a threatening look on his face. Then he slowly walked toward the Mabjanene Mountains to speak to the spirits of the ancestors, as was his custom whenever he was greatly disturbed by anything that undermined the culture, traditions, and customs of the Batlokwa people, of which he saw himself as the custodian.

The next day in the village I was scared to death when a cousin suggested that I was bewitched. She said she thought this because whenever she saw me, I was always reading a book. The other girls of Ranhlokana, however, were always happy to see me during school vacations. Sedima smiled and teased me. "I hear you are now a black European. You speak

NEW DEVELOPMENT

English. Do you still know me?" she asked. My youthful answer was to chase her around and around her mother's hut, like a cat after a mouse.

My sensitivity to the conditions of the tribe had sharpened by the time I came back to Molemole on my winter school vacation in 1949. The tribe needed a school, I felt, under Chief Machaka, the ruler of the Batlokwa of Molemole. So I organized a meeting at the royal kraal with other students and teachers, the members of the Batlokwa Students' Association, and we persuaded the chief and the tribe that a school had to be built.

Many men spoke. "The school will bring white people to this tribe. We do not want them here. They have taken our land. They will take our children from us, too," said one of the old villagers.

"Times have changed. Education is the key for the future," said a man who had many children at school.

I stood up and looked at the gathering and said, "I am one of the sons of this land whom you sent to boarding school far, far away to the land of Ngungunyane. Now I am back! Many of the children of Molemole are at boarding schools in this country. You are spending money; selling your precious cows, oxen, bulls, sheep, goats, fowls, beans, maize, corn, millet, peanuts, eggs, and whatever, to raise money to educate them. Why? Can one of you tell me why you are sending so many children far away to be educated outside this tribe?"

"I think he speaks wisely. He speaks the truth. Yes, answer him! Someone must answer this man," said Headman Makaepea.

"How can a schoolboy speak truth? He is still a child. Let him go away. Let him go back to Lemana," shouted Headman V. P. Manthata.

Then Chief Machaka said, "Batlokwa, some of you must be careful what you say when you speak in this meeting. This meeting is for everybody. Everyone speaks here. Everyone is a man here. Men from the Bodika school! Any man who refers to another as a boy here will be fined. A heavy fine. Do not forget that our fathers taught us that in a public meeting every man can speak until the sun sets in the west. If we need time to speak, we shall have it."

Despite this warning by Chief Machaka, the paramount ruler of the children of Tšhaka-Maimela at Molemole, Headman Manthata stood up and said: "Batlokwa, Chief Machaka is looking for trouble. This boy is dangerous! Our paramount chief is causing big, big trouble by allowing these schoolboys to address tribal meetings in this royal kraal. These boys must go to school, and leave this tribe alone. I am one of the headmen of this tribe. I warn this tribe—do not allow this boy to speak any longer. He is dangerous! He must go back to Lemana."

Manthata was a junior headman under Chief Machaka. The tribe always complained that he did not want to see the people progressing like himself. He did everything in his power to obstruct the efforts of those who tried to help Chief Machaka in developing schools and other modern projects.

Chief Kgarahara Machaka rose to his feet again, furious and stern, and said, "This is not a white man's meeting, white men who close people's mouths when people wish to speak. If we do not finish speaking on this matter today, we can come back tomorrow and speak and speak and speak until we are tired. White men, like you, Manthata, have no concept of freedom of speech. They even arrest people for speaking," declared the royal tiger of Mabjanene.

Chief Machaka was still speaking when Manthata again stood up to insist that I leave the meeting.

I said, "It is true that I am a man. You all know that I am a man. It is also true that the Christians and whites say we are boys. This is not a meeting of Christians and whites. It is a meeting of men of the tribe of Puledi Masenyane and Maimela. I respect Headman Manthata. I am a graduate of the school he built in his village—Manthata School. He should speak like a man of the age-group and regiment of Mankwe-a-Morwakgwadu—the age-group to which he belongs.

"Today I wish to tell this tribe what education means to me.

NEW DEVELOPMENT

I mean the education I am receiving at high school. It means hope and brotherly love, responsibility and unselfishness, sensitivity to the plight of our people, sincerity, optimism, upliftment of one's fellow men. Education means liberation from oppression, life and not death. Patriotism!" I said. Fists, clubs, knobkerries, and other walking sticks were waved in the air, clearly demonstrating the tribe's desire to build the royal school.

Sebitšo Mahlako, one of the chief's righthand men, requested that the chief announce the tribe's decision on the royal school of Batlokwa.

"Speak, Tiger," he said. "Speak, you the multicolored tiger of Molemole and Mabjanene! Speak, give us the law! Give us the school! Speak, Moleya; speak, Nkwe Maimela; roar, and speak. The people have spoken; your children cry for schools, and food and life! Ruler of our men, speak! Your children will hear!"

Monyemangene rose, looking very, very angry, and he said, "There can't be two bulls in one kraal. Batlokwa, you all know that Manthata is not the chief of this tribe. The blood of Puledi Masenyane and of Kgwadu-a-bo-Madibatwana is chief of this soil. Let the owner of this land and people speak!"

Monyemangene was one of the most senior and strong headmen under Chief Machaka. He challenged Headman Manthata to walk out of the meeting himself, rather than try to stop the educational progress of the tribe. Before I returned to school, the tribe was already gathering stones for a foundation for the proposed school building.

The first weekend after I returned to Lemana, I received a long and important letter from Eduardo Mondlane, who was now studying in Johannesburg, at the Jan H. Hofmeyr School of Social Work. He told me a great deal about the school, its teachers, and students. He also enclosed the handbook of the school and invited me to apply for admission. I did so after consulting with my teacher and friend J. L. Rammala, who explained to me what social work was all about: "A profession of men and women who comfort and care for the sick, the crippled, the incarcerated, the troubled, the dying—a profession of those who are truly their brothers' keepers."

Later that year I received a letter from Mozambique. It was written by Mondlane.

Dear Collins,

This is to let you know that I am here at Gaza, Mozambique. I am writing in my mother's hut. The smoke stings my eyes as it blows into them. I was deported by the South African government.

They deported me from the University of the Witwatersrand, where I had transferred from the Jan Hofmeyr School of Social Work. They arrested me at the university like a criminal, handcuffed and kicked me like a dog, called me names. Even insulted me by my mother's private parts.

They accused me of being a foreign native who was trying to pollute the minds of Mozambicans living in South Africa. When I questioned them further, they told me that they did not wish to have any black students from outside South Africa studying in their universities.

My heart is sore. I wanted to complete my social science studies at the University of the Witwatersrand before coming home to free my people from Portuguese rule.

When I arrived in Mozambique, I was arrested and interrogated. They continue to harass me. I wanted to see you before I left to urge you to study social science before anything else. It was painful to go without having seen you and spoken to you, man to man, as we did at Lemana, about our future, the future of South Africa and of Mozambique. But it was impossible. I was bundled up and thrown out. They cursed the man who fathered me, and his father, chiefs in the land of Gaza and Ngungunyane. They even cursed the Swiss Mission church that brought me over to South Africa, calling them devils, kaffir lovers, Communists. I simply looked at them in disbelief and accepted my fate, knowing,

NEW DEVELOPMENT

however, that God is not dead, and that their days are numbered, both here and there. I intend to go to Lisbon to study social science there. If God wills, I will proceed to the United States of America for advanced studies. Whatever you do, study social science first. Someday, somewhere, we shall meet in this or the next world to come.

The struggle continues.

Yours,
Eduardo

8
City of Gold

Mother sipped water from a calabash, rolled it in her round cheeks, splashed it into the air, and chanted incantations to the spirits of our Living Dead, the Eternal Presences, my great-grandfather, Moshweu, and his son, Moraba, my grandfather. She spoke to her father, Moraka Matsapola, and to my father, Mothibi. I was going from my tribe to the city of gold, Johannesburg, after finishing at Lemana in 1949. My sister Mokgadi handed me my provision basket. It was full of food for the road—chicken, wild greens, sorghum porridge, ground nuts, and beans.

As I walked toward the red truck that would take me to the Pietersburg train station, I heard my mother say, "May his roads be opened. May he arrive in Johannesburg safely, and return in peace. May he grow, and grow, and grow, like an elephant, O Mothibi, my children's father." Then more libations followed from my sisters and my father's second wife, Ngwakwana-a-Machethe.

As I climbed into the back of the truck, which was heavily loaded with cornmeal bags, my father's sister began to ululate as my people do when warriors leave for battles in faraway places. The whole village reverberated with voices as the ten-ton truck roared and lurched forward. Within one hour I was at Pietersburg town, about forty miles south of Molemole, to board the train that would take me to Johannesburg to study the profession of angels—social work.

It was always exciting for a young tribal man in South Africa to travel to Johannesburg. I was dressed to kill: green shirt, Churchill hat stuffed with a rim of paper because it was too big for my head, dark brown shoes, and a khaki tie. I must have looked like a perfect yokel.

I watched the long sooty train roll into the quiet Pietersburg Station from Messina, the northern copper town that lies on the banks of the crocodile-infested Limpopo River. It was seven o'clock in the morning. The sun was bright, the air still. The train was packed with men from many lands on their way to the mines of gold and death. They came from Mozambique, northern Rhodesia, Nyasaland, southern Rhodesia, and the northern Transvaal. Hundreds of them! There were women, too, traveling to their men in the cities to get pregnant and then return to their reservations. Women in multicolored headdresses from Vendaland. Women from the land of Gaza wore their traditional beaded skirts, which made their thighs appear swollen with desire, while the Batlhaloha women mingled freely with them in their traditional red and green dresses, which made them look like butterflies.

More men from the tribal reservations in the northern Transvaal joined the train at Pietersburg Station, where cheap black labor was obtained by the gigantic gold mines and manufacturing industries for the building of a strong South African economy.

Our first stop was at Mokopane, Potgietersrus, in the land of Matebele-Makwankwane-a-hloka-kgomo-a-dja-motho-bana-ba-Mamolalela-ka-lewa, the ferocious Mandebele, Mzilikazi's remnants from the land of Phunga and Mageba, the children of King Shaka, the scion of Senzangakhona. They had remained in this area when Mzilikazi and his mighty impi traversed southern Africa from Zululand to the empire of Changamire in search of peace of mind and life itself. Matebele-Makwankwane were mighty warriors who killed in rivers, in caves, and on mountaintops, devourers of men and beasts alike. Mzilikazi and his Matabele followers mauled and demolished whoever stood in their way until they reached and settled in Zimbabwe, leaving some of their descendants at Mokopane in the northern Transvaal.

The white conductor waved the green flag and called out to

the dozens of lean men and women who were boarding the train at Mokopane Station: "All aboard! Naboomspruit, Nylstroom, Warmbaths, Hammanskraal, Pretoria, Germiston, Johannesburg!" Bony men and women in tattered clothes climbed into the already packed train. Poverty and hunger were etched on every face. The soot and smoke flew into the third-class coaches where the black passengers were packed. The white passengers sat comfortably in first-class compartments at the back of the long train, where no soot from the engine reached their eyes.

With me in my compartment was Hamilton Maitša, an official mine escort from my tribe. He traveled with mine workers, taking them to the mines three times a week from the Soekmekaar Recruiting Depot to Johannesburg. He was a short, heavyset, bright-eyed, pitch-black worker, employed since 1936 by the Witwatersrand Native Labor Association. From him I learned many things during the journey.

Maitša pointed out Deputy Prime Minister J. G. Strydom's house. I was now in the town of the man who used to roar at his audiences wherever he addressed political meetings: "*Waar staan ek nou*—Where am I standing now?"

"You are standing on the platform," the audience responded.

"No, no, no! *Nee-ek staan op die nek van die kaffers*—I am standing on the necks of the kaffirs," Strydom would say, amid deafening cheers and clapping of the white members of his Nationalist party.

We stopped at Pretoria, the home of apartheid, unjust laws, segregation, oppression, and minority white rule. I thought of Malema, that handsome son of our tribe, who had slipped into the furious ISCOR furnace five years before.

Suddenly Maitša called out, "Look, look there! On the left, on the hill! There is General Smuts's home. Very, very big! Look at those fat oxen and bulls!"

"Does he really live here all the time?" I asked.

"The old fox lives everywhere. In Pretoria, in Johannesburg, in Cape Town, and in heaven. One day he may live in hell!"

Maitša stood up and appeared to be very disturbed. I asked him if there was something wrong. He said he was always troubled when he passed Smuts's farm. "I can never forget the bloody massacre of our people who fattened the vultures at Bulhoek. Smuts not only killed our people in Bulhoek, he killed them also in southwest Africa, the Bondelswarts. He killed them like dogs for dog tax; over one hundred men, women, and children slaughtered! Smuts sent a force of four hundred men armed with machine guns and bombing planes to slaughter our people there. He mutilated their bodies. Hundreds more were injured. Smuts! He fed birds with the flesh of our race!"

Soon we entered the luxurious Witwatersrand reef area, where gold lies buried in the bowels of the earth. The land was rolling and green. Houses increased like mushrooms everywhere, and I began to realize my dream—I was about to enter Johannesburg.

From the train window I saw streets filling up with people. On each side of the tracks black men worked with picks and shovels, hammers and chisels, breaking rock to build railway lines and the road. They sang to make their task seem lighter, while fat white men stood by, hands on hips, gesturing and pointing and screaming in Fanakalo and Zulu, *"Thatha-lapha-beka-lapha,"* which means "take from here and put there." So many black faces! I began to think that the city of Johannesburg was perhaps the city of black faces and gold. But this was not yet Johannesburg, it was Germiston.

The train rolled into the Johannesburg station at 5:30 P.M. There I expected to be met by Dr. Ray E. Phillips, the white American missionary-sociologist who headed the Jan H. Hofmeyr School of Social Work. But he was nowhere to be seen. I pushed my way through the milling black crowds on the platform. Thousands of our people going home from work swarmed like bees into congested trains.

Everywhere there were signs saying: FOR WHITES ONLY, FOR NONWHITES ONLY. Apartheid everywhere; segregated platforms, segregated benches, segregated coaches, segregated subways, segregated telephone booths. Everywhere symbols of oppression loomed as grotesque images of racial hatred. I was stunned by the naked expression of the white man's hatred for his fellow man and his air of superiority. So this was Johannesburg, the Johannesburg I had longed to see for all these years! The biggest and richest city ever built in South Africa!

I felt a different kind of tension than I had known before. I asked the way to Eloff Street. I thought I could get a streetcar or a bus from there to the Bantu Men's Social Center. There was none. As I waited on Eloff Street, streetcars screeched by over steel tracks; buses passed bearing WHITES ONLY signs. Slowly I realized that no bus or streetcar was going to stop to pick me up. Every vehicle bore signs that said WHITES ONLY.

Throngs of black men and women walked past speaking different languages, many with eyes looking strained and desperate. A rickshaw came. It stopped in front of me. It was drawn by a heavyset black man, strong, colorful, and witty. This was the first time I saw a rickshaw. I could not bring myself to ride in a vehicle drawn by a human being. What is it that reduces men to the level of beasts of burden? Drivers in cars blew their horns and went their way. A fat white man hopped onto the rickshaw, and it moved on. I forced myself to move southward along Eloff Street.

What would happen to me here? Would I make it in Johannesburg? I remembered the many warm people I had left behind in the land of Tšhaka-Maimela. Oh, how I missed them! Yet, as I walked along Eloff Street, I thought I had never seen such a beautiful city. The center of the city seemed like a golden valley. The clothes in the display windows looked like attire for angels, the food, fit for the gods. The skyscrapers enchanted me. I stood at the corners of the streets and gazed at them while time and passersby went on.

Finally I arrived at the Bantu Men's Social Center, built by American philanthropists for blacks in the heart of Johannesburg. Our people passed their leisure time here day in and day out enjoying billiards, table tennis, jiving, volleyball, basketball, chess, ballroom dancing, music, boxing, and other cultural activities. Educational, religious, social, and political conferences sponsored by various black organizations were often held here and were attended by anyone, irrespective of color or race.

I was assigned to one of the three guest rooms, which I shared with two other first-year students. There was a bed with a comfortable mattress, a writing table, and a chair for each of us. For the first time I lived on premises with hot and cold water.

I was still sleeping the next morning when my old classmate from Lemana days, Edward Fyfe Sono, knocked hard on the door of my peaceful small room. We embraced each other warmly.

"I thought I was lost," I said. "Molemole is far from here. How is your family? Are you teaching already?" Sono responded that his family was well, and he would show me his school as he showed me Johannesburg and Sophiatown. I followed Sono, gazing at everything as we went. Huge streetcars appeared and stopped in front of a skyscraper. I was amazed at how vast things were in Johannesburg. Then I said to myself, Son of Mothibi, this is not your place. You will not be happy in this place. I felt apprehensive.

Sono looked at me as if he had heard my thoughts. "I was born in this city," he said. It was built with the sweat and brawn of black men who have no rights of citizenship. It was a city of golden streets for the white man, and of alleys, sorrow, death, police brutalities, and passes for blacks who could not ride these streetcars or buses. They could not live in any of the skyscrapers or own a business in any part of this city. The white man said it was against his law, the unjust law passed by the white parliament, a governing body in which no black man had a voice or a vote. But Sono predicted that the day would come when the tables would turn and South Africa would return to its lawful owners—the true sons and daughters of Africa.

We passed the Anglo-American Corporation Building. The one opposite it was the Magistrate's Court, where thousands of our people were tried daily for pass offenses and other infractions. Here our people suffered, were sentenced to work for cruel farmers after being convicted of nothing—or of crimes they did not commit. They were loaded into huge trucks, which went as far as the Bethal area, Middelburg, and Rustenburg, where they were unloaded to work on white farms, on which many of them died and were buried.

I asked if the Anglo-American Corporation owned many diamonds, much gold, iron, platinum, and other kinds of minerals. Sono said the company exploited our black people, who dug the minerals in the bowels of the earth.

Sono stopped on Market Street. "Look," he said. "This is the Office of the African National Congress, and that is the office of the Transvaal Indian Congress over there!" I wondered if Dr. A. B. Xuma was in, but Sono said he was no longer in office. Sono told me that Dr. Xuma had been dropped from the presidency of the ANC the month before I arrived. After ten years of leadership, he had been replaced by Dr. J. S. Moroka, who lived in Sophiatown, near Sono's home. We boarded the PUTCO bus on Diagonal Street and headed for Western Native Township.

After twenty minutes, we arrived at the fenced-in ghetto for black people, a city within a city, a city of revolutions, of vast uprisings, and cruel exploitation. This area had been a bastion of defiance against the colonial invaders since the 1880s, when the white man discovered gold in Johannesburg. Africans lived in identical three-room houses, consisting of kitchen, bedroom, and living room, erected by the municipality of Johannesburg. All Africans were tenants of the municipality, never owners of the houses. There was no electricity or plumbing. Cold water was drawn for use in the house from a water tap installed on the wall of the outhouse. Here the Sonos lived, a family of ten persons, all in this depressing matchbox house. In these unplastered and unheated structures, children were born and grew up.

Sono had been to my house in Ranhlokana, and I had looked forward to the day when I would meet his family. His mother was friendly, and so were his brothers and sister, Florence.

Sono's mother explained the facts of life for black people in Johannesburg. I listened and felt as if I were back home, at Molemole, in the land of Tšhaka-Maimela, listening to the good storytellers of Mabjanene. Sono's mother spoke to me about our leaders, who lived in Western Native Township and Sophiatown. "The fight is on, my child," said the daughter of Hlong-wane, Sono's mother, referring to well-known African leaders. "Even Dr. A. B. Xuma lives here, my son."

Sono showed me his small vegetable garden in the backyard, and I asked him when we would see Dr. Xuma's house. I hoped we might see Dr. Xuma, too. I wanted to see the man who had led our people throughout the last ten years of struggle. Sophiatown was nearby. Sono explained that Dr. Xuma had been dropped from the presidency of the ANC because he had no practical program of action for dealing with the white rulers of South Africa, and because he had said "Please, please, please" to the white man far too long. Sono told me Dr. Xuma had been ousted by the younger generation of leaders, the youth leaguers, who worked hard within the African National Congress for more progress. "They threw him out: A. P. Mda, Walter Sisulu! The spirit of Lembede lives on!" Sono exclaimed. He sounded as though he was one of those who had worked for the ousting of the American-trained medical man.

I asked Sono about Dr. Moroka, the new president of the ANC. Sono said he didn't know him personally but those who knew Dr. Moroka well said that he was too soft on whites, that he was a great friend of white people, and that he had many white patients at his surgery—you know, of course, that he is a medical doctor. In short, he was a black moderate of the old guard, who wasn't going to be too useful for our cause.

Sophiatown was a gilded ghetto of upper-middle-class moneyed Africans, Coloreds, Indians, Chinese, Japanese, and Malays. It was a predominantly black suburb five miles within the boundary of the city of Johannesburg, situated opposite the hostile white suburbs of Newlands and Westdene, where the Afrikaners lived. Here in this budding, black, bourgeois home of different racial groups, Dr. A. B. Xuma lived with his

American-born black wife, Madi Hall Xuma. The homeowning community consisted of teachers, businessmen, doctors, traders, nurses, factory workers, and laborers. It was here in Sophiatown that our people built beautiful homes on land of their own choice, purchased at a time when Africans and other nonwhites could still buy land. Our people lived here in the dignity of their souls. They had begun to regard themselves as an integral part of the developing middle-class society, a suburban people led by men such as Dr. Xuma, Cachalia, S. Letlalo, Mabuza, and others.

In the midst of elegant houses, the symbols of urban pride and permanency, stood Dr. Xuma's home. Massive, colorful, majestic, and valuable in every sense, it was a palatial home among other luxurious African homes built out of our people's desire to live and develop in Johannesburg. I could not believe my ears as Sono told me that the South African government was anxious to demolish these fine homes on the ground that Sophiatown had become a "black spot" in a white area, and consequently had to be wiped out. Every time our people developed an area in or near white areas, even if our people were there before the whites came to build their cities and towns, the white regime would force our people to move. The government moved in troops and bulldozers to dump our people miles away in undesirable and undeveloped areas while the white people took over our land and the area we called home.

I could feel the tension in Johannesburg, brewing like a mighty caldron about to pour out its burning contents and engulf everything in its pathway. An uneasy feeling gnawed at me as I walked through the valley of skyscrapers. The violence and rumbling anger was barely audible—like thunder in a distant storm approaching.

Part Two

The Turbulent Years

9

Profession of Angels

As I prepared to leave my village for Johannesburg, there was much concern and uncertainty expressed about my chosen profession. Back there, the youths of Molemole who aspired to professional training ordinarily became teachers, preachers, or agricultural officers—not social workers. My oldest brother, Moraba, was very strongly opposed to my choice. Fortunately for me, my guardian angel, Molatelo Ramusi, did not stand in my way; he agreed to furnish me with pocket money and material needs.

When I arrived at the Jan H. Hofmeyr School of Social Work on their scholarship, I found that they had a fund for students in need. I was given a few pounds at the end of each month to buy clothes, books, and toiletries, and the school was part of the Bantu Men's Social Center. Dr. Ray E. Phillips was the director and founder. He was a stocky white man with a massive bald head, a theologian and sociologist from Yale University, and the author of many books on South Africa which dealt with the sufferings and plight of the urban black people of our country. The school drew its staff of fifteen white teachers and one black teacher mainly from the University of the Witwatersrand. Most other full-time staff members were liberal whites who came to work at the school because they admired and supported Dr. Phillips, the missionary-sociologist of the American Board of Missions.

The students came from as far away as Zimbabwe, Zambia, Namibia, Botswana, Swaziland, Mozambique, Lesotho, and the whole of southern Africa. The school also admitted coloreds and Indians. The only racial group barred from the school was whites—South Africa's racial laws forbade any mixture between blacks and whites in schools. Joshua Nkomo, Winnie Mandela, Eduardo Mondlane, and other internationally renowned leaders are among its graduates. Here I would spend three full years training as a social worker.

I met people from various tribal reservations from outside South Africa as well as within who were fascinated as I was by Western culture. What at times disgusted me about some of my fellow students was the way in which they denied their own cultural backgrounds and languages because they felt inferior to other nationalities. I, however, was proud of my tribe at Molemole, my cultural heritage, my language. I wanted the whole school to be aware of my background and felt more should have taken notice of the school's motto, Gamma sigma—Know thyself.

Along with our other courses we had etiquette classes which included teaching us how to walk like dignified, educated, cultured men, how to dress, how to greet others and have Western table manners. I was especially delighted by the part about how to treat ladies—how to walk side by side with them, opening doors and pulling out chairs for them. I had been brought up in a culture where women walked some yards behind their men, carrying heavy luggage on their heads and babies on their backs while the men walked at a leisurely pace in front, resting a walking stick on their shoulder. To surprised Westerners, I explained that a man must always be unencumbered and ready to protect his woman, with his stick held in a ready position should a lion or other wild animal or robber attack. But sometimes this arrangement produced curious results.

There was a man from Ranhlokana village, named Matome-a-Mokoti, who walked in this manner with his kinky-haired, scrawny, pretty wife. He told her that if a lion attacked him, she should not run away but hold on to the lion's tail while he beat it with the walking stick and killed it. Lo and behold, a lion unexpectedly appeared. The brave young wife did as her husband had instructed her—she threw the luggage away and held on to the tail of the lion with the baby securely tied to her back. Matome-a-Mokoti, when he realized what was happening, disappeared faster than lightning into the thicket. His wife was rescued by the timely arrival of young braves of the tribe, who killed the lion and mercifully saved her and the baby from being eaten. Her husband was never seen again.

I was so taken with Western etiquette that during my first school holiday at Ranhlokana, I wanted to share my newly acquired knowledge with my fellow tribesmen. An occasion arose at the first meeting on the proposed new school. Having initiated the idea for the first Batlokwa Tribal Elementary School, I was elected chairman of the building committee. The church hall where we met was full of enthusiastic tribesmen and women. There were very few benches. Most of the women stood while the men sat comfortably. After the official opening of the meeting, I stood up to address the people: "Gentlemen, please offer the ladies seats. Ladies first! Please offer the ladies seats first." Before I could add another word, all the braves of Molemole stood up in unison, and old man Ramatswi shouted from the front seat with his fist in the air: "Did you call us to belittle and despise us in front of our women? Is this what education has done to you? To cause you to despise our manhood? To place women over us? At our expense?" The giant fumed, and I had to apologize quickly before the men walked away.

At school we were also taught to play indoor games and do physical exercises with female students wearing minitunics and bikinis. Their seminakedness was more tempting to me than the bare breasts of the belles of Molemole.

Ballroom dancing—the waltz, fox-trot, tango, cha-cha, quickstep, and jiving—were all taught and reminded me of the beautiful tribal *dinaka* dances I used to dance at Molemole. During dancing ceremonies when a woman fancied a male dancer she would select one of her neck beads—*lekgakge,* the love bead—and place it around his neck as an invitation for him to pursue her. Whenever a girl adorned my neck in this manner, I would jump into the air. I would dance very hard until the earth shook with my thunderous stamping, whether she was beautiful or not. As long as she had hung the love bead around my neck to touch my chest, my heart, I would dance like crazy, knowing that when the sun set, I would find the maiden waiting for me behind a bush or hut on my way home.

There we would neck. I would caress her until I was consumed with desire, but because of her education at the Bjale initiation school, she would stop me before I seduced her, to preserve her virginity for her wedding night. At times I was in such demand that three to four maidens would hang the love beads around my neck at one dance. They would visit and walk with me as a group and play with me in a teasing manner. How proud I felt! These dances at the school of social work brought back very pleasant memories for me.

My studies included sociology, law and legal problems, Christian ethics, penology, social work, psychology, and research. But what held my interest most was practical fieldwork. I was shocked to find that black families literally starved while their neighbors had an abundance of food. In Molemole, everyone shared whatever they had with each other. Here, in the city of gold, people actually lived in holes, in pipes, and on the pavement without anywhere to turn.

I opened a file on a black family in Phomolong, Johannesburg, where I was assigned to my first case. I arrived there eager but not knowing what to expect and found the door of the two-roomed tin house open but no one at home. After hesitating, I walked in. A small, emaciated, knock-kneed girl wearing an oversized, threadbare school uniform approached me with the savvy look that one sees in urban children. She stood at a safe distance from me as she inquired what I was doing in her home, suspecting that I could be a thief, or might even molest her. After I patiently explained to her my good intentions, she relaxed and told me that she did not know where her mother was, but that her father was in prison for shoplifting, and she was hungry. Her face was drawn and her lips cracked. She had just brought her schoolbooks home so that she could ransack the neighbors' trash cans for a morsel of food—something she did daily. I felt a lump in my throat. What was I involving myself in? How was it possible for such a situation to exist?

When I returned to the office, I related that bitter experience with tears streaming down my face. I knew I was not supposed to become emotionally involved in my clients' problems, but I was touched by the incident—one of the many I would encounter in my fieldwork. I made a vow to motivate my clients to find any means to provide for themselves. But I was to discover many social pathological problems which confronted the black man in South Africa. Problems too big to overcome on his own.

At school I was profoundly impressed by the warmth extended to us by our white lecturers, who invited us to their homes and treated us as their friends. I began to consider those white liberals as true friends who wanted to mold me into a cultured, formally educated, respectable, and proud man of my black community. I was being westernized but not divorced from my own culture and my own people. I had much to think about, much to study and to ponder.

Although I socialized with the rest of the students, lived, danced, and played sports with them, I preferred to be with men from Ranhlokana and Molemole who worked in mines or industries or built roads in Johannesburg. Many resided in the Denver, Jeppe, or Wemmer men's hostels. Despite the availability of apartments at the school, I preferred to live at the hostels. Being there helped me to feel that part of Molemole was still with me in Johannesburg. It helped me to adjust to the fearsome city and to see the problems posed to the men working there.

This was where I observed at close quarters men who labored as cogs of the South African industrial development, men whose sweat contributed greatly to what South Africa is today. One such man was a close relative of mine, Isaac Madumedume, who lived at the Jeppe Men's Hostel for single men for over forty years. Because women were not allowed to enter this hostel, and he could not legally bring his wife and children to the city to live, Isaac secretly took another wife in the black township of Orlando. He had left his lawfully wedded wife at Ranhlokana village. Every Sunday he dressed in a doublebreasted navy blue suit and a "butter's bee" hat—a gray, small-brimmed hat with a black ribbon. He loved to wear navy blue overcoats in winter, and he always carried a blue and white cane. On weekdays, he was employed as a worker in a factory which made building materials.

Isaac took me for a visit to his home in Orlando, but because he was a lay preacher in the Lutheran church, he was not willing to disclose to me that the home we visited was his own. In fact, he never divulged the truth about his second family to me to the end of his days. What pains me now is that I cannot visit the family at Orlando because I cannot remember the street where they lived. I was still new to Johannesburg when he first took me there, and I didn't know how to find my way around.

Johannes Ramokgopa was a cousin who lived in the Wemmer Hostel for many years and worked for a company that manufactured ball bearings. Many of the free moments I had at night or over weekends I spent with him, talking and learning about the people, working conditions, and the city of gold. Johannes introduced me to many parts of the city and to relatives who lived around Johannesburg. He was very attached to his wife and children back home at Molemole. He struggled hard and managed to educate his children. However, I witnessed a situation that made me very unhappy. His newly married bride, the youngest of his wives, stood outside the hostel gate daily trying to catch a glimpse of her husband. She was not allowed to enter the hostel grounds.

One day after school, as I walked past his hostel, I found her standing outside the gate, looking wistfully at the crowd of men passing in and out, hoping to see Johannes or to get word to him that she was there. When she saw me she explained that she had just arrived from Molemole on the morning train. They had been married for just a week when he had rushed back to his job, leaving her behind. Because she was young and in love with her husband, she followed him by train just to be with him, and to get pregnant while their marriage was fresh and new. Charming, delicate, and lovely, she waited and hoped. So there she stood for hours and hours, hoping to attract his attention as he passed in or out of the gate so that he could take her away to the black townships to look for a room where they could go and live for a week or two and make a child. Thereafter, forced to return alone to the tribal reservation at Molemole, she would allow the child to grow in her womb and be born some 250 miles away from the city where her husband remained working.

Makuka Sehowa was a friend who headed the trousers department in a clothing factory owned by a New York firm which manufactured most of the suits and shirts in South Africa. He lived at the Denver Men's Hostel, where I spent many hours talking with him about Johannesburg. He took me around to visit members of our tribe who worked in white homes. It was here that I learned how many of our men managed from time to time to bring their wives to the *dikhichini*—"kitchens"—to stay illegally in the backyards with them while on a baby-making visit.

My nephew George Masipa had married a young girl at Molemole, but he did not have enough time to stay with her for their honeymoon. He had to rush back to where he worked for a Chinese doctor at Parktown, Johannesburg. A week or two later, the new bride, Moloko, arrived, and he had nowhere to take her. They came to see me at the school, and it was she who told me in a humorous manner about their plight. "Uncle," she said shyly, "do you have a room here in the school where my husband and I can stay and make a baby as fast as we can? I came here without a pass, and if they catch me they will take me to jail, where I will never have a chance to make our baby."

I was sympathetic, but living in a men's hostel, I couldn't

be of much immediate help. Fortunately, my fieldwork provided me with the chance to ask around. I found a place at Orlando, in the home of one of my poor clients, where my nephew hired a room for ten pounds a month. Because the home was so expensive, they had to make "a quickie baby." After two weeks, when they were satisfied that she could be pregnant, Moloko left for Ranhlokana before the police could arrest her. But after a month she realized that she was not pregnant, and she rushed back to Johannesburg to make another try.

On and on she went, in and out of Johannesburg, risking arrest for illegal entry each time she came. She tried for two years, until finally she became pregnant and went home to bear twin baby boys, appropriately named Tshokolo, meaning "suffering," and Kgotlelelo, meaning "perseverance." My nephew's wife did not return to Johannesburg until the twins were old enough to permit another sibling; then the long race for pregnancy started all over again. She commuted between Johannesburg and Molemole every second month, trying to conceive. It took another three years of traveling back and forth before she again became pregnant. She bore another set of twins and named the girls Thabo, meaning "happy," and Tebogo, meaning "thanks." The couple were thankful and happy to be blessed with such beautiful sets of twins after a long and patient effort to have a family. I was happy that I had helped in the small way of finding them a room to solve a problem faced by our people daily—a problem that interfered with normal family life and worked hardship on the most meaningful part of our very existence.

I felt new pain when I perceived the full impact of apartheid and recalled the tormenting words of Fryer at Lemana. Advocates of this diabolical system were determined to refashion South African society according to their Calvinistic Afrikaner ideals of racial segregation coupled with their Hitlerian theories of racial purity. Sex between whites and blacks was outlawed, even between those who were legally married before the Population Registration Act of 1950 became law. All mixed marriages were outlawed. Individuals were classified by race, and to avoid race mixture the Group Areas Act of 1950 was passed, establishing racial zones for occupation and ownership of land and trading rights in urban areas. At the same time, critics of the new Nationalist party government were silenced by the Suppression of Communism Act—anyone voicing protest could be arrested and charged under this act.

I watched South African history unfold while I studied at the Hofmeyr School. The year 1950 was the second year of Dr. Malan's Nationalist party rule and second year of apartheid. I observed black reaction to the weird world that was made by whites in Johannesburg.

My younger sister Moratwa, who had walked so many dusty miles to bring me food while I was at Lemana, was married to a man named Mosehlaphala. He was employed by the Witwatersrand Native Labor Association in Johannesburg as a mine cook, and he lived in a mine compound, where he was housed with thousands of other mine employees, who slept on concrete bunks. They had communal latrines—as many as thirty men sat side by side while defecating. No wives or girlfriends were allowed inside the mine or on the grounds. Homosexuality was rampant inside the compound and prostitution just outside the gates. Venereal diseases were rife among the men, and family life disintegrated when men left their wives back home. This happened to my sister. Mosehlaphala's heart broke, and he died.

Mosehlaphala had been active in black politics, and despite his illiteracy he was a great student of international politics. He knew all the leaders, black and white, and could discuss world affairs like a political analyst. It was from him that I learned a great deal about our leaders—many known throughout South Africa and some internationally renowned.

"I tell you, brother-in-law, you will see them all. They all come to the Bantu Men's Social Center. Yes, you will come to know all of our leaders. Dr. Xuma is finished. He was educated in America and England; he was a black man with a white soul—a European! A black European! He was not aggressive enough. What we need in the ANC is a spirit of Black Nationalism! Africanism! A new spirit of militancy which Xuma is not able to give: The spirit of Lembede . . . Dr. Moroka's leadership is no good either, but he is not the people. He is not the ANC. There is a young generation within the congress that is impatient with the old guard, the congress establishment, and the new generation will win." The new generation wanted to change South Africa and kill apartheid with civil disobedience, strikes, stay-at-homes, boycotts. Yes, extralegal tactics, mass action, noncooperation would be their strategy.

"Our program of action," Mosehlaphala said, "must give us freedom in our lifetime. Apartheid must be crushed. Away with domination, slavery, oppression, and racial discrimination. Nothing can stand in our way. We shall use any means at our disposal."

I left the hostel with much on my mind. I felt disturbed that a man who had so much faith in the ANC did not have complete faith in its leadership, whereas I had accepted without question everything that the ANC's leaders said and stood for ever since I had learned about them at Lemana.

That same week I met Chief Albert J. Luthuli when he came to visit Dr. Phillips at the school. Chief Luthuli was then president of the ANC in Natal Province and a leading light in the movement. In my excitement, I fired a number of questions at him. He seemed amused at my eagerness to learn, and I felt embarrassed that I had pounded him with so many questions. But the chief smiled at me and, placing a reassuring hand on my shoulder, he said, "Son of tigers, we are not savage beasts. All Africans shall fully participate in the government. The wealth of this country shall be equitably shared among all the people. And by Africans, I mean all the people of South Africa, black and white, irrespective of race, color, religion, or creed. South Africa belongs to all who live in it. We are all of us sons and daughters of Africa, of South Africa, and of God. Anyone who chooses Africa as his home is an African. All we seek is democracy, so that we can all live in peace and harmony in this land of ours. We are not racists."

To hear this view expressed by Chief Luthuli was an eye-opener to me, particularly because it was coming from a tribal ruler from the land of Zulu Malandela, the land of Phunga and Mageba, the land of the scion of Ndaba, Shaka. Although I was brought up under the authority of African chiefs, I had never met a chief who spoke so eloquently about whites being Africans.

After this meeting with Chief Luthuli, I joined the ANC. I was not quite convinced about the position of the whites, yet I had been educated in their mission schools and was receiving education from missionaries and liberal white professors. I had no real difficulty with the idea of cooperation between black and white when I thought of such whites as these.

The ANC was an organization of nationalists of varying ideological persuasions. I met many of the members of the ANC Youth League in Johannesburg at the Bantu Men's Social Center, at the ANC offices, or at political rallies. Almost all of them became my friends and colleagues. Little did I realize that many of them would be imprisoned, exiled, or killed less than ten years later. Among these leaders were Nelson Mandela, a leading member of the Thembu Royal House, then an attorney and vice president of the ANC, soon to become leader and founder of the *Umkhonto We Sizwe*—Spear of the Nation; A. P. Mda, attorney, teacher, politician, scholar, philosopher; Oliver R. Tambo, attorney, teacher, and a future president of the ANC; Walter Sisulu, past secretary general of the ANC; Robert Mangaliso Sobukwe, the quiet giant of peace whose bravery and intelligence were a beacon; Robert Resha, a soldier, leader, and astute politician; Nthato Motlana, a medical practitioner several times detained by South African police. The list of names read like a *Who's Who* of South Africa.

I watched black men at work. I realized how vital they were to the creation of the mighty South African economy—even in their often degrading roles. Pule Tabudi, a man from Molemole, lived at the Wemmer Hostel and worked for the Johannesburg municipality in slums like Alexandra township. He collected night soil—refuse from the latrines—which was carried in buckets to large trucks driven by white men. I was so impressed with the stories he told about the collection that one evening I decided to witness it myself. Tabudi told us that on a previous evening, while collecting the night soil buckets, boys insulted them, calling them *sampongani*—scavengers. In retaliation the men conspired to teach the rascals the lesson of their lives. They collected and emptied half of each bucket of night soil at the gates of all the residents of Alexandra; it did not matter that innocents would also suffer—after all, these boys belonged to the township and were sure to suffer the stench and discomfort that was to follow. This way they avoided a riot and did their job.

When my cousin Maphala was next free, I convinced him to come to Alexandra township to watch the night soil collectors at work. It was a spectacle of suffering and humiliation all in the name of earning a living. The collectors wore burlap sacks that had holes for the head and arms. The men could not wear ordinary clothes while running behind the night soil truck with the heavy buckets—the feces and urine spilled onto their bodies from the moving truck. If they failed to keep up with the white driver, they were left behind and forced to walk a long distance to deposit the buckets, which would be loaded on another truck by other collectors.

Teams consisting mostly of Zulus worked at road digging and construction. I loved watching them as they dug with anger. If given a chance, they would push the picks into their oppressors with the same vigor. I witnessed black men singing their road and digging songs while driving huge machines, tearing rocks and soil. Most referred in a cynical way to the hard, unfeeling, cruel heart of the white man, and the weakness of his muscles. Their songs, in effect, said that while blacks were digging and sweating to build the roads, streets, and skyscrapers of Johannesburg, the white man baas lazed around, holding his bulging stomach. I realized that the alternative to their dirty, smelly, and humiliating jobs would be starvation from unemployment and finally expulsion from the city to the tribal reservation—and certain death. This awareness kept me awake nights. I began to teach adults to read and write so that maybe their literacy could make their burden lighter. I lived in the hope that they would be allowed to enjoy living in the South Africa that they helped to build.

10
Defiance

The government and mining magnates recruited thousands of black men to come to Johannesburg to mine gold. Masses of our people came to work and helped build Johannesburg into a huge and prosperous city. After the white man discovered our gold lying virtually untouched in the bowels of the earth under the city of Johannesburg, calamity befell the seed of Mashila-a-Gatisha, Sekhukhune. The white man claimed it as his own—the gold, the city, the mineral rights, and the land. We, the original and rightful owners, were dispossessed. Black landowners were from that time onward regarded as "squatters." A few blacks acquired freehold properties, but the masses of our people were simply settled as squatters.

Black workers were herded into ghettos referred to as "urban locations." These were nothing but urban reservations built by the municipality of Johannesburg to provide cheap labor pools for mines and other industries. There were two such reservations in Johannesburg: Pimville and Orlando, located fifteen and twenty miles southwest of the city. However, most Africans were housed in mine compounds, barracks, and hostels. From this compound and barracks system the wicked and vicious migrant labor system developed, and the South African economy burgeoned.

The Pimville and Orlando urban labor locations proved inadequate to house the flood of migrant laborers who came to work and live in Johannesburg. The Second World War brought the problems of the migrant labor system to a head. The housing shortage became acute, and thousands of home-

DEFIANCE

less men and women were compelled to defy the existing laws and take matters into their own hands. They followed a Zulu warrior, James "Sofasonke" Mpanza, from the land of Zulu Malandela, and the scion of Senzangakhona; the son of Ndaba and Mageba, who led our people on a march from the mines of Orlando and Pimville to reclaim the land and build their homes, the shanties of shantytowns. They followed the call of the broad-shouldered, strongly built, good-humored, horse-riding hero of heroes.

The shantytowns were built along the southwestern rail line from Orlando to Pimville. Here our people were confined by the dark ghetto walls erected by white society, in towns of leaking asbestos and corrugated-iron sheets, towns where thousands lived along a riverbank of urine and shit. Infectious diseases were rife because of lack of sanitation facilities. Tuberculosis, smallpox, pellagra, and other diseases associated with starvation and poverty came from this area.

The shantytowns grew while our people continued optimistically to say, "A person's home is where he is able to get a little sleep," "The sun will rise," "The end of our suffering will come soon," and "Nothing goes on forever." Churchmen sang the hymns of old—"Lead, kindly Light, amid the encircling gloom. Lead thou me on." The oppressed masses prayed, offered libations for deliverance, and sang:

> *This load is heavy,*
> *Too heavy, too heavy.*
> *Men can't lift it.*

The children sang:

> *There comes a policeman, Mother!*
> *Run away, Mother,*
> *Run away, Mother.*
> *Please don't let 'im catch you.*

Farther to the southwest of the Orlando shantytown was another heartbreaking ghetto—Moroka-Masakeni, the town of hessian shacks, a town born of defiance and anger. To the southeast stood Albertynsville, with its leaking corrugated-iron and asbestos sheets, just like the houses at Orlando, Moroka, Pimville, and Jabavu, shantytowns where our people lived in mortal fear, day and night.

James Mpanza mounted his sprightly horse and moved from corner to corner amid ululations, giving guidance and counsel. The praise singers chanted his praises with many names—some called him Ndaba, others called him the scion of Senzangakhona. The people called out, He is the devourer of men and beasts alike,

> *The unshakable Sofasonke!*
> *The thunderer while sitting . . .*
> *'Tis he whose spears resound and cause wailings.*
> *Sofasonke, lion of Mshishi!*
> *Take your land and ride your horse.*
> *So many enemies were never seen before.*
> *Take your shield; take your spear.*
> *Take your cannon and keep the land,*
> *Fire, Sofasonke, fire!*
> *Reclaim our land!*

The whites panicked at the resistance, and increased numbers of black people defied the influx control laws. They took more land, settled on it with their families, and told the white city fathers to go to hell. The local authorities' attempts to stop the defiance proved futile. The white man made threats, but the black people refused to be intimidated. Orlando, Moroka Shelters, and Albertynsville emerged as some of the largest shantytowns ever seen in the black world.

Assigned by the school to do my practical fieldwork at the Masakeni shelter at Moroka, seventeen miles southwest of Johannesburg, I found our people living in overcrowded, deteriorated housing and suffering high infant mortality, crime, and epidemics. Howling winds at night would blow away the shacks, leaving women and children wading in pools of cold water that stood in our people's homes week after week. Yet in their despair, I noticed signs of hope as I worked among them. There was cooperation. The shacks were tidy and clean. There was faith in the future, although many were without homes, job, food, clothes, peace, or rights—living in misery beyond description—a sharp contrast to the vision I had previously had of Johannesburg as a city paved with gold.

These men and women became the backbone of the South African economic development, filling the bankers' vaults and attracting the multinational corporations to South Africa. Like the white South African community, foreign corporations exploited their cheap labor and ignored their suffering.

People left the shantytowns for work in the city as early as 4:00 A.M., on bicycles or by train, leaving their children behind with no one to care for them. But the citizens of the shantytowns were determined to form a community of faith. Here the seeds of the largest defiance campaign of the ANC were planted. Here the community of the oppressed and the exploited revolted.

By this time I was part of the suffering blacks of the Johannesburg ghettos. I resided in the Denver Men's Hostel during the last two years of school and spent many hours visiting in the Wemmer Hostel, discussing the latest developments. The Defiance Campaign was on everyone's lips. The ANC and the South African Indian Congress (SAIC) began a campaign against racial laws. The newly elected president general of the ANC, Dr. J. S. Moroka, wrote a letter in January of 1952 to Prime Minister Malan demanding that he and his government abolish the unjust laws of apartheid, failing which, a campaign in defiance of these laws would begin. Malan and his government turned a deaf ear.

The campaign began on June 26, 1952. The pass and curfew laws had become the enemy of the black man. Under the Group Areas Act of 1950, the government had removed black people from Sophiatown. Black leaders were banned on charges of Communism under the Suppression of Communism Act. The Bantu Authorities Act attempted to turn the clock back by settling urban Africans into ethnic zones and appointing puppet tribal chiefs of the white man's own choosing. They were going to kill thousands of our already diminished number of livestock under the stock limitations regulation. They said black people had too many animals. They took away our land, and would now further impoverish our people by killing our cattle.

The ANC and SAIC worked in conjunction to defy these laws. Dr. Yusuf Dadoo, president of SAIC, defied the ban he'd been placed under and spoke at a meeting, as did David Bopape, secretary of the Transvaal branch of the ANC.

By the end of the first day of the campaign, the South African police had arrested 103 persons in Witwatersrand, 30 in Port Elizabeth, and 3 in Durban for defying curfew regulations and entering locations without permits. Moses Kotane, member of the ANC and secretary general of the Communist Party of South Africa, also defied his ban and was sentenced to four months' imprisonment. Blacks defied everywhere. They stood in white lines to buy postage stamps at post offices; they entered whites-only waiting rooms at the Cape Town Railway Station and refused to leave. On Eloff Street, in Johannesburg, I walked behind Nelson Mandela and a group of fifty others selected by the ANC to defy the curfew. It was twenty-five minutes past curfew. We were met by police who ordered us into vans. Nelson Mandela and Samuel Mokae were assaulted in the arrest.

Our case was heard in July. We were defended by Dr. George Lowen, Q.C. At the end of the trial, the magistrate said, "The accused should have been asked individually for their passes, and clearly this was not done. I find them all not guilty." A breakthrough had been made, but it would prove to be an exception.

The campaign continued in spite of heavy penalties. Thirty-two women defied in New Brighton by entering the whites-only entrance of the New Brighton Station. Dr. Moroka was arrested on August 14, 1952, at Thaba Nchu, Orange Free State, and charged under the Suppression of Communism Act.

In November, he stood trial in Johannesburg with twenty others for "advocating or encouraging the achievement of communism." By the middle of October, the number of arrests had passed the 5,000 mark. In November, the first Chinese Defier, Keem Lau-Kee, a shopkeeper, entered a Pretoria location without a permit. He was arrested.

Black people were on the march. Fines were increased to 300 pounds and imprisonment to three years; this did not scare us. More people joined the campaign, including some whites. Patrick Duncan, son of the first governor general of South Africa, joined us, as did Manilal Gandhi, the second son of Mahatma Gandhi. Duncan, Gandhi, and their party of Defiers entered the Germiston location on the evening of December 8, 1952. Duncan had broken his leg and walked on crutches with Manilal Gandhi at his side. Within minutes a huge crowd of blacks were following them and singing:

> *This load is heavy.*
> *Too heavy, too heavy.*
> *Men can't lift it.*
> *Men can't carry it.*
> *This load is heavy.*

Patrick Duncan spoke: "I wished to show that there were at least some whites who are prepared to cooperate on a basis of loyalty with the two congresses. *Mayibuye Africa!*—Let Africa return!"

By the end of 1952, the ANC and SAIC had mobilized some 8,500 people. Chief Luthuli continued to work for freedom in nonviolent ways, even though he was banned, beaten, persecuted, and arrested. He defied banning orders and continued to rally the people.

Following the campaign, 156 leading members of the congress alliance, including Mandela, Sisulu, and Chief Luthuli, were arrested on charges of high treason under the Suppression of Communism Act. The penalty for treason was death by hanging. I prayed for him and poured libations to our ancestors. The people rallied behind them. Mandela, Sisulu, and Luthuli were acquitted on all counts. We had succeeded again.

The Criminal Law Amendment Act was rushed through Parliament early in 1953. Anyone protesting against color discrimination could now be fined 500 pounds, or imprisoned for five years and whipped ten strokes. In the same session the Public Safety Act was passed, giving the government power to declare a state of emergency and to arrest and detain people without a trial. Violence against blacks escalated as blacks continued to resist. I watched from Johannesburg—city of gold, city of tears.

11

My Jewel

Amidst the defiance my education and social life continued to expand into the community. In my final year at the Jan H. Hofmeyr School of Social Work, I was assigned to work at the Moroka Community Welfare Center at Masakeni, some twenty miles southwest of Johannesburg. Baldwin Mavungu Mudau, my supervisor and friend, was always thinking of ways to uplift the spirits of the people—ways to make the burdens of life in the shantytown a little easier to bear. We put our heads together and organized a dance to raise funds for the preschool children of Moroka.

Every one of us was busy doing something to contribute toward our big social event. A huge crowd turned up from all the townships and Johannesburg. Among them was one young woman my age—tall, graceful, and soft treading. Her eyes were black, her eyelashes long. She was dressed in a navy blue taffeta dress, and as she walked heads turned, mine included. I watched spellbound as she glided and swung on the dance floor in her silver-blue high-heeled shoes. Her soft voice harmonized beautifully with her babylike gentle face.

There, I found a jewel!

Halfway through the dance the ladies who ran the day care center announced that they had organized a raffle. The young lady placed her bet. I followed. The prize was a shaving kit, and I asked her what she would do with it if she won.

"I will give it to the man who will one day be my husband," she said.

SOWETO, MY LOVE

I laughed and asked if we could dance. She moved with grace and skill, waltzing and jiving. When the results of the raffle were announced, Thabo Morare had won. I escorted her to pick up her prize, congratulated her, and introduced myself.

> *I am Molapatene, Mafa, Kotoleleele,*
> *Matšhipi's brother, son of Maubene*
> *Who feeds on bravery.*
> *Do not play a fool at Mabjanene,*
> *The son of Mauba is too brave.*

She responded.

> *I am Thabo Mary Jane Morare.*
> *I am Mopo, Mopo Sethetele,*
> *The children of the big . . .*

She paused, "I do not want to sound vulgar, I am only chanting our family name." She smiled and explained that part of the praise of her people was a little embarrassing.

A year later I learned that the word she had omitted was *vagina*.

The following Monday I went to visit Thabo at the Moroka Jabavu—White City Clinic, where she was a nurse. She was on night duty. I marveled at her as she walked toward me. She had stolen my heart. Yes, I had fallen in love, wildly, madly in love for the first time in my life. I left the clinic walking on air.

The next time I saw Thabo, it was at the Johannesburg Music Festival Competition, which was held at the Bantu Men's Social Center two weeks after we first met. There she was towering above the first line of the Jabavu Choristers, smiling at me from the stage. I touched cousin Maphala on his shoulder and whispered into his ear, "Is she not beautiful, Cousy?"

On her first weekend off duty, I decided that the time was ripe for me to invite Thabo to the roaring caves and the mead-

MY JEWEL

ows of the St. Peter's Valley Rivulet for a picnic. When we arrived at my favorite spot in the love valley, Thabo took off her shoes, and with me hard on her heels, we jumped from rock to rock, water to rock, and rock to water, splashing in the cool water. I eventually caught up with her and claimed my kiss. She nestled against my chest, melted in my arms, and kissed me like I had never been kissed before. I kissed her again. Thabo pushed gently away from me. "You haven't known me long enough," she protested.

"Oh, Thabo, my darling, Thabo," I whispered between kisses. "I have known you every waking hour of every day and in my dreams every night for the last two weeks. I imagined you embracing me, locked in my arms in love, your tall beautiful frame melting inside me." She was becoming increasingly uncomfortable. "Please!" She pleaded for me to stop, but I couldn't.

"This memory will last for the rest of my life," I urged.

"This is impossible. You are placing me in a most embarrassing position. Young men should not go about behaving as you do to young ladies—strangers!" Thabo said.

I caught my breath. "Am I a stranger? Still a stranger to you, my *Chum?*" I asked.

"I am sorry to disappoint you. You remind me of the Professor." The Professor was her previous boyfriend. She had left him for making the same demands.

I spent all my free time courting Thabo and looked forward to the day I would have completed school and found employment with sufficient income that I could afford to marry her. When my graduation ceremony came, Thabo was there to grace the occasion. My dreams had been realized. Cousins Maphala and Ramokgopa, and Molatelo Ramusi (my guardian angel) were there to share with me the joy of success. Good fortune smiled on me, and I was immediately employed at the Entokozweni Family and Community Welfare Center in Alexandra township.

After working for seven months, I was finally in a position to propose marriage to my jewel. I asked my family to begin the traditional African marriage negotiations, which require *bohadi* (dowry) to be paid by the boy's family to the girl's family as a gift in consideration of the valuable addition of a wife to our family and the Babirwa clan—my clan. According to tradition, there could be no valid marriage between Thabo and me without payment of bohadi, but because Thabo's family were Christians, I sent my emissaries with no money or valuables, thinking they would not be expected.

My "guardian angel"; my cousin Motlatšo Isaiah Maphala; and Robert Miyen, a friend and fellow social worker, traveled 600 miles to open marriage negotiations by asking for "a calabash of water," as my people say whenever they come to ask for a lady's hand in marriage—the calabash from which we eat and drink.

Thabo's father, Sekgweng Morare, replied, "I have no mouth; I cannot speak. I have no eyes; I cannot see you. I have no ears; I do not hear"—he, in fact, required the traditional fee for "opening the mouths" of the girl's people. So my emissaries withdrew to confer among themselves. In recognition of the clan's relation to tradition, they delivered 5 pounds cash and again asked for the calabash of water.

Thabo's father pretended to have no daughters and insisted that perhaps the girl they wanted lived next door. He encouraged the family to pretend that they did not want Thabo to be married. So the representatives of the two families talked back and forth until the Morare family conceded and settled for the sum of 100 pounds as bohadi. When the agreement was reached, the families rejoiced and a sheep lost its life to feed my emissaries from Molemole.

Preparations for the wedding feast began in Thabo's village. The voices of the Batlokwa and Morare praise singers mingled in the yard on our wedding day, December 12, 1953. Thabo was a special bride in this place. She was born and brought up at Tiger Kloof, where she had also worked as the school nurse before going to Johannesburg. A red carpet was laid for her on the path to the church. My mother stood ululating at the church door, chanting the praises of our clan, the Ba-

MY JEWEL

birwa. My father's sister took over to praise my name. Then, at 11:00 A.M., Thabo and I were married. The ceremony was performed by the Reverend Aubrey Lewis, superintendent of Tiger Kloof Institution and principal of the high school.

Aunt Malekanyane took over and praised my name. Then Sono's mother shouted, "We have taken her! We have taken her!" She announced to all present that Thabo was now married to our family, while Cousin Maphala and my guardian angel were jumping and kicking the dust in the manner of my people, who jump and dance in front of the bridal couple to show happiness at a wedding. The crowd sang and danced to the traditional wedding songs as we came out of the church.

I pounded the earth, kicked the dust, and danced. Thabo treaded softly amid the ululating voices of women from our two clans, the Elephant and Babirwa clans. I was happy. Thabo was happy.

After lunch the traditional naming and counseling ceremony began. We assembled at Thabo's parents' home. Aunt Malekanyane rose and walked to the table where Thabo and I sat. She looked into the face of the bride and said, "The name of our new daughter-in-law is Ma Selaelo Ramusi. From this day you are no longer Thabo Mary Jane Morare, you are Ma Selaelo. You are the woman of your house, a mother. You are no longer a girl. Leave your girlhood behind, my child. We welcome you into the Babirwa family. The name of your first child will be Selaelo. Even if it never comes, you are its mother."

Then she turned to me. "Do you hear me, son of the Babirwa clan? Do you see me? Look at me! I am your father's sister; therefore, I am your father. You brought us many miles from Molemole-a-Masehlo to fetch a wife. Don't disgrace us, my child. Treat your wife decently. Treat her well. A wife is a queen, my child, a queen. She will bear us soldiers of Africa. I have seen her family for myself. It is a good family. Honor your wife. If you get tired of her, you bring her to me. I am your father. If she gives you trouble, speak to her. If she does not listen to you, don't kill the daughter of the Elephant clan. Come to me. I am your father. She is my daughter. Don't forget who we are." She paused to allow the words to sink into my consciousness. After praising Mothibi, her brother, and myself, she produced the sum of 5 pounds and said: "With this five pounds I hope you will buy a cow and milk it for the children in your home."

Then Thabo's paternal aunt, Christine-a-Ndlazi, rose. "Thabo, my child, do you hear me? Do you hear me, you daughter of the Elephant clan, you daughter of my mother's child? Listen to me! I am your father's sister. I am, therefore, your father. Look after your husband and his family. It will be good for you to feed them and to care for them. We never thought that you would marry so far away from home. Love took you to faraway lands. We taught you everything in this home. Follow the example of your father and mother. Where the front hoof has stepped, the hind hoof will step. Like mother, like daughter. A woman is hands. That is what we taught you. Listen to the advice of your mother-in-law and of your new family members; if you don't, you may find yourself in deep waters. Remember the good ways of your parents and follow their good example. Work hard in your new home. . . . Don't give a chance to other women to take your husband and make him happier than you. Keep him happy in his home. Don't allow them to give him more care and affection than yourself. Don't lose him to other women who will give him nice pieces of fried liver in their homes to entice him away from you."

She wiped some sweat. Then she turned toward me and said, "To you, my son, I say, look after this child of my mother's child. I brought her up. Love her. Care for her. If she gives you trouble and makes you angry, please don't kill her. No! Return her to the Elephant clan. We will talk to her and bring her back to you. We will teach her to become a better wife to you. I have nothing. I only have this five pounds for you, my children. Buy what you like for your house." Ma Selaelo was in tears. The words were piercing. It is the custom

MY JEWEL

when brides are counseled that they cry to show that the words are not falling on deaf ears.

Then her mother began slowly, as if in pain. "Do you hear me, Thabo? I am your mother. Today you have grown. You are married. I am proud of you. Respect your people-in-law, old and young. Respect your mother-in-law. Respect your husband. If you fail to respect them, no one will respect you. If no one respects you, we will be ashamed to come in your house. Share whatever you have with your people-in-law. Remember, my child, children of one man share a grasshopper's head. No matter how little we have we must always share. Consult your people-in-law in whatever you do, so that there can be peace and harmony in your home. Feed the Ramusi children, feed them, my child. Don't lock yourself behind doors and eat alone like a child of a witch. A person is a person through other people, my child. You must remember that the grave of a woman is at her people's-in-law. . . . Honor the aged members of the Babirwa clan. . . . If you respect your people-in-law, you will be a queen, my child. The wealth of every queen is her people. Your father and I have some gifts for you." She started singing a hymn and the crowd joined in.

Thabo's father stood, looked toward the north, and said, "We are Bapo, we are Bapo Sethetele, the children of the Elephant clan. Our people have said: If a child cries for a *mokhure* whistle, make it and give it to her. You have your whistle today. Keep it. Your mother has told you that the grave of a girl is at her people's-in-law. Let it be so. . . . You are married to the Ramusi family. You must persevere to the very end. We have never seen divorce in this home. It must not start with you."

He turned to me. He scrutinized me as if seeing me for the first time, and he said, "Son, this is my daughter in whom I am well pleased. Take her to your people and love her. Care for her, my son. She is the pride of my youth and my loins. Honor her like your own mother and sisters. If she wrongs you, let me know, my son. I will speak to her. She is the jewel of my heart. Your mother and I have spoken. God bless both of you. We have some kitchen furniture for you. It is our gift to you both. We have this cash and other things for you. Use them in your home." He sat down, looking somewhat dejected and disturbed by his own words.

My cousin Ma-Moloko Masipa started singing a traditional Batlokwa song that is always sung when a man brings a wife home to cook and help feed the family:

> *Our mother has come.*
> *Hunger, you will shit!*
> *Our mother has come.*
> *Hunger, you will shit!*

The crowd joined in the singing and dancing before the bridal group. My mother came over to us. She looked at Ma Selaelo, then looked at me proudly. "Let me talk to you first, Mafa-a-Molapatene. Let me speak to the blood of the Babirwa clan. Son, look at me. I am your mother. Today you are a man, a man of men. You are no longer a boy. Leave your boyhood behind. Build this daughter of Morare a home. Be proud that you have married a girl from a decent home like this one. Treat her well, my son. A wife is a jewel, a piece of porcelain, breakable. Handle her with care. Protect her. She is your child and your mother. She is your sister. She is your all."

Then she turned toward Ma Selaelo and said, "Welcome into the Babirwa clan, welcome into our family. Welcome into our home, my child! You are our daughter, you are his wife, you are our wife, my child. Today, you are his wife and mother. Treat him well. If he does not treat you well, please let me know. He is my son. I will help you. I will speak to him. Ma Selaelo, please respect your husband and his people." The counseling was accompanied by music and traditional chants of family praises. Many relatives stepped forward to give us advice and gifts. After the ceremony we continued with traditional wedding dances in front of the bride's home until it was time for the second reception at the assembly hall, where

MY JEWEL

we danced until the early hours of the morning. And so we were wed!

I had managed to secure a house in Dube, Soweto. It was a matchbox kind of house, gray and unplastered, with no electricity, gas, or running water—only a tap attached to the outhouse twenty yards behind our home. A Primus stove and a coal stove were our means of heat and cooking. Thabo did her best to make it hospitable.

Dube township, like Pimville and Orlando townships before it, was a segregated black ghetto in the heart of Soweto, born out of dispossession of the people of Sophiatown, Pimville, Eastern and Western Native townships.

The Dube Men's Hostel, on the northern side of the township, accommodated the migrant laborers from the Bantustans. A one-plate coal stove and a common cold-water shower room were shared among sixteen men. There were no dining rooms, no visitors' rooms, no reading rooms, no privacy for the inmates, and no recreational facilities. An ugly barbed-wire fence separated Dube Hostel from the village. No women or children were allowed on the premises, where their men were caged like wild beasts in the land of their birth.

After my marriage I continued with my studies. I was, by then, halfway through my second-year courses as a corresponding student of the University of South Africa. I was studying English, sociology, anthropology, and North Sotho. Work and study presented their own problems, but Thabo was my inspiration. I was usually physically and mentally exhausted by the time I got home. Often I fell asleep at the dinner table, and she would encourage me to get into bed with a promise of waking me up after two hours' rest. I was grateful to be married to an understanding woman, my beautiful, loving Thabo.

Other practical problems of studying were overcome as I read by candlelight at night and in buses, trucks, and trains, under trees, and even on bicycles as I traveled in villages doing my social work. I remember traveling on a donkey in Sekhukhuneland and reading Keats's "Ode to a Nightingale." I was about to begin Wordsworth when the donkey, exhausted, stopped trotting. I borrowed a bicycle and cycled slowly down Leolo Mountain, toward the valley of Steelport River, reading and reciting "Tintern Abbey." A friend and I decided to write a study guide for other external students on reading on donkey back, in treetops, on carts, on foot, and on bicycles.

I had also taken a job with the mobile eye clinic of the Bureau for Prevention of Blindness. I traveled ahead of the doctors to look for cases of trachoma, and every time I found a high incidence of the disease, there was invariably a lack of water and food. My work took me back to Molemole, where I had the great joy of seeing my people undergo treatment and regain their sight.

I loved social work, but I loved Thabo more. Our first son, Selaelo, was born on November 14, 1954. Mother came to live with us to look after the baby while Thabo continued to work. I graduated from the University of South Africa in 1956. By the time I left the university, I was the editor of *Bona* pictorial magazine. I had been attracted to it because it was to be published in the languages of the black people of South Africa—North Sotho, South Sotho, Tswana, Zulu, and Xhosa. The salary was attractive. A professor had urged me to apply for the position, and I got it.

I hadn't been with the magazine long when the white editor in chief began bringing me pictures and articles on feasts celebrating the removal of black people from Sophiatown and Alexandra township to Meadowlands and Diepkloof townships, which caused them to lose their freehold rights to the land. I was alarmed by the pictures showing fictitious black chiefs in leopard skins and ostrich feathers attending these "feasts," where tribesmen were dancing in jubilation for their new houses. I was horrified to discover that *Bona* was a sister magazine to *Dagbreek*, *Die Ster*, and *Vaderland* under Die Nationale Pers. I refused to publish the articles, handed in my resignation, and walked out without looking back.

MY JEWEL

I got involved with the Black Social Workers' Association and became president of the Transvaal organization during 1955. I helped found the South African Non-European Social Workers' Association and traveled to many of its conferences. In 1957, after spending one year at the University of the Witwatersrand, I rejoined the University of South Africa as an external student in the law school. At the same time I was articled to the firm of Morris, Alexander, and Hirsch for a period of three years; there I did mostly civil work. Toward the end of three years, in order to gain more experience in criminal court trial work, I ceded my articles of clerkship to a Johannesburg firm of attorneys, Harry Solomon and M. & J. Marks.

I was able to avoid carrying a regular pass book in Johannesburg until that time. I managed to escape arrest by carrying business cards from the Jan H. Hofmeyr School as identification documents, which certified that I was an "exempted native," exempted even from curfew regulations. But these were valid only as long as I was a student at the Hofmeyr School. Otherwise, my work could have been taken away and I could have been sent back to Molemole to starve in the tribal reservation. Thabo and I would have had no legal right to reside as husband and wife in Johannesburg. But I was lucky. I said to myself, The gods of my fathers, the Ever-Present Eternal Presences of Babirwa, are with me! God Almighty is with me! God bless our family—our home!

12

Giant Rising Up

Shortly after the birth of Sekgweng, our second son, I opened the door of our house to greet Mabusha Masekela, my cousin, who had come to see our newborn. Masekela was born and brought up at Molemole, a grandson of King Mamokutupi Ramokgopa and a trained social worker from the Jan H. Hofmeyr School. When I met him he was already the executive secretary of the Donaldson Orlando Community Center in Johannesburg. He was a middle-aged, heavyset Motlokwa man of tremendous energy and intellect. He ended as a businessman and a politician of no mean reputation.

Both of us were concerned about the question of African unity and national relations between blacks and whites. We attended a meeting of a newly formed organization, the Pan Africanist Congress (PAC), in the Western Native township. When we arrived, we found the meeting charged with intense anger, black anger, raging from every corner of the room. As the meeting wore on, it became apparent that there were more enemies to fight than the apartheid government. The old guard of the ANC, SAIC, the South African Colored People's Organization (SACPO), and the South African Congress of Democrats had been ineffective. The white liberals and their organizations seemed only to be feigning friendship to the black man while drawing the sting out of the African Revolutionary movement. Even Masekela, usually a man of few words, felt the bitterness. "We have run out of cheeks to turn. We are tired of begging and pleading, and tired of trying to be nice to those who oppress us. To hell with them! We must fight!"

GIANT RISING UP

Two names dominated the talks: Muziwakhe Anton Lembede and Robert Mangaliso Sobukwe. Lembede, who was long dead by this time, was the founder of the African Youth League of the ANC in the 1940s, while Sobukwe had been the sustaining influence of Pan Africanism since his university days. Sobukwe was a lecturer in African languages at the University of the Witwatersrand. He was known as a tenacious man with a specific mission in life.

Sobukwe and I rode the train together on weekdays. The Monday after the PAC meeting, I was anxious to discuss events and learn more about Lembede, the father of Pan Africanism and orthodox African nationalism, and about this rage against the ANC for its policy of cooperation with liberal whites, coloreds, and Indians in the fight to free the black man. The Pan Africanist Congress was formed as a splinter group by those who felt the educated "African elite" of the ANC had betrayed the millions of illiterate and semiliterate Africans. The Pan Africanist Congress was a militant and progressive-radical movement which would ensure that no deal was struck between the upper-echelon African leaders and the white liberals or rich Indians that would undermine the goal of freedom for the masses. "Mind you," Sobukwe said, "they do all this on the grounds of the alleged unreadiness, backwardness, and illiteracy of blacks!"

I was, for a while, somewhat torn between the two ideologies. After I told my cousin Maphala of my talks with Sobukwe, he said, "I am old. I have seen many things come and go. The African National Congress is powerful, big, and highly respected. I have been hearing about this destructive splinter group of yours because of its exclusive nationalism. I know that the nationalistic ideology is dynamic, and that in the long run it may even win. But the ANC will never die." My mind turned to Chief Luthuli, and I wondered how he stood in all of this confusion and anger. It appeared to me that the real difference between the PAC and the ANC was the issue of who were the rightful owners of the land. In that light, I came down on the side of Lembede and Sobukwe. Pan Africanism had captured my imagination.

The Pan Africanist Congress was formally launched on Jan van Riebeeck Day, April 7, 1959, at the Orlando Communal Hall, amid jubilation and shouts of "Africa for the Africans," "Imperialists, quit Africa," *"Izwe lethu-i-Afrika"* (Africa, our land), "Freedom in our lifetime." Sobukwe was unanimously elected president, and Potlako Leballo emerged as the general secretary. From the moment he assumed leadership, Sobukwe persistently refused to compromise his ideal or to be co-opted. Revolutionary optimism was the secret of his life. He was a devout believer in the slow but inexorable advance of African nationalism.

The next morning I arrived early at Dube Station to make sure that I did not miss Sobukwe and the 7:20 train. At 7:15 he appeared, all smiles and pleased to find me waiting on the platform. We took our usual seat in the crowded train that daily took almost a half million people from Soweto to their work in the city.

Robert Sobukwe was born in Graaff-Reinet, a small Afrikaner town. His father was a missionary, whom he despised for his subservience to whites. After graduating from the University of Fort Hare and starting his own family, he felt it was time for change so that his children could live in an Africa free of apartheid. Sobukwe wanted to build an organization that was in touch with and represented the masses. "We breathe Africa, live Africa, dream Africa—a free and humane Africa, where the masses of our people will live in peace. . . . But we will no longer be controlled or dehumanized by anyone."

Sobukwe no longer believed in the politics of compromise practiced by the ANC. "Every time our people have shown signs of uniting against oppression," he said, "their white friends have come along and broken that unity. . . . The white missionaries have done the same thing. . . . Our people now hate the white man because they associate him with oppression. If you remove the association, you remove the hatred. Once the white domination has been overthrown and the white man is no longer the boss, but an individual member of society, there will be no reason to hate him . . . but history has taught us that a group in power has never voluntarily relinquished its position. It has always been forced to do so." It would be a long fight, but one he hoped would follow the examples of Ghana, Algeria, Egypt, and other places in Africa.

In a matter of weeks, Sobukwe became a household name in Soweto, and the atmosphere pregnant with historic possibility. Already black people began to boycott stores where African customers were treated badly, and they started to picket. Seeing hope in the movement, I called upon the spirits of my fathers and their fathers, and poured libations to my ancestors, the Eternal Presences of my clan and tribe, and our long-departed rulers and chiefs. I prayed for the spirits to be with us and make us a free people.

Nineteen fifty-nine was a year of extraordinary events. The Pan Africanist Congress planned a campaign against pass laws, while the all-white South African Parliament passed legislation to introduce apartheid in universities as well as create tribal universities. The doors of education which had, up to then, been open to black students, would now close. Nineteen fifty-nine was also the year when the man of peace, Chief Albert Luthuli, the national president of the ANC, was banished to his tribal home of Croutville, Natal, in an effort to keep him from organizing his people to resist injustice. The Parliament also passed one of the most vicious pieces of legislation ever placed on the statute books, the so-called Promotion of Bantu Self-Government Act—the Bantustan Act—of 1959.

Lecturers and professors of the University of Fort Hare, both black and white, protested and were dismissed. Eleven opposition members, white liberals of the United party, resigned in protest against apartheid and created the Progressive party. Patrick van Rensburg, a young Afrikaner diplomat, resigned his post in the Congo and moved to London, where he led a campaign to boycott South African goods. It was the year 300 white men were prosecuted under the Immorality Act of 1957 for not only sex across the color line but also mere kissing, fondling, or even looking at black women with lust.

Both the PAC and the ANC were planning mass demonstrations against passes at the same time, so we moved ours ahead to strike first. Sobukwe rallied the African people and appealed to them to conduct the campaign in a spirit of nonviolence. Our defiance campaign would have a twist different from that of the ANC's—unlike them, once we had presented ourselves for arrest we would accept no bail, no defense, no fine. We would not acknowledge a legal system under which we had no rights.

On March 21, 1960, Thabo and I arose at 5:00 A.M. and awakened our children to see history being made. The campaign began by cutting off the voice of apartheid. In each house, the government had installed a radio-diffusion device over which they transmitted their propaganda. After speaking to God and the spirits of our Living Dead, the Eternal Presences of our clan, I cut the wires and carried the device outside. I and my neighbors took our radio-diffusion devices to the home of Joseph Makema, the senior announcer of the South African Broadcasting Corporation, to be burned in public in his yard. The sun rose and passes were left at home while men gave themselves up for arrest. The revolution was on.

The day was one of brazen tyranny forever crimson stained in the history of South Africa. By sundown the police had killed 72 people at Sharpeville and Langa and severely wounded 180 others. Not satisfied to arrest those without passes who surrendered to them, the police opened fire on unarmed nonviolent protesters while the words of Sobukwe still hung in the air.

Some thirty miles away, as the people of Soweto burned and destroyed all visible symbols of apartheid and oppression, the people gathered at Sharpeville to search among the dead for their loved ones. Corpses covered with newspapers lay scattered about where the police bullets had felled them.

A warning was issued to the government of South Africa and to the prime minister:

> *Verwoerd, beware!*
> *Beware of the black man!*
> *Be careful of the black man!*
> *The black man is coming!*

When the news of the innocents massacred at Sharpeville and Langa reached the world press, the Johannesburg stock market fell, and protests against apartheid poured in from every part of the globe. The previously indifferent world was shocked by the brutal display of violence used by the white regime against unarmed black demonstrators.

Philip Kgosana of the ANC organized 15,000 blacks to march against Parliament in Cape Town. The government panicked and suspended the demand for passes for a little while. As black anger mounted, the whites appeared helpless and petrified, but this was only a lull before the storm. Police reorganized throughout the country; they arrested, wounded, and killed peaceful protesters everywhere in the land. The government announced in Parliament that both the ANC and the PAC were banned under a newly enacted law that outlawed organizations considered dangerous. The leaders of PAC were all arrested—Sobukwe, Mothopeng, Masekela, Leballo, along with hundreds of others all over the country. They appeared together in Johannesburg Magistrate's Court, and Sobukwe addressed the court on their behalf.

"Your Worship, we challenge this court because we fear that we will not be given a fair and proper trial. We do not consider ourselves either legally or morally bound to obey laws made by a parliament in which we have no representation. We shall therefore apply for no bail, no defense, and if convicted, we shall pay no fine." Sobukwe and his co-accused were convicted and sentenced to serve three years in prison.

Sobukwe was sent to Robben Island, where he was kept in solitary confinement and tortured. Every year, his three-year jail sentence was increased by one year by special act of Parliament. After nine years he was transferred to Kimberley, where he lived under house arrest until his death nine years later in 1978. He returned to the house of his parents only as a corpse, eighteen years from the day when he entered the court and said, "No bail, no defense, no fine."

His words stayed with me. I visited him many times at Kimberley. Every time we parted he would look hard at me as he used to do in our corner in the Soweto train, and say, "Ram, go well, son of Africa; go well, son of my father. I am sick, but I am fine." Meaning his spirit was strong and undaunted.

Sobukwe will be remembered in the history of South Africa as the maker of a psychological revolution. Two years before he died he declared: "At Sharpeville and Langa we overcame fear of the consequences of disobeying colonial laws. It became respectable for us to go to jail and emerge as what Kwame Nkrumah called 'prison graduates.' We thus stripped the white man of that particular weapon against us. Now the white man has to fall back on his ultimate weapon, the gun. Soweto has been a lesson in overcoming fear of the gun. Now that he relies on the gun, and we too can get it, confrontation is inevitable."

Sobukwe had helped South African blacks over the largest hurdle in the struggle for freedom—fear and the slave mentality. His use of noncooperation as launched in the 1960 Sharpeville and Langa campaign informed and dominated all the freedom struggles of the people of South Africa. The policy was relentlessly pursued by Stephen Biko and members of the Black Consciousness Movement organization from 1968 on. In its various phases noncooperation touched off the massive student demonstrations of the early seventies, ignited wave upon wave of workers' strikes in the midseventies, launched the 1976–77 Soweto uprising and the present revolutionary upheavals. Sobukwe is dead and buried, but his spirit marches on and the struggle for liberation continues.

13

Mthembu

I am convinced that God never leaves his people without a champion, a warrior to meet their needs. Although the South African regime could jail Sobukwe's body, they could not jail his spirit. Chief Luthuli was banned. Another champion arose and took up the battle. Mthembu! Nelson Rolihlahla Mandela. Mthembu was his royal clan name. Rolihlahla was his praise name. The people chanted his praises:

> *Rolihlahla, demolisher of hedges*
> *Zodwa Zintshaba,*
> *Begrudged by his enemies,*
> *Madiba! Madiba intonga,*
> *The royal giant from deep blue waters*
> *Hala! Sopitsho!*
> *Pitso's father!*
> *Ngqo Lomsila!*
> *Vela Zimbentsele!*
> *Dlomo! Dlanga!*
> *Mthembu!*

It was 8:00 A.M. when I looked at my watch in Beacon House, West Street, Johannesburg. There was music in the air. West Street was overflowing with singing voices in congested police trucks. I listened intently. The singing grew louder: "*Izongunyathela Afrika*—Africa will trample you!" They thundered and roared.

I moved to the window and saw the trucks that drove past my office each day to the courthouse conveying prisoners to trial. The prisoners sang. Their voices were clear with defiance. I closed my eyes and listened.

A big blind black man with a white walking stick stood on the pavement and listened as if the wind were whispering into his ears. The prisoners roared in unison beautiful refrains, pounding on the floors and roofs as if the vehicles would burst. They chanted songs of freedom: *"Paasop, Verwoerd!"*—a warning to the white minority government. I heard myself humming, "Africa will trample you. Verwoerd!" I stopped when I entered the Magistrate's Court building. I was standing at the entrance to Courtroom O when Mandela stopped right in front of me and asked me to take a case on his behalf.

The charge against his client was that she brewed African beer in her home without a license. An African housewife prosecuted for making traditional beer for her beloved husband!

As an articled clerk and an apprenticed attorney in my final year, I was permitted to defend cases in court. I assured the client that I would do my best for her. Again she smiled warmly. Mandela shook his client's hand, shook my hand, and left. That was the last time I saw Mandela as a free man. Shortly thereafter he went underground to organize the May 1961 general strike as well as Umkhonto We Sizwe—Spear of the Nation.

Mandela was among the few black lawyers I met after my arrival in Johannesburg. In due course I came to know him well. He was born in Umtata, Transkei, on July 18, 1918, a member of the Royal House of Mthembu. A graduate of the University of Fort Hare, he was a patriot and devoted leader of the ANC, loyal to his president, Chief Luthuli. He became my mentor as he practiced law in partnership with Oliver R. Tambo, now president of the ANC.

When Mandela left me with that file and that client in front of the court, he had decided to abandon not only his legal practice but his family life. The time had come when the government of South Africa had compelled him to leave Winnie, his beautiful wife, and his two pretty daughters, Zenani and Zindziwa. He did so following the Sharpeville-Langa massacre and the sentencing of Sobukwe and his followers. When the South African government declared the country a nationalist republic in May 1961, through a whites-only referendum, without consulting a single black, Mandela called a general strike in his own name. The Black Pimpernel—Madiba! Madiba intonga! The royal giant from deep blue waters was seen in mountains and rivers. The royal tiger of Umtata strode the narrow paths of South Africa by day and by night, living in hiding, disguised, today here, tomorrow there, the invisible elephant of the land of diamonds, tears, gold, apartheid, and death!

> *Mthembu! The thundering, lightning of Mthirara*
> *and Nguboengcuka, the horny one,*
> *the straight-tailed bull Ngqo Lomsila,*
> *the stinging stick . . .*
> *Rolihlahla Mandela-Vela Zimbentsele,*
> *the multicolored lion of Amatola,*
> *the gentle ruler of men and beasts alike;*
> *Zondwa Zintshaba—begrudged by enemies of his*
>   *fathers,*
> *The eagle of the African skies.*

On March 25, 1961, Mandela represented the ANC at the All-in-Africa Conference, which opened in Pietermaritzburg after many years of enforced silence as a result of banning orders. He was elected to head the National Action Council, formed to execute the demands of the conference. The resolutions included a demand that representatives of all races in South Africa meet in a national convention to determine a new democratic constitution for the country. If the government failed to convene such a gathering, demonstrations would be staged for three days—a stay-at-home strike would coincide with the establishment of the Republic of South Africa.

Mandela wrote the letter to Prime Minister Verwoerd, on behalf of the National Action Council, warning him, "We are not deterred by threats of force and violence made by you and your government, and we will carry out our duty without flinching." Verwoerd never favored Mandela with a reply. Mandela wrote another letter to the leader of the parliamentary opposition and told him, "A call for a national convention from you could well be the turning point in our country's history. We will have to either talk it out or shoot it out. . . . It is still not too late."

Still Verwoerd did not reply. Instead he threatened to act against anyone who supported the calling of the national convention. He referred to the supporters of the convention as agitators and Communists fit for punishment.

As the strike neared, the police made large-scale raids to intimidate our people. Ten thousand black men were arrested, but the Black Pimpernel could not be netted. White civilians were sworn in to be special police. The government called out police, commandos, army, citizens' forces, and Saracen armored units. Meetings were banned all over the country. Strike leaflets were seized, and printing presses were raided. Gun shops sold out their stocks to whites.

Mandela was not deterred. He reiterated the call for the stay-at-home strike and called for the people to show their determination to end the pass laws, minority rule, and unequal wages: to destroy apartheid and establish rule by one man, one vote, to demand freedom in our lifetime as the ANC had demanded for years.

My admiration for Mandela increased daily as I read his directives to the oppressed from the underground. The stay-at-home strike was scheduled for May 29 through May 31, 1961. As the twenty-ninth neared, the press moved in from around the world. Helicopters hovered over black residential areas, and searchlights flashed over houses and yards. Such a call-up had not been seen in South Africa since the Second World War. All police leaves were canceled, while armed guards were posted to protect power stations and other sources of essential services.

May 29 arrived. Hundreds of thousands of blacks risked their jobs and homes in solidarity with Mandela and his council to stay home, and they continued to stay at home on May 30 and 31. Mandela was pleased with the response. He praised the students of the University of Fort Hare, the University of Natal, Lovedale, Healdtown, and other secondary and primary schools for their support and demonstrations. He also gave special praise to Asiatic and colored students.

The strike was a tremendous success, especially in light of the forces marshaled by the government to suppress it. Hundreds of thousands of courageous men and women defied their employers, the police, and the army. Mandela declared: "The government is spoiling for a massacre. . . . Desperate people will be provoked to acts of retaliation. In my mind we are closing a chapter on this question of a nonviolent policy."

On June 26, 1961, Mandela issued a statement in which he called for violence, noncooperation, boycotts, and the isolation of the South African government, diplomatically, economically, and in every other way. The tide was about to turn. The new epoch in South Africa's history was about to begin. Men and women would no longer submit. The hour had come at last.

For seventeen months Mandela sent chills everywhere in the bigoted society of the privileged, while living and organizing underground. He gathered freedom fighters after announcing the formation of Umkhonto We Sizwe in November 1961. He planned sabotage, not in the spirit of recklessness but as the result of a calm, sober assessment of the tyranny, exploitation, and oppression that had gone unchecked for too many years. The view on violence had changed.

> In our National Liberation Movement, the ANC has always avoided loss of life and conducted our demonstrations in an orderly, peaceful manner. We avoided any recourse to violence. That is what we did in the past. The South African government was not impressed. It continued to introduce new harsher laws, to increase its weapons, Saracens, army tanks, and other vehicles and mobilize its forces against us.

It has been government by force of arms—government by intimidation! I am thinking of an alternative method of dealing with them. The National Liberation Congress has to find another way of stopping the soldiers and police from coming into our communities with impunity. Years of nonviolence has brought us nothing but more repressive legislation and deaths. Our rights have been trampled underfoot.

"Mthembu!" I chanted his clan name to urge him on. He raised his right fist and shook it. "The time is nearing when our people will no longer talk of nonviolence. They have been talking about the day when they would fight against the white man and win back their land."

"PAC seems to be gaining ground rapidly. . . . They say they will liberate our oppressed masses from white domination within three years' time," I blurted out.

Mandela concluded that violence was inevitable. "I have asked myself: How long can I continue to preach peace and nonviolence when the South African white minority regime practices force and violence? If everything else fails, if channels of peaceful protests are barred to us, I am afraid we shall have to embark on violent forms of political struggle."

In December 1961, he published the manifesto of Umkhonto We Sizwe: "Soon there shall come a time when we shall only have two choices—to submit or fight. That time is coming in this country. I am sure our people shall choose to hit back with all means at their disposal in defense of our people, our dignity, our future, and our humanity."

Umkhonto became a closely knit organization for sabotage. The ANC could not be used for such purposes because its express policy was nonviolence. Its national president, Chief Luthuli, had won the 1960 Nobel Peace Prize for the organization's role in passive resistance. The people respected the chief; they would not go against him even if their doubts about the feasibility of nonviolence were growing and their hopes for a peaceful solution dying.

The ANC, under the guidance of Chief Luthuli, believed in

turning the other cheek, in loving their enemies. They were following the precepts of Christianity taught by whites who themselves practiced murder, robbery, and rape. Mandela made up his mind to approach the ANC with one request: that it depart from its fifty-year-old policy of nonviolence by approving properly controlled violence, and by not taking disciplinary action against members who undertook such activity. This closely knit organization of saboteurs would be guided by the ANC. As Mandela formulated Umkhonto's plan of action, he made it clear that he felt that the country was fast moving toward a civil war. Although he did not want war, he felt it was imperative that blacks be ready when it came.

Umkhonto struck first on December 16, 1961, the year that followed the Sharpeville-Langa massacre. There would be no repeat of what had happened there: no more brutalities, arrests, imprisonments, and torture of our leaders like Sobukwe and others, who suffered for pleading for sanity from an insane system of apartheid. Umkhonto We Sizwe hit government buildings in Durban, Johannesburg, and Port Elizabeth the same day it issued its manifesto. Mandela headed the national high command, which determined the targets and tactics, raised the finances, and trained manpower. Local sabotage groups were directed by regional commanders.

The whites responded violently. The government threatened to take strong action and made many desperate and determined efforts to crush Mandela and Umkhonto. But Mandela, the elephant of Amatola, the lightning of the heavens above, Hala! Dlomo! Ndlanga! Madiba! Mthembu! caused every effort to fail. The people chanted his praise. The government combed the area, using all the forces at its command to capture Mandela, but the Black Pimpernel survived.

Even Chief Luthuli, who still believed in nonviolence, recognized the legitimacy of armed struggle. He conceded, "Our goal is a united Africa in which the standards of life and liberty are constantly expanding. . . . This goal, . . . pursued by millions of our people with revolutionary zeal, by means of books, representations, demonstrations, and in some places armed force provoked by the adamant policies of white rule, carries the only real promise of peace in Africa."

Chief Luthuli tried to hold back the inevitable bloody conflict, pleading with those in power to come to the conference table, to grant the natural rights of men, the vote and other rights which the regime in their determined insanity continued to deny. While the people called him the last of the truly great peaceful warriors, the government was deaf to his pleas. Mandela in effect said, "If you cannot hear our chief, perhaps you can hear better when the bombs begin to explode."

I watched the government go mad the day bombs started exploding in Johannesburg, Port Elizabeth, and Durban. Mandela was smuggled across the border early in 1962. He flew to Ethiopia and other African countries, Europe, and North America. Umkhonto was creating shock waves with each blow. Umkhonto surprised the regime everywhere, as freedom-loving men and women rejoiced.

The conflict escalated. Each dawn revealed that Umkhonto supporters had acted by night and were gone. They struck even by day and vanished. Even as they blasted installations and buildings, these men and women asked time and again what it was that drove the whites, what committed them so earnestly and irrevocably to destruction of black people.

Mandela returned to South Africa and was captured on August 5, 1962, in Natal. He had been betrayed by an informer, and Pretoria rejoiced. He was charged with two offenses: inciting people to protest against the law, and leaving South Africa without a valid passport. He appeared in the Johannesburg court chained like a wild beast on August 8, 1962, Verwoerd's most wanted man, the royal son of the land, the gentle ruler of men and beasts alike; Mthembu, Dlomo; Dlange; Hala; Zondwa, Vela Zimbentsele; the elephant of Amatola; Madiba intonga; the gentle crocodile from deep blue waters. Protests demanding his freedom came from many parts of the world, but Verwoerd and his government hardened their hearts like Nebuchadnezzar. Mandela was sentenced to five years' imprisonment.

In court I felt proud and privileged to hear Mandela say: "I have no doubt that posterity will pronounce my innocence, and that the criminals that should have been brought before this court are the members of the Verwoerd government." Three times as he was leaving the court Mandela chanted, "Amandla!" and three times the people roared in response, "Ngawethu!" The power is ours!

As the police drove him away to prison, the people showed their support for Mandela when they ignored bans on demonstrations. They danced and marched along the streets, singing one of the songs of freedom, the song of Mandela: *"Tshotsholoza Mandela!"*

Mandela was taken to Pretoria Central Prison, where he began his sentence, but he was transferred to Robben Island Maximum Security Prison, where he was jailed for nineteen years before being removed to Pollsmoor Prison, where he remains today.

The military wing of the PAC, POQO, emerged during 1963. Sabotage continued in the absence of both Mandela and Sobukwe. Threats of ninety days' detention without trial did not deter Umkhonto and POQO from taking action. The arrest of thousands of followers did not deter them. The people's reply to white terrorism and militarism against black people had, therefore, begun a serious and genuine armed struggle in our land—the revolutionary war of liberation.

The South African regime banned both the ANC and the PAC on March 30, 1960, and declared a state of emergency throughout the country. The regime boasted that it had smashed the backbone of the black liberation organizations, but the truth was that POQO and Umkhonto We Sizwe spread a Mau Mau style panic amongst the whites. They both had underground branches, which regrouped into small cells of armed units. The standard weapon used by POQO was the *panga*, the homemade machete. Units of POQO staged a number of armed insurrections against police and other government supporters. Two whites were killed during the attacks at Paarl, a city near Cape Town.

Nineteen sixty-three had been designated by PAC as the Year of Destiny, when a massive campaign to overthrow the white regime was planned. The South African regime panicked and appointed a commission headed by Judge Snyman, of the Supreme Court of South Africa, to investigate the uprisings, particularly at Paarl. The judge issued an interim report, warning white South Africa that PAC was planning attacks similar to those at Paarl on a nationwide scale during 1963. The government responded by amending the Sabotage Act to provide for the infamous "ninety-day, detention without trial" law, and the so-called Sobukwe Clause, which empowered the minister of justice to detain Robert Mangaliso Sobukwe, the PAC leader, at his pleasure after Sobukwe completed his three-year hard labor sentence for leading the Sharpeville campaign against passes. The courts were stripped of their power. Any commissioned police officer could order the detention of a political suspect for ninety days at a time, renewing the detention indefinitely.

Minister of Justice B. J. Vorster ordered a massive roundup of suspected members of PAC. By the middle of 1963 more than 10,000 POQO suspects were behind bars, and 100 blacks were hung by the Pretoria regime. But the people were not deterred. Sobukwe's words were still in the air: "There will always be others to take our place." And those who took his place armed themselves with pangas, spears, machetes, axes, clubs, machine guns, bazookas, cannons, and songs. They fought, marched, and sang:

Sobukwe needs soldiers,
Soldiers of Africa.

On July 12, 1963, the South African police raided the house of Arthur Goldreich in the Johannesburg suburb Rivonia, where they arrested Govan Mbeki, Walter Sisulu, Raymond Mhlaba, Ahmed Kathrada, Dennis Goldberg, and others. The Rivonia trial began on October 9. Mandela was taken from his cell to join those on trial for organizing and assisting an armed invasion of South Africa. Elias Motswaledi and Andrew Mlangeni were there too.

On April 23, 1964, Mandela spoke in court, with the authority of a ruler of men, of the Umkhonto military organization and his role in its formation. He had garnered support and received guerrilla training all over Africa for the fight for a democracy in South Africa, which the white man feared. Mandela urged his people to make a final choice of freedom, a leap toward self-rule, a turn from oppression, racial domination, and slavery in their fatherland. As Mandela walked away from the dock, he raised his right thumb—a sign of solidarity with his people who had come to his trial, and those all over South Africa and the world whose belief in the ideal of freedom stood with him.

On June 12, the court delivered its verdict and sentenced Mandela and others to life imprisonment. Chief Luthuli defied his ban and spoke out in support of Mandela and his followers. He denounced Pretoria and appealed to Britain and America and all governments to bring full-scale sanctions against the racist regime to end the hateful system. The ANC and the London-based antiapartheid movement called for Mandela's release and began an international campaign for him and other political prisoners.

The followers of Mandela continued to urge him on. The armies of Umkhonto We Sizwe have increased. Forty thousand young blacks left South Africa and joined the Umkhonto We Sizwe and POQO liberation movements. Praise singers still chant Mandela's name: "Persevere Mandela, hero of heroes, the whole nation is marching. You will hear from us."

> *Hail to you, Mthembu,*
> *Indefatigable Mandela!*
> *Elephant of South and North,*
> *Star and sun that never sets in Africa,*
> *Hero of heroes!*
> *Persevere!*

14

America: A Taste of Freedom

My first encounter with cultural anthropology came when I was studying for my bachelor of arts degree at the University of South Africa. Melville Jean Herskovits's name stood high on the list of the learned cultural anthropologists in America. I was captivated by his books, *Man and His Works, The Myth of the Negro Past*, and many others. As a boy I had danced to the music of the thundering drums of Molemole. I had grown up in the world of black African tribal traditions and culture, which the colonialists had tried hard to stamp out, but couldn't.

After I completed my B.A. in African administration, anthropology, and sociology, African culture took possession of me. I was a Motlokwa, of the lineage of Tšhaka and Madibatwana, Moleya. The colonialists and missionaries had tried hard to instill in me negative feelings toward my own culture while cultivating Western values and culture in me. After reading Herskovits, I questioned the teachings of the colonialists and the missionaries, and I questioned myself. I was black and educated. To which culture did I belong?

I was walking back to my office one day from the Johannesburg Magistrate's Court when I was still studying law by correspondence at the University of South Africa, when an idea occurred to me. Could Herskovits still be alive? I went to the U.S. Consul General information service just behind my office to make inquiries. The lady behind the counter said, "Well, of course, Professor Herskovits is alive! He is teaching at Northwestern University, in Evanston, Illinois."

AMERICA: A TASTE OF FREEDOM

With his address in my pocket, I walked back to my office and typed a letter to him, and within three weeks I received a reply.

Dear Mr. Ramusi:
Of course I am still alive and teaching anthropology at Northwestern. It would be a pleasure for me to teach you if you could obtain a passport from your government to come to the United States of America. Both your tuition and travel expenses would be met by the program of African Studies of this University, with pleasure.

Yours,
M. J. Herskovits

It was always a problem for a black person to obtain a passport to travel outside South Africa. Just getting the birth certificate necessary to begin the process would be difficult. My birth was not registered. Fortunately, my cousin Motlatšo Isaiah Maphala solved that problem for me by making a sworn affidavit about my date of birth. The Security Branch police officer interrogated me in connection with my application for the passport. I told him that I was a tribal man interested in going to study for a Master of Arts degree in cultural anthropology in America. He looked into a file, which I later realized was a dossier of my life. He said, "Your parents have never been to school; your sisters, your brother Moraba have never been to school. Your brothers Nkwatlapi and Matsapola had very little education. You are the only one in your family to go through high school, the School of Social Work, and the University of South Africa." I was shocked to realize how much the government knew about me.

He stopped speaking and looked hard at me, as if he was about to assure me that his white South African government would never allow me to go out of the country to study. But he said, "If I had a son like you, I would thank God. You are going to get your M.A. degree! Your mother must be very happy. You will be hearing from us in due course." I could not believe my ears.

SOWETO, MY LOVE

I waited without further word until the day before I was due to fly out of the country. Then I finally received my passport, after paying the security deposit of 400 rand. The intervention of E. F. Potgieter, my anthropology professor at the University of South Africa, must have helped. He was the man who had introduced me to Herskovits's works.

Accompanied by Thabo Ma Selaelo, I went to Pretoria to get my passport. I introduced her to the passport officer and said, "She will be following me. Please help her." He chuckled and said *"Tot siens*—till we meet again."

On August 3, 1961, I said good-bye to Soweto, to my family and friends, to Johannesburg, to apartheid. I had Harlem, New York City; Kansas City; and Chicago in my mind. America! The land of the free and the brave. I was eager to see the country of Booker T. Washington, W. E. B. Du Bois, and George Washington Carver, the country to which our people had been dragged in chains as slaves, those unoffending people who had been captured like beasts when they had waged no wars against the white people of America and Europe. I was on my way to the land of Sojourner Truth, Harriet Tubman, and Frederick Douglass; the land of the Indian people who had lived there before the coming of the white man.

Professor Herskovits had sent me my airplane ticket. My first taste of freedom came at the Jan Smuts Airport in Johannesburg, when the plane was delayed for two hours because of an oil leak. The airline offered free drinks to all passengers during the delay. Because of the liquor law, black people were not permitted to drink without special permits. When I was offered a dry martini, I informed the airline hostess that it was illegal for me to drink. She smiled and said, "No, dear, you are no longer in South Africa. You are now free. Inside this plane you are in an international zone. You can drink what you like." I drank to freedom.

As the giant jet was about to take to the air, I looked through the window and saw my beautiful wife, children, mother, sisters, and friends who had come to see me off. I could hear in my mind praise singers of my clan speaking to the long-departed warriors, the Eternal Presences of the Babirwa clan.

AMERICA: A TASTE OF FREEDOM

We arrived eight hours late at Idlewild Airport in New York. As the plane touched the ground, I thought of the Indians on whose soil the plane was now rolling. I thought of the African soil, and my mind went back to Molemole, to Soweto, where people walk with smiles in the streets. I thought of the drums of Kubjana-Ramokgadifela, and the mighty *busilo* drum of Mabjanene that sounds and pounds in the depth of the night, and the dancing, bare-breasted belles of Molemole. I was in the city of skyscrapers, New York.

Eduardo Mondlane and his wife, Janet, had waited for me at the airport for many hours, but the plane was so late that they could wait no longer and went back to Syracuse University, where Dr. Mondlane was then professor of sociology, after having served several years on the staff of UNESCO as a research officer.

John Henrik Clarke and LeRoi Jones, accompanied by two other friends, met me at the airport. Although I knew that our African people had been stolen and brought to the United States in chains under guns and whips as slaves hundreds of years ago, I was taken aback when I saw their black faces waiting to welcome me to America on behalf of the black community of Harlem. Black folks, right there in the airport, going wherever they pleased, doing whatever they pleased! Walking about freely like white people! I was amazed. Clarke introduced himself to me. I embraced him and shook hands with all of them.

We walked to the car, which was parked in the street. Like the cars in Soweto, it refused to start. We pushed. Sweat began to run down my forehead. At last it moved. "Well, that's all right," Jones said. "Welcome to New York. We greet you in the name of the People of Africa in this land. Welcome, brother!"

Now, I saw the New York skyscrapers and great bridges with my own eyes. I marveled at man's achievement in the New World. When we arrived at a bookshop in Harlem, we stopped. Inside the walls were decorated and covered with pictures of black leaders from all over Africa. Books, books, everywhere! Books by Africans on Africa! I gazed at them, incredulous. So many books on Africa I had never seen before. My eyes ran everywhere. High above all the other pictures was one of Dr. Kwame Nkrumah. Next came Jomo Kenyatta, Patrice Lumumba, Sekou Toure, Tom Mboya, Chief Albert Luthuli, Robert Mangaliso Sobukwe, Nelson Mandela, Oliver Tambo, Kenneth Kaunda, Julius Nyerere, Nnamdi Azikiwe, Kamuzu Banda, Marcus Garvey, Col. Nasser, and many others. The bookstore was an institution of black culture and pride. It was full of books dealing with the black world and the black experience.

As my eyes moved from the portrait of one African leader to another, admiring them, I noticed the picture of President Dwight D. Eisenhower. An enlarged photograph of the warrior-president was attached to a dilapidated, rickety door in one of the rooms of the bookshop. I said to my guide, "Why is this picture of the president down here?" He kicked the picture and said, "He is in the shithouse." As he kicked the door, it opened. I saw that indeed it was the door leading in to the toilet.

Then Jones turned to me. "Now the people are ready. They want you to come and greet them." I found that they had already erected a platform on the pavement in front of the bookshop. Jones ascended the ladder, went onto the platform with a book in his hands, and looked across the street. He saw a white man passing by and began to shout and waved the book at him. "White man, goddamned white man, white man, you are damned." He kept waving the book at every white person passing by. The more white people passed by, the more he shouted, "White man, white man, goddamn!" I was suddenly in a world where a black man could curse a white man and still be free from harassment by the police.

Jones turned to me and asked me to speak. I froze. For the people of Harlem, I was a messenger newly arrived from home, but I didn't know what to say to such a charged gathering. Fortunately, the woman next to me realized I was unprepared for the rally and said, "Don't say a word. Tell them you are tired." I ascended the platform. "I bring you greetings from home."

AMERICA: A TASTE OF FREEDOM

"Speak, brother, speak," they called out in unison.

"I come from home. Greetings from your people at home. From your brothers and sisters, from your mothers and fathers, from your uncles and aunts."

"Yes, he is from home, from home! Let him tell us how our people are living at home. Speak, brother, speak!" they said. "We want to hear how it is back home!"

"I just came from home today. Today! I am tired. I will tell you everything tomorrow. All these years at home we thought you were lost forever. Now, I have found you! I have found my brothers and sisters! You are not lost! You are still alive! Thank you." I stepped down. Someone took me by my hand and said, "You look hungry. Come!" I was taken to a house around the corner from the bookshop, where I was given tea and food.

"We are Black Jews in this home," said my hostess. I was surprised at black people calling themselves "Black Jews." The food was good and the tea refreshing. I mused to myself, I had never met a Black Jew before. What a combination, to be both black and Jewish!

Clarke and Jones took me to the Harlem YMCA. I was accommodated there for the weekend as the guest of the people of Harlem.

When night came, I smiled. I was going to see Harlem and New York by night. I was going to exercise my newfound freedom of movement and experience nightlife in the neon city of skyscrapers without a pass and without fear. I saw the Hotel Theresa. I remembered Fidel Castro and his famous speech delivered from there. I thought of the people of Cuba and Soweto. I thought of freedom. Sugar Ray Robinson Corner. At last I was on the very soil on which the man with the golden gloves lived. Duke Ellington's Joint—the band's home. I touched the walls and windows of the hall in which he played his illustrious music, and moved on. Count Basie Restaurant. I went in and sat down. A hog was turning on the spit over a glowing fire; the music was superb. I ate and sang and danced until my muscles ached. I walked the streets of Harlem until daybreak and felt at home. Harlem was like a dream come true, an unbelievable dream, the home of urban black culture and life in America. I loved Harlem. I loved its people. It was during that first night in Harlem when I realized that black people in New York were still Africans in life and culture. They sang and danced like the people back home.

The next morning I saw the songbird in her nest, Miriam Makeba, the singer from South Africa, who now lived in Manhattan. She and Hugh Masekela lived in the same apartment. He was a student at the Manhattan School of Music. When I saw Masekela, I thought of Molemole. He belonged to both the Bakwena clan and the Crocodile clan and was of the lineage of Kgwadu and Madibatwana and Mamokutupi; Motlokwa-a-Machaka Maimela, my nephew.

One of the most moving experiences of my stay was the visit of a black resident of Harlem with me in my YMCA room. He arrived early Sunday morning, before I left for the University of Kansas at Lawrence. "I am your brother," he said. "I heard you speak at the bookshop on Friday. Welcome to Harlem."

"Good morning to you, son of my father," I greeted him.

"I'm Allen Tom. That's a slave name. Let me tell you something about Harlem, brother, about the black people of America, about the white man here, about black life. This is Harlem, brother. This is Harlem, where our people live and die. You will hear screams of fire engines night and day. You will smell smoke, see flames, women jumping up and running out of burning buildings in their nightgowns. Soon you will be tearing blankets from burning beds, and carrying children and old folks from flaming rooms, and you will wonder what the hell is happening in America," he said.

I said, "Last night I walked and walked and admired the beauty of Harlem by night. I thought Harlem was a little heaven."

"Brother, stick around for a few days and you'll see what a nightmare it is to live in these firetraps. You'll see children dying in high flames and smoke from apartments on fire. Brother, the city of New York has turned Harlem into a huge slum, an isolated, enormous ghetto." He shook his head.

AMERICA: A TASTE OF FREEDOM

"Are there any whites living in Harlem?" I asked.

"The only whites who live in this hellhole are the dregs—the bums who can't make it anywhere. They can't make a living and are too maladjusted to keep a humble family structure together. Brother, it is a hell of a lot of bullshit for us living here in Harlem. Bullshit. The white man is treating the people of African descent like animals. They think we are content to live from one day to the other with booze and drugs, fucking wherever we can find it. They have turned Harlem into a fucking hell."

He started talking as if to himself. "We don't know who we are! Who am I? Maybe I am the king of Kumasi, maybe my great-great-grandfather was king of the Congo, maybe I am of the royal blood from Senegal, Nigeria, Ghana, or some other African kingdom. Who can tell? Who knows?" He looked at me as if I might know something that would help him, but seeing me silent and unable to answer he repeated, "Yes, brother, yes. Who knows? It is now three hundred years since our people were stolen and brought into this country in chains. We are still in chains right here in Harlem. Women suffer. Children suffer. We all suffer. God knows, it is a hell of a damned mess here in Harlem!"

He expressed a deep attachment to an Africa he had never seen but from which his ancestors had been brought against their will, leaving him disinherited, cut off from his true identity. He was almost in tears when he left. After he was gone, I looked out a window and Harlem still looked fine to me. There was nothing like the horrifying hovels, shacks, sacks, shanties, holes of Pimville, Orlando, and Moroka. There were no police patrolling the streets looking for pass offenders.

That Sunday afternoon Clarke and Jones saw me off. I flew from New York to Lawrence, where I spent a month at the University of Kansas undergoing orientation. I was surrounded by a large group of students from all parts of the world—from the Orient, from the West, the Arab world, and others from Africa. I had to share a room with a student from Brazil. When the time came for sleep, I panicked. I was finding it difficult to sleep in the same room with a white man. I started to sweat and tremble as soon as I got into my bed. I rolled and tossed long after the lights were off. The South African way of life had distorted my development so badly that the mere proximity of a white body could create a difficult situation for me. I had never before slept in the same room with a white person. It was two weeks before I began to relax.

While we were at the University of Kansas, we visited the home of President Truman. It was 1961, and he was already very old. He met the entire group of international students and showed great interest in those from the South American countries. I was disappointed when he did not show any interest in South Africa. I wondered how a great president like Harry Truman could fail to show any interest in the land of apartheid.

I visited Topeka, the city where the separate but equal doctrine was challenged and overturned by the *Brown* v. *Board of Education* decision. I looked at the courts and the schools and wished that Bantu education would die in my country and all the separate institutions perish with it. At the end of the fourth week, I left for Evanston to commence my studies in anthropology and African culture at Northwestern. It was a beautiful old midwestern university built on the shores of Lake Michigan. There were about ten or so black students there at the time, and most of them came from Africa.

My very first glimpse of the North Shore impressed me. Lake Michigan was calm. Boats floated on the steel blue waters, while birds and airplanes flew above, and girls in bright-colored bikinis ran across the university grounds from the shore. They reminded me of the bare-breasted belles of Molemole. I thought of my tribe back home and chuckled at the thought of white bare-breasted belles of Evanston running all over the university grounds.

As soon as I had settled down, I made inquiries about Professor Herskovits. At last we met. He was bespectacled and short, professorial in disposition and appearance, but there was a youthful air about him. When classes commenced, he be-

AMERICA: A TASTE OF FREEDOM

came one of my main teachers in cultural anthropology. Oh, what a teacher!

It was a joy and a rare privilege to sit in his classes. He was an orator, a scholar, and a wit. He would walk up and down in the classroom and say, "No matter how hard the colonialists tried, they could not stamp out the culture of Africa." I felt reassured, and proud of my own culture. With each class discussion my pride in Africa grew. "Africa is the home of man and the civilization of man. Darwin said so. Sonia Cole said so. J. D. Clark said so. Leakey said so. Dart said so. I say so," Herskovits said. I smiled with deep appreciation and thought to myself, So our Africa is mother of mankind and his civilization. But how did the Western world get to look down upon the culture and peoples of African descent? One day I posed this question to Herskovits in the classroom.

"Ethnocentrism," he answered. "It is nothing but the ethnocentrism of the white man that seeks to degrade the cultures of Africa and its peoples."

I posed yet another question. "But the Western people call our culture primitive and backward—are they correct?"

"That is again a question of ethnocentrism and racism on the part of the Western man. To be primitive is to be first, not backward or bad. There should be no value judgments in explaining and defining culture. The culture of Africa is the first culture in our world; the first culture, I say. It has continued, and changed while continuing. This continuity and cultural change must be understood if we are to grasp the new reality of Africa in all its meaning." I was now on the road to understanding. Herskovits was removing the cultural dilemma in which I had found myself. The African culture survived against all odds.

I began to understand that the culture of my people had retained various deep-seated African patterns of behavior and thought, even during the colonial period, despite the most intensive exposure to other ways and despite war, punishment, scorn, and intensive attempts at westernization.

My roommate for the first four months was a Spanish man,

José Blanco. My sweating and trembling in the presence of a white had come to an end by the time I started sharing a room with him. I was getting used to living with white people. The tribal man in me was also more at ease. My professors were doing it—transforming the tribal man into a universal man, far away from the land of his fathers.

One day soon after my arrival, an elderly man visited me at my residence. I went to the door and found a tall, handsome man with a broad smile, holding on to a bicycle. "Look, I am your father, Eric Grimwade. Good morning, my son. Welcome to Evanston."

"You, my father? But you are white," I said, puzzled.

"Yes, my son, your mother and I would be very happy to have you at our home. Here is my address." He spoke with a beautiful English accent, like the Englishmen of Britain.

Surprised, I asked, "But who are you?"

"As I said, I am Eric Grimwade. And I would like you, my son, to come home as soon as you can. Your mother, brothers, and sister are very anxious to meet you. Long before you arrived, we knew from the university about your coming, and we picked you as our foster son." I promised to visit my new American home soon. I discovered that it was a practice for residents in Evanston and the vicinity to call at the foreign students' adviser's office and pick up the names of students they wished to adopt.

I was invited to speak in various communities around Chicago—including Evanston, Glenview, Wilmette, and Winnetka. This was also when many countries in Africa were gaining their independence. The colonial regimes were challenging our right to govern ourselves. They could not accept that Africans had a right to manage or mismanage their own affairs; I found myself forced to defend the cause of black Africa. I defended it vigorously.

One day I was invited to speak at the Glenview Community Church, together with three other African students, from Ghana, Nigeria, and Tanzania. The fact that I came from South Africa did not prevent me from defending and explaining other African countries when they were under attack. I was invited to come back alone to discuss Africa with the men's club at the church. I accepted. I was pleasantly surprised when the members offered to pay my wife's fare to join me. Several months earlier Thabo had been offered employment in America, but we were unable to pay the transportation costs. The church paid her airfare from Johannesburg to Chicago, and she began her work as an exchange nurse at Presbyterian-St. Luke's Hospital.

When she arrived, I was invited to bring her to my foster home. A big welcome party was given in her honor. Thabo and I spent many days and evenings becoming part of a white American home. We met many South African whites who tried to justify the things that white men do to blacks. I saw that they lacked understanding or pretended to lack awareness, blinding themselves to the real issues.

One day a white South African professor visited. Some friends of my foster family came to meet him and asked him many questions about South Africa. "Professor, why is it that you people in South Africa will not allow such educated and cultured persons as our two friends here to vote? We have known them, and others from South Africa; surely they should vote. Why do you deny that right?"

The professor tried to get me to tell the Americans that as black people were not educated, it would be undesirable to entrust the vote to them. What he did not explain was that not all whites allowed to vote were themselves educated. I reminded him of countries in Africa that had obtained freedom and allowed their people to vote when their citizens were, by and large, unable to read and write. He then changed the subject and started to praise his South African white minority government for having overeducated the blacks. I told him, "For that reason, Professor, I believe that my people deserve the franchise." The Americans laughed. The professor also laughed. I felt angry. My wife shook her head and said, "These South African whites are in trouble."

As I settled down in Evanston, I made many friends in the

community, both black and white. I felt fortunate. I remembered the proverb of my people: The buttock of a guest is made at home by the host. I became immersed in a humane environment both within the university and outside its walls. I went all over Chicago and its suburbs, lecturing on South Africa to groups in schools, homes, churches, and universities. I never worried about a pass or about police.

Everywhere I went I was asked if there was anything in particular the American people could do to help in South Africa. One day I said, "I believe you can help. You can help schoolchildren with school fees, books, and clothing. The children of Soweto are in need of educational support." As I said these words, there was dead silence in the room. I told the audience the story of my own youth and how I kept on dropping out of school. I told them about my guardian angel, without whom I would have been lost. I told them of the hundreds of children in secondary schools, boarding schools, and universities, in need.

"Give me a name," someone called out from the audience.

"Wait, wait a minute. Give me a chance to write to the teachers and some parents that I know at home for names of students who may be in need of this help. In due course the information will come. Give me your names, addresses, and telephone numbers. I will communicate with you again when the names arrive." The teachers at home wrote, forwarding names of the students in need. I then distributed the names to those who wished to help. The Americans helped my people on a scale I had never dreamed of—thus started a two-year project.

Soon after I submitted names to the Evanston and Glenview benefactors, Molemole students heard from their American friends. There was direct contact between the people who gave and those who received. Americans opened their hearts. Housewives, doctors, professors, this congregation, that community, even high school students paid for one or two students to be educated. It was beautiful to see such generosity!

Seeing Americans helping my people this way, I began to

question our own condition in South Africa. I became immersed in this deep, emotional, beautiful living with a free and caring people. Now that doubt in the essence of my own humanity was gone, I turned my mind back to South Africa, Pietersburg, Pretoria, Johannesburg, and Khurukhutšhu Mission Station, and recalled a host of people who had constantly battered my humanity. I remembered that I used to ask myself, Why is it that I am so mistreated by white people? Did I deserve it? How could they treat me like this if I was not less than human? I thought I must be guilty of something brought about by my blackness. Was white right? What kind of a world was this? What could ease this strain, take this load from me? So I had begun to apologize for the system that dehumanized and oppressed me. I had undermined my own humanity, doubted myself because I had been treated like that for so many years. I dehumanized myself and my family—not overtly, but I did.

I was again the son of Mothibi-a-Ramathathe and Motswetla-a-Rasekgothoma, Batlokwa, of the lineage of the Babirwa clan, Mafa-a-Molapatene Kotoleleele, Matšhipi's brother, the long leg of Mabjanene, the son of Maubene, who is too brave, as my people would chant my praises. I was black and beautiful, the seed of Moshweu, the dark destroyer of the Babirwa clan, and Moraba, the warrior who returns to the battlefield when other warriors fear to die. I was fully human.

I got to know Hank Leffellaar and his wife in 1962. They lived in an apartment next to ours. I was surprised to learn that he came from Holland. He was the first Dutchman from Holland I had ever met. He was different from the Boers—his countrymen who oppressed our people in South Africa. Hank was a man of quiet disposition with a fine mind for details. He showed remarkable interest in the happenings in South Africa. Gradually we became so close that we began to live like brothers. When Miriam Makeba appeared in Chicago at the amphitheater, my wife and I organized a big party for her at the home of Hank and his wife. We had Christmas together, and night and day we discussed things that were close to our hearts. Then and there I decided that I would see Holland one day. I wanted to see the country that could produce both Hank Leffellaar and Jan van Riebeeck, Simon van der Stel, and the Boers who tortured us back home in South Africa.

Another one of my friends in Glenview was Nathaniel Robinson. He was a loving and hardworking black man. I once asked him to tell me why he and other Americans were helping the people of Molemole and Soweto, and he said, "We are doing it for ourselves, our country, our humanity, and our God!" A tear trickled down my cheek as he spoke. In appreciation, I thanked him.

Isaac Rangata, who was in charge of the Khurukhutšhu Mission Station, was my cousin and friend. He was blind and poor, but blessed with a beautiful singing voice. One day he wrote me:

Dear Cousin,

If you meet any kind people who can help there, kindly let them know that I would be grateful for any assistance to put up a roof over my head to prevent the howling winds from pestering my children.

Isaac

Within days, a gift from Glenview Community Church was on its way to help the son of the Crocodile clan. His reply was brief:

Dear Cousin,

Thank the people of the Glenview Community Church for me. Thank them many times for me. Tell them that the name of the house is Helen Miller House.

Isaac

Helen Miller, a member of the Glenview Community Church, started a fund to help the blind evangelist at Molemole.

I was invited to lecture at New Trier High School by Dr. Kay Rasco. The topic was to be Alan Paton's book *Cry, the*

AMERICA: A TASTE OF FREEDOM

Beloved Country. I told stories from the book itself. The students were moved. I looked into their eyes. I looked at Dr. Rasco. I tried to go on. Tears gathered in my eyes. I said, "That is the story of my land, South Africa. That is the story of the land of apartheid, the land of Sekhukhune, and Zulu Malandela, the land of Kgwadu-a-bo-Machaka Maimela, the land of Tshidi Moroka Morolong, the land of man's inhumanity to man. Cry, Beloved Country, cry," I said as I left the room.

Before I left America for Molemole and Soweto, Dr. Rasco invited me to speak to her English class again. This time I did not cry. My perspective had changed enormously. The change was brought about by my studies of Africa and its people. I was also bolstered by the knowledge that the black people of South Africa had friends in the United States.

Eduardo Mondlane had come to Northwestern University to say good-bye to his alma mater, his professors, his friends. When I saw him enter Africa House, I jumped to my feet and lifted him high into the air. We agreed to meet after the seminar to talk about the past, present, and the future. He told his audience Africa has a long way to go, economically, educationally, and politically. "We go forward. There is no stopping. Mozambique must be freed. The time has come; the spark of hope will glow; the journey to freedom starts; the dream cannot die. Freedom or death! Mozambique shall be free!" He was returning to the land of his fathers to liberate it from five hundred years of colonial torture and discrimination.

As Mondlane spoke, Professor Herskovits's face lit up with approval and joy. Finally, Mondlane declared, "Friend, allow me to say good-bye. I go to the tribes of Gaza and Ngungunyane. I have heard the singing of the wind. Freedom in our lifetime! Freedom now, freedom for the sons and daughters of Mother Africa! Revolution now!"

Mondlane had changed. That pious man was now speaking openly of returning to Mozambique to free his people through armed insurrection. In his speech, he had said, "The only language the Portuguese will understand and respect is the language of guns and bullets. We have prayed and pleaded. Our father prayed, protested, and begged before us. The hardened hearts and minds of the Portuguese regime were not moved. Now bullets and guns shall be the new language of our times."

It was when I saw Mondlane the next morning that I learned how he was deported from South Africa, arrested, and interrogated by the Portuguese police about his efforts to organize a Mozambique students' association; how the Portuguese authorities had thought of nipping his black nationalism in the bud by sending him to a university in Portugal; how at the University of Lisbon, the son of Gaza and Ngungunyane defied surveillance and continued along the path of revolutionary ideas.

As he was telling me the moving tale of his past, he stood up, started to pace the hotel room, and said, "It was there at Lisbon University that I met and became friends with African brothers from other territories, such as Dr. Agosthino Neto, Marcelino dos Santos, Amilcar Cabral." He sat on the bed and looked into my eyes. "Brother," he said, "the fate of Africa is in their hands." After spending a year in Lisbon, he came to Oberlin College and obtained a B.A. degree in 1953. Then he came to Northwestern University and got his M.A. and Ph.D. in sociology, and he spent another year at Harvard University doing research in role conflict. Now he was a professor of sociology at Syracuse University.

As if in pain, he caught me by my right hand and with tears in his eyes, he said, "Good-bye, son of Africa, good-bye, son of my father, good-bye, son of my mother. If we meet again in this life, then praise be to the God of our fathers, and if we meet in the world to come, we shall meet again. I am leaving. I am going to assemble our people at home into a revolutionary guerrilla army to smash the Portuguese and their allies. Let us fight to the end. Let us have faith in our cause. Freedom is now within our reach, brother. Now nothing else matters."

As I said good-bye to my friend, a fear that I would never see him again gripped me. That was the last time I saw Eduardo Mondlane alive. Seven years later, he was assassinated in Dar es Salaam. "Someday, somewhere, we shall meet, in this or the next world to come. The struggle continues." Those were the last words I heard from him, in a letter from the land of Gaza, Mozambique. They were the last words he said as we parted. May the Lord bless him and keep him until we meet again in the land of the Living Dead.

While studying for the M.A. degree at Northwestern University, I was also studying for my law degree by correspondence with the University of South Africa. I completed both the M.A. and Attorney's Admission Diploma in 1962. I was then offered a scholarship by Professor Herskovits to continue with my graduate work at Northwestern in anthropology.

In February 1963, I received a letter from the Incorporated Law Society of the Transvaal, which controls the admission of attorneys to legal practice in that province. The secretary's letter reminded me that in order to be admitted as an attorney in the Transvaal, I would have to apply within two years of service of my articles of clerkship. From their records, it appeared to be more than two years since my articles of clerkship had expired. I was advised to go back to South Africa immediately, failing which I would have to do the articles of clerkship all over again. Another three years!

I decided to return. Professor Herskovits was in Evanston Hospital with a serious heart ailment. I was informed that I could not see him because of doctors' orders. I explained that I could not possibly leave America without seeing the man who had brought me there, the man who had taught me so much. My "guardian"! Mrs. Herskovits interceded in my behalf, and my wife and I went to see him in the hospital. He was cheerful and humorous. He wished me well as I departed. I can still see his big smile as I was leaving him. Two weeks later, Professor Melville Jean Herskovits was no more. The American embassy broke the news to me in Pretoria. May he sleep well with the Eternal Presences of his fathers.

I said farewell to Hank Leffellaar and his wife, knowing

that they would continue to be a brother and a sister to my beloved Thabo, who was remaining behind to complete her nursing exchange program before rejoining me in South Africa. Hank and I embraced each other as brothers. I departed with Holland on my mind. I decided to go to see the land from which Hank came.

En route to South Africa, I stopped in Holland and stood in the streets of Amsterdam to behold the soil on which Jan van Riebeeck must have walked before sailing to South Africa to bring a race that brought tears to our land. I moved about in the University of Leiden, where Hank Leffellaar, de Groot, Voet, and Van den Linden studied law. I found a people quite different from the ones who tortured us in South Africa. So, the Dutch people of Holland could smile! They smiled like the beautiful ones of Molemole in the land of Kgwadu and Madibatwana.

I arrived in Soweto on the first day of March 1963, eager to tell about America. I found there were already 400 students who had received financial aid from my American friends. It was moving to see so many benefiting from a few friends they had never met. Many came to see me and showed me the gifts of books, and clothing, in addition to scholarship aid. Some had received blankets, and I thought of the tattered blanket I took from my mother's hut the first time I left. The people of Molemole began to refer to me by many names—father of fathers, husband of widows, father of orphans, father of the fatherless, friend of the children of Tsherane and Kgwadu and Madibatwana.

I leafed through the pages of the books sent in the name of the people of Glenview and Evanston, who had heard my speeches. Never had I experienced such joy, such unmitigated joy as when I returned to the bosom of my people and felt again the reassuring measure of their love and trust! With this tremendous upsurge of love, I began to comprehend the link between my sense of responsibility and their expectation of my accountability to them. Thus, what started during my sojourn in Evanston, Illinois, was transformed into the beginning of a long commitment when I returned to Molemole and Soweto. The happiness of the students and parents who had received gifts from the Americans gave me strength.

Thabo returned to me in Soweto and Molemole at the end of 1963. It was heartening to learn from the daughter of the Elephant clan that the correspondence was continuing between the benefactors and the beneficiaries, that the people of Glenview and Evanston were continuing to help our people even after Thabo and I had both left the land of Lincoln behind.

In nine months' time, we were blessed with the birth of a third baby boy. We named the baby Mothibi Glenview Evanston Ramusi, blood of our blood, flesh of our flesh! A tribute to freedom and humanity, to our American experience, which stood like a monument in our minds!

Part Three

The Revolutionary Years

15

Back Home

I went back to South Africa fully aware that the white establishment would try to dehumanize me and drag me into the bottomless pit of oppression and racial discrimination, as they had done before. I had decided to go back to Molemole, to Soweto, to my people, to my land, because they were too valuable to abandon.

When I arrived at the Jan Smuts International Airport, I was greeted by a host of security police, who were there to find out who had come to meet me. My guardian angel, Molatelo Ramusi, stood by my two sons, who had remained in his home while I was in America. I smiled as I greeted these representatives of the Babirwa clan. They had both grown tall and handsome. They asked me many questions about America and its people, and they wanted to know when their mother would be coming back home.

We got into the cars and left for Pretoria. The security police followed us for the thirty miles. They trailed us as if we had committed a heinous offense. My children watched it all and laughed. My mind went back to Chicago. I remembered the happy days in which I had lived as a free man, without fear of the police. I looked through the rearview mirror and saw the security police taking a route toward the east while we moved west. As we headed straight to the home of my guardian angel, I let out a long sigh of relief. Selaelo, my nine-year-old son, looked into my eyes and said, "Do the American police bother the people like our police here, Daddy?" I assured him that in America I was free to go and come as I pleased and the police never bothered me or any of the many people I visited. I knew my sons could not even imagine what it was like to be free.

The following week Molatelo accompanied me to a government building to surrender my passport so that I could collect the 400-rand security deposit he had paid for me when it was issued. It was oppressively hot during March in Pretoria. When we arrived at the government building, we found an old Afrikaner security guard standing at the elevator. When we tried to get on the elevator, he stopped us. "No, no, no! Kaffirs are not allowed to use this elevator. Walk!" he shouted, as if shouting was the only thing he was ever taught to do when speaking to black people.

"Are we to walk ten floors up? Is this—?" I did not complete my question. He was on me, pushing me away from the elevator.

"Kaffirs are not allowed to stand in front of this elevator. Walk! There are the stairs!" he snarled at us.

"Please let my brother go into the elevator! He is old. I will walk up the stairs. Please!" I tried to suppress my rage. Inside, I was at the point of bursting.

Molatelo said, "This man is my brother, son of my father's brother. He has just returned from America, from overseas, where he was free. Please let him go into the elevator. I will remain behind. He is an educated man, a lawyer," Molatelo offered, thinking this piece of information might make the guard change his mind and allow us to use the elevator. The old Afrikaner was not impressed.

"*Loop julle*—Walk, you! Move from here! This is not America. This is the Union of South Africa. No! This is the Republic of South Africa. White man is boss!"

I was back in the land of humiliation. So my brother and I walked up the ten flights of stairs. Breathless. Enraged. Exhausted. Demeaned.

At last, when we returned to the ground floor, I stopped in front of the security guard and said, "I hope one day my child will show mercy to your child long after we are gone. I hope your child and my child will live in the times of humane hearts." I walked away, feeling a little better.

I had arrived in South Africa on Friday, March 1, 1963. On the following Monday, I called at the offices of the secretary organizer of the Incorporated Law Society of the Transvaal to inquire about my status. I was informed that I would have to do my articles of clerkship de novo—another three years, as if I had never been articled before. I was puzzled and hurt. With pain in my heart, I went back to Johannesburg and entered into a new clerkship with the same attorney who had articled me before. I decided to research the law, to find out if I could apply for admission in spite of the opposition of the law society. My research led me to the conclusion that I had an excellent chance of success. I consulted more than nine advocates on the Johannesburg and Pretoria bar councils. They all discouraged me. Some of them were Queen's counsels and senior counsels; some had been my teachers at the University of South Africa Law School. Ultimately, I found one who agreed to take my case before the Supreme Court. He was Advocate L. W. H. Ackerman of the Pretoria Bar Council, a teacher of law at the University of South Africa, and later a judge on the Supreme Court. In 1987 he resigned and became professor of law at Stellenborsh University, one of the largest in South Africa.

When the matter was called before Judge Cillie, it was postponed. I thought I had lost the case before it even started, since I'd recently heard that late applications from whites had not been turned down. I could not understand why they were opposing my application. I had asked them to give me the names of any recent applicants who were admitted late without opposition from the law society, and I was assured that no persons had done so. I had searched high and low for such cases, but without success. My advocate could find none either. But they were there. And the law society knew it.

My advocate rose to make the application to the court that I be admitted forthwith. Judge Cillie asked him to sit down. He then addressed the advocate for the law society.

"Mr. Eloff," the judge said, "can you tell me why you are opposing this application for admission?"

"Because, my lord, my instructions are to oppose the application. The applicant should have made his application within the period of two years from the date of the completion of his articles of clerkship, or within a further period allowed by the court. He did not do so. Instead, he went to America for some obscure reasons."

"The applicant states that he has been to the United States of America to continue his studies at the Northwestern University in Illinois. There he obtained the degree of Master of Arts in anthropology. Is that what you say was obscure?" asked Judge Cillie.

I felt encouraged. My advocate appeared happy. My guardian angel did not understand much, because the hearing was conducted in English. Then Judge Cillie asked, "Mr. Eloff, have the Transvaal courts ever entertained such an application?"

"Yes, my lord," conceded Mr. Eloff.

"Can you give the name of any of the cases you know?"

"*Ex Parte Kloppers*, a judgment of the full bench, Judges Hill and Ludorf. It was heard on the twentieth of May, 1963."

"Was he admitted?"

"Yes, my lord."

"By the full bench?"

"Yes, my lord."

"Now, tell me, can I, sitting here as a single judge, go against that decision even if I disagree with it?"

"No, my lord."

"Then why are you opposing this application?"

Now the moment I had been waiting for had come. I looked at my guardian angel and smiled. I wished he could have understood the question.

BACK HOME

The judge adjourned the hearing until the following morning. It had taken a mere twenty minutes.

When the verdict was about to be announced the next morning, the names of the white applicants who had been admitted without opposition by the Incorporated Law Society of the Transvaal came into my mind. And so did the name of J. B. Vusani, a black man who had been turned down in the Cape Province. But I was to be more fortunate. Judge Cillie announced, "I have come to the conclusion that I am bound by the decision of the full bench. But even if I am not so bound, I would still follow it because I can find no reason to doubt its correctness. Under the circumstances, therefore, the court grants an order, firstly, that the late application of the applicant is condoned. He is given an extension of the period in which to apply for his admission. He is today admitted as an attorney of this court, and he is given leave to apply later on the same papers for his admission as a notary public and conveyancer."

I almost fell on my back right there in court. I was being given a fair trial in this country of injustice. I won!

"Is the applicant here? Let him come forward."

I stood up. An oath was administered to me. The judge congratulated me. I felt like a newborn baby! I knew that my moment to serve my people had at last arrived. I would be able to walk into the courts and appear for victims of apartheid and racism. There were already cases waiting for me. I had to run to catch the 12:00 train for Johannesburg to be on time for my first court appearance. At 2:00 P.M., I walked into the Johannesburg Magistrate's Court with my head high, to defend two black women who were charged on an offense under the pass law. At 2:15 sharp, the magistrate ascended the bench, and the court orderly announced, "Silence in the court!"

The prosecutor's Afrikaans sounded throughout the courtroom: "The crime with which both of you are charged is that you entered the magisterial area of Johannesburg without a permit." The allegation was that the women were living with their husbands and children in contravention of the influx control laws. Both women pleaded not guilty, and I rose to inform the court that I was appearing for both of them. Thoko Mabinda was a thirty-year-old mother of three and a housewife of immeasurable beauty with a nine-month-old baby strapped on her back. Nobantu Mthembu was the mother of a one-year-old infant who at twenty-five years of age looked as if she could be fifty-five. She ascribed her premature aging to her never-ending troubles caused by the pass laws.

The husbands of both the accused perched themselves on the benches of the section of the courtroom reserved for blacks who came to listen to the cases. Fear was on their faces. I was feeling uncomfortable with the prospect of defending these women on a matter so serious it could result in breaking up their families.

Just before the prosecutor's first witness testified, he made the following statement to the court: "Your Worship, the state would be willing to withdraw all charges against both the accused if they would agree to leave Johannesburg within three days and return to their Bantustan. The Transkei reservation from which they have come." The prosecutor further explained to the court that the women had in fact arrived in Johannesburg and applied for permission to reside there. After they were both refused permission to live in the city with their husbands and children, they paid an official to change their passes so that they could appear to qualify to reside in Johannesburg. He said that such a thing was fraud, that the charges being brought in this case were of fraud.

The Afrikaner prosecutor was still angrily banging on the table and shouting threats against black "violators" of the pass laws when the two black children began to cry at the top of their lungs. They screamed as if in protest against the trial. The court was forced to adjourn without any evidence being offered. The case was postponed for a week.

Both women disappeared after they left the court and were never seen before the magistrate again. But worse things were still to come as I became a warrior for my people in court.

16

Warrior in the Court

In South Africa if a black woman loses her husband by death, divorce, or desertion in an urban area, she will be forced to leave her home because of the pass laws. If she has no children, the government authorities will try to accommodate her in a hostel for women only. If she is ill, too old to work, or has children, she must face a life of destitution in a Bantustan—the tribal reservation. It does not matter whether she has a job and employers who want her services. Removal to the Bantustan is tantamount to starvation.

Jane Msele had lived happily with her husband in Johannesburg for over forty years when her husband died. Soon after, she received a letter from the local government representative requesting her to report to his office, where she learned that she would have to pack up her goods and leave her home. "I felt as if a train were running over me when that white man was telling me to leave my home," she told me. "The government is trying to force me to divorce the Msele family after my husband's death. I won't do it. I can't." According to the custom and traditions of the Zulu people, to whom she belonged, a woman is not permitted to leave her husband's home after his death. "Let the government arrest me. I will not leave my home. I am the daughter of generations of Zulu warriors, daughter of Shaka, Dingaan, and Zulu Malandela, kings and rulers of the African soil. I will stay in my home," she insisted.

A week after her last visit to the local superintendent's office,

Mrs. Msele received a formal written notice requiring her to vacate her house within thirty days, failing which she would be criminally charged and evicted.

Thirty days elapsed, and Jane Msele was still in her house. The police arrested her for refusing to leave.

I conducted a thorough legal research into the housing regulations, pass laws, and women's rights. A month later the case was tried in the Orlando Magistrate's Court. Mrs. Msele walked slowly on swollen feet and breathed with difficulty as she entered the courtroom. She stood quietly and listened to the prosecutor read the charges against her in Zulu and Afrikaans. Tears rolled down her cheeks. I feared that she might break down. She pleaded not guilty.

It was alleged that Jane Msele had contravened Housing Regulation 15(K)(1) of Government Proclamation No. 1036, dated June 14, 1968, which stated that if the registered tenant does not occupy the house with his dependents, the tenant is subject to eviction after thirty days' notice. Countless numbers of deserted, divorced, and widowed women had been victims of this law, sent back to the Bantustans to face certain starvation. But what no one had argued before was that this housing regulation was directed specifically at the registered tenant—it had nothing to do with the dependents per se. In fact, the only concern Regulation 15(K)(1) had for the dependents was that in the event of the tenant's death, the dependent was to be given first preference in reassigning the lease. So Mrs. Msele not only wasn't legally subject to eviction but should have become the new tenant.

I argued this in my cross-examination of the prosecution's first witness, the superintendent of the Orlando West Municipal Office. The state had brought an innocent and wronged party before this court. The magistrate, Mr. Van Vuuren, immediately delivered his judgment. He found the accused not guilty and ruled that in the future such cases would not be heard in his court. As he was the magistrate who heard practically all the cases involving widows, divorced women, and deserted wives who were removed from their homes, this meant that these women would at last be left alone. There would be peace in the valley of Soweto!

When I left the courthouse to join my client, scores of widows, deserted wives, and divorced women who had attended the trial were waiting for me to ask if I would take their cases. Mrs. Msele placed her hand on my shoulder saying, "It has given me much happiness to be defended by my kith and kin. I am so glad. I'm very grateful." She walked out of the court with her head held high, smiling.

Not all my cases were successful, however. Martha Mbatha, a widow and devout Christian, entered my office as an icy wind blew. Her face was drawn, its color that of dead leaves. Her husband had died recently; she had no children. The authorities told her she must leave her home and go to the Bophuthatswana Bantustan—a Zulu reservation. "I can't go on, child of my mother.... Help me!" she pleaded to me in Zulu.

She and her husband had built their home in Soweto using their own hard-earned funds. She was denied possession of the house by authorities who told her that they would give the house to her brother-in-law, who lived in Bophuthatswana Bantustan, although he would not be permitted to live in the house either. The government would sell it for whatever price they saw fit and give her brother-in-law the money. He would also inherit her, although he was already legally married. Mrs. Mbatha and her brother-in-law protested that they could not accept this decision because they were both Christians. Mrs. Mbatha refused to move to the Bantustan. "That would be tantamount to suicide," she said.

Two weeks later Mrs. Mbatha brought a copy of an eviction notice to my office. I was about to laugh at it, because it reminded me of the case of Jane Msele, which had established in the Orlando court that such a position was illegal. But then I noted that Mrs. Mbatha was to appear in the Dobsonville Magistrate's Court, not Orlando. I was alarmed. I found out that the state was moving cases from Orlando to Dobsonville in an effort to bring them before a magistrate who was not aware of the correct new legal position. Moreover, the case was classified as criminal.

I appeared several times in the Dobsonville Magistrate's Court ready to fight the case, but each time I showed up, the prosecutor asked for a postponement. This went on repeatedly until one day I appeared at the appointed time only to find that the prosecutor had already called the case and disposed of it. Mrs. Mbatha was convicted, in the absence of her legal representative, of residing in the magisterial area of Johannesburg without a permit issued in accordance with the pass laws. She was told that the real offense was that of refusing to leave her home or the area after being so ordered.

I appealed the case for Mrs. Mbatha. In due course it was heard by the appeals judges in the Transvaal Provincial Division of the Supreme Court of South Africa. The court decided that because Mrs. Mbatha had been married under African law and custom, she had no right of ownership over her house. In addition, Mrs. Mbatha was herself chattel, or property, to be inherited by the heir to the estate of her late husband, as decided by authorities—her brother-in-law. It didn't matter that she was now Christian.

The morning following the hearing, the client came into my office to learn the outcome of the appeal. I could not look in her eyes. Her face had sunk from much suffering. I closed my office door and told her what the judges had decided. She listened intently. Slowly she groaned, "Where is God? Where is He? Where can I find Him now?"

Never shall I forget the cries of Mrs. Mbatha, or her tears when I informed her of the decision. I talked to her about the God of our fathers, the living God, the God of comfort, the God of Shaka, the God of Africa, when suddenly she cried out loud, "God is dead!" She stood up crying and left. That was the last time I saw Mrs. Martha Mbatha.

Anna Rantalane traveled 125 miles from the western Transvaal town of Stilfontein to ask for my assistance. The mother of five children, she had been deserted by her husband, who had disappeared into the mines. Anna Rantalane reluctantly sued for divorce. As soon as the local authorities heard of Mrs. Rantalane's circumstances, they decided that she, together with her children, would have to leave the Stilfontein urban area.

Government officials confirmed that they had deprived her of her house at Stilfontein, ordered her white employer to terminate her services, ordered the teachers to cast her children out of school, and given her six one-way tickets to the Bantustan of Basotho Qwaqwa, where she had never been and knew no one. They told her to take a vacant plot of land and build herself and her children a hut in the tribal reserve. This order left her and the children with no means of livelihood. When she refused to leave, she was detained. I visited her in her jail cell and defended her, and many others like her, to the best of my ability. When the case was over, and we were victorious, the magistrate was moved to say to her, "Mrs. Rantalane, I would like you to know that I feel very sorry for what happened to you."

Anna Rantalane's big eyes blended so well with her beautiful big lips and broad nose that when she smiled one could hardly believe she was the same person who had stood before the court at the start of the case. I drove her to her children in the black township where she was staying with friends. She took out a calabash, drew some water, and poured libations. She spoke to her ancestors, thanking them for victory.

I had seen the destruction of all the institutions of our culture by the white man. I had seen our people dehumanized, humiliated, scorned, and enslaved by whites and by government authorities. I had seen them brutalized, beaten, and thrown into police vans, tossed into jail cells and disposed of at the whim of the white regime. Many of our men and even some of our children had been detained and died in the cells. But it seemed to me the cruelest thing the white regime had ever done was to destroy black family life. How many black families could I save from destruction? What of the many thousands that I would never see? The white man lived freely with his wife and children. No one tortured him this way. Why did he torture the black man so? I was turning this over in my mind when Ben Mogorosi came all the way from Cape Town to see me about his problem.

Mogorosi grew up in Bethlehem in the Orange Free State, where he was born. He had been a truck driver there for five years before moving into Johannesburg, where he drove for one employer for ten years. When the firm relocated to Cape Town, Mogorosi went with it and remained in the same job for another fifteen years as a reliable, hard-working employee. Two years after he married, the firm closed, and all the employees were forced to seek new jobs. But Ben Mogorosi was told by the Afrikaner pass officer that he would not be permitted to seek new employment and would have to return to Johannesburg. He spent a year trying to establish his legal right to remain in Cape Town. Two years before we met he was finally arrested and deported to Johannesburg. That was also the last time he saw his wife, who remained behind in Cape Town.

When Mogorosi arrived in Johannesburg and applied for a work permit, he was informed that he'd lost the right to such a permit when he left so many years ago to work in Cape Town, and that he was to return to Bethlehem, where he was born. At Bethlehem he was ordered to go to the nearest Bantustan town; he'd lost all rights to residency in Bethlehem as well.

Once the best-dressed man in Cape Town, with an immaculate appearance, Ben Mogorosi now paced back and forth in my office in tattered clothes, rumpled as though he had slept in them. His worn shoes curled in the front, and an old rope, broken and retied in two places, held his pants up. Mogorosi had gone from one office to another for over a year trying to establish his legal right to continue to live and seek employment in Cape Town. Everywhere he went authorities sent him away, denying him any right to live and work in the area and warned him to get out of town before he was arrested. Nervous, overcome, and so tired of telling his story repeatedly as he moved from one prospective employer to another, from one pass officer to another, and from one lawyer to another without adequate assistance, his voice now trailed off as he retold the same story to me. Ben Mogorosi, like thousands of other black men and women, had been rendered stateless and homeless, his family life destroyed by the pass laws.

A little research showed that the rights taken away from Mogorosi were, in fact, protected under Section 10(1)(b) of the preapartheid Urban Areas Act of 1945. I immediately decided to travel to Cape Town to defend this man. After moving from administrative office to administrative office without success, I brought an urgent application on behalf of Mogorosi to the Supreme Court of the Cape Province to compel Cape Town to permit him to live and work there. The Cape Town municipality was so shaken by our bold threat of litigation that within a week of our intended Supreme Court action it granted Mogorosi a residency and work permit. Ben Mogorosi was finally reunited with his wife.

17

Our Guests

My thoughts often turned to America, freedom, and the good friends I wished could visit me in South Africa. I would show them my home, Molemole, Soweto. I wanted to remember these proverbs of our people: A dish that crosses fences today will cross fences tomorrow—this is the way our people express gratitude to those who have been of help to them. Hands wash each other. A person is a person through others. I wanted to express my gratitude, as well as the gratitude of my people, to the Americans for their gifts of money, clothing, books, love, and hospitality.

The telephone rang one day in my law office in Johannesburg. "Hold on for Mr. Hank Leffellaar," said the voice on the wire. It was like a dream. I had not heard from Hank for over a year. He was calling from Johannesburg.

"Welcome to the city of tears," I said. We hung up and I was at his hotel within minutes.

The receptionist announced my presence to him, but for a long time nothing happened. She rang Hank's room again, and I was given a telephone to speak with him. He asked why I was not coming up to his room, and I told him it would be better if he came downstairs. I did not find it polite to explain to him that it was not permissible for me, as a black man, to go up to his room. There was great joy when we met. I was accompanied by a friend, Peter Selepe. The three of us drove to my office downtown on Commissioner Street.

Later that day I took Hank to an Indian restaurant. He was

the only white person in a big room full of Africans, Coloreds, and Indians. During the meal Peter told us how he and 155 others had been arrested out of the blue at four o'clock one morning. "I was never told why. For twenty-eight days I was kept as prisoner in a cell without a charge and not allowed to call or write a letter. The trial was conducted in a synagogue in Pretoria because there was no place else large enough to accommodate all the prisoners. The trial lasted for four years. We were all found not guilty." He laughed aloud.

Whenever I went to fetch Hank at his hotel, the girl at the reception desk would say to him, "Your chauffeur is here," even though my car was obviously not a taxi. She knew very well that in South Africa taxis must carry signs indicating that they are for the conveyance of whites only or nonwhites. She could not imagine us being friends.

Hank's visit pointed up the tragic facts of South Africa. I had to hide my friend everywhere we went. He had to lie down on the floor of the car whenever we approached dangerous places or groups of people. This was the only way I could take him anywhere. Hiding the friend who had done everything in Chicago to make my wife and me at home. Hiding him because I did not want the South African authorities to harass him for visiting with a black man.

I took him all the way to Soweto in the trunk of my car. It was a great relief when I brought him safely back to his hotel. I took him to Molemole. On our way he was rudely searched by an Afrikaner policeman at the filling station at Warmbaths. He was pulled out of the car like a bag of potatoes, ordered to open his suitcase, and interrogated. I knew the white police sergeant, for I had cross-examined him in a case in which he was a state witness against my client.

The questioning was intense. The replies were given in Dutch. I witnessed it all and felt sorry for my friend. Not only was the Afrikaner policeman mistreating my friend, he was mistreating a top journalist. Hank was the traveling editor of a group of Dutch newspapers and a man from the land of the policeman's forebears. In a way I thought it fortunate that such an eminent man had experienced what the people in South Africa go through daily. He would return to Holland and speak as the spoon from the pot, as our people say. In the end there was nothing the policeman could do legally to prevent me from giving Hank a ride to Pietersburg.

We arrived at Molemole, and I introduced Hank proudly as my long lost brother. My mother was happy to meet him. Within hours after his arrival, Hank appeared to be completely at ease among my own family and tribe. I took him from home to home, introducing him to various members of the community.

I will never forget the conversation between Hank and Isaac Rangata, the blind preacher of the local Lutheran church. It was Rangata who was able, in a few minutes, to explain the plight of the people of Molemole and of South Africa to my friend.

We found Rangata in his house, sitting at a wooden table and wearing a dog chain as a symbol of his dignity. It was the chain of his seeing-eye dog, the dog that led him wherever he went. He weighed well over 300 pounds and spoke with a heavy, musical voice. Rangata referred to the forcible removal of the Batlokwa in 1958. "They brought my people from their old places over here, and the soil is not the same," he said. "They told us that we would not suffer, but we did. When we arrived here they told us that we could not keep more than three heads of cattle per family. They told us that they would plow our lands with government tractors, but they didn't."

"How do the people plow without cattle?" Hank asked.

"The government charges our people two pounds and ten shillings per morgen [about two acres] when they plow for them. The people have no money. What are they to do? I get a small pension from the government because I am blind. It is not enough to buy me cornmeal. What can we do? We shall never forget although we keep on saying, *'Dankie, Baas!'* Yes, we say, 'Thank you, Boss'; 'Thank you, Boss'; repeatedly to the white South African government for everything. 'Thank you, Boss' for laws against us! 'Thank you,' for taking our land; 'Thank you, Boss' for the pass laws; 'Thank you' for forcing us from our homes; 'Thank you' for imprisoning us. Yes, we keep on saying, 'Thank you, thank you, thank you, Boss'; 'Thank you' for our being suppressed."

He looked up toward the ceiling like someone studying its lines. A gentle smile emerged on the blind preacher's mouth. "We have become dehumanized because of the conditions under which we live here. The black man has to build an extra skin, another skin which appears to be impervious to the daily insults to his humanness. He has to develop an almost boundless capacity for suffering, sacrificing, and agonizing for one's family and people. We have become more beautiful inside our souls, more sensitive. We have developed deep insides that cannot be violated, that cannot be touched. Our inner thing is strengthened. We care more deeply, with overwhelming strength. Are you listening, Hank?"

"I am listening," Hank said.

Rangata struggled to his feet, removed the dog's chain from his neck, placed it on the table, and continued. "Mr. Leffellaar, let me tell you what our late chief did for this tribe to avoid having passes issued to his people. I mean Chief Kgarahara Edward Machaka. On a certain day when a team of officials were coming here from Soekmekaar to issue passes to women, the chief ordered all the women to disappear from the villages, so that when the pass officials arrived they should find no women around. He also advised the men to disappear to the fields and be nowhere nearby when the officials arrived. The chief explained that women had no pockets in which to keep the passes."

Rangata began to chant the praises of Chief Kgarahara:

> *Let us go to Bandolierkop,*
> *Bandolierkop of Sokana,*
> *To see the British army fight . . .*

Rangata was still chanting the heroic praises of Chief Kgarahara Edward Machaka as Hank and I were leaving. "The number-one enemy of the black man is the pass. Go well, Hank. Tell the Dutch people the truth!" he said.

I was pleased to see Hank so happy among our people at Molemole. He spoke about his experiences there for days after, until he left South Africa.

On the day of his departure, we sat for many hours at the airport and talked. He told me how deeply he had been touched by his visit. He spoke with very strong emotions and with tears in his eyes. "I was privileged to be here. I have seen the conditions under which the black people live. I am now, more than ever before, convinced that the rights of the black people of South Africa have been violated. They are entitled to their rights and their dignity above everything else. What breaks my heart most is that we could not eat together in any public eating place except that Indian restaurant, the fact that I could not openly visit your home. I came to visit you as a friend, and yet I was not permitted to show that I was your friend. This is the thing I feared most when I arrived in Johannesburg."

One week after Hank's departure my nightmares began. Every night I saw an American guest in my dreams. In my worst one, Nathaniel Robinson, accompanied by his pretty wife, Ola Mae, arrived from Chicago at Jan Smuts International Airport. They had been our friends during our Northwestern University days. Nathaniel was stationed at the Glenview Naval Base just outside Chicago, where he worked as a kitchen hand during the time we lived at Evanston. He expressed great interest in South Africa. Our friendship grew until our two families lived like one.

There he was. Six and a half feet tall—black and handsome! I watched him being searched like a criminal at the port of entry. He cleared. I was excited to see him walking toward me. We embraced warmly. I led him to my car and headed to Soweto, where black people live and think and plan for the day we will be free. Soweto, where blacks move and dance in invisible freedom lanes—Soweto, my love!

As we were about to enter Soweto, a police car stopped us,

and the captain, Botha, demanded passes from Peter Selepe, Nathaniel, and me. Nathaniel produced his passport. "I am sorry, sir, you cannot enter Soweto without a special pass. You must have a permit to enter a black residential area." The captain stiffened his neck.

Nathaniel said, "What is the problem, sir? I am black. I am going to black people's homes. What could be the matter?"

His mouth fell wide open when the Afrikaner police captain tried to explain how in South Africa, black Americans are classified as whites.

Peter laughed out loud, and Nathaniel protested, "I am sorry, sir, I cannot be a white man under any circumstances. Never. I ain't crazy. I'm American. I'm the guest of my brother here. I came all the way from the United States of America to visit with him and his family."

Captain Botha said, "You could stay at a hotel downtown." The policeman raised his eyes to study Nathaniel's reaction, ignoring what he had just said.

Nathaniel was determined. "I came here to visit my brother, Mafa Molapatene Kotoleleele Ramusi. I am going to his home! Take me to his house! Take me to Soweto! I will stay nowhere else! Take me to where my people live." Nathaniel was now moving southward toward Soweto. On foot!

Captain Botha stopped him. "I am sorry, sir, you cannot go into Soweto. Just go to a hotel. You are an honorary white while you are in this country."

Nathaniel scoffed. "Me, honorary white? Bullshit!" Now he was losing his temper.

Captain Botha continued. "You know, Mr. Robinson, many black Americans have visited this city, Johannesburg, and lived happily as honorary whites and returned to their country without any trouble." The policeman was really trying his best to pacify my friend, while I stood and watched it all without a word.

Nathaniel shouted, "That is bullshit! Bullshit! Take me to jail! Take me back to the airport! I will never, never, stay in this city as an honorary white!"

Nathaniel was still busy removing his luggage from my car when I woke up. I was glad that it was only a bad dream.

Andrew Washington, a tall, lanky, urbane white American, was another friend who came to visit. I had met him at Hank's apartment the night the songbird—Miriam Makeba—took Chicago by storm at the famous Gates of Horn Club House. Andrew had asked Miriam Makeba, Thabo, and me so many questions that I soon realized he had a fund of knowledge about our native land. I was to become Andrew's friend for the two years I lived in the Windy City. Gradually his home was like my own. We both loved meat—fat and tasty beef, mutton, and pork—and Andrew could cook all dishes the way we most enjoyed them. He took me to many sporting activities and important musical events and usually paid for the tickets. He and I were very close friends by the time Thabo arrived in Chicago, so I was not surprised when Andrew telephoned, informing me that he was coming to South Africa and wanted to spend a few days with me.

Peter and I met him at the airport and took him around the City of Gold and Soweto by night, so that he could see the social life of black South Africans in their own environment. But entertaining a white friend again proved to be fraught with difficulty.

On the third night after his arrival, we were on our way to Molemole when, after passing the town of Nylstroom, I became aware of a car trailing us. I reduced our speed to allow it to pass. It also slowed. I accelerated, expecting to outdistance it, but it also increased its speed. I explained to Andrew and Peter about my suspicions. Then the driver accelerated, cut in front of me, and forced me to stop. It was then that I realized it was a police car. We were all petrified when two robust policemen jumped out of their vehicle to confront us: *"Kom julle uit!"* They snarled at us, demanding that we get out of our car. *"Pas, kaffers!"* One shouted at us to produce our pass books at lightning speed lest we be molested. Peter and I produced our books.

OUR GUESTS

"*Nag Pas, kaffers.*" The stocky policeman shouted at us to produce special night passes.

"Aa . . . aah . . . my Baas . . . Ek . . . ek . . . ee . . ." I stammered. Then I committed the grave error of answering in English when the Afrikaans version of what I wanted to say evaded me. "My boss, I don't have a night pass."

The hefty policeman who addressed us turned red when I answered him. He smashed me in the jaw with his right hammerlike fist, but I would not go down. The second policeman went for Peter when he was trying to come to my rescue. Both pulled their firearms and pointed them at us. Andrew stood outside the car petrified. He was asked to climb into the car after he was interrogated about who he was, from whence he came, and where he was going with "two black terrorists and criminals." On hearing that he was an American, their attitudes became friendly toward him but more hostile and threatening toward us. Peter and I were ordered at gunpoint to get into the trunk of my Mercedes. After we were pushed inside, the trunk lid was locked.

"How dare they travel in the same car with a white man? Who do they think they are? Probably this is a stolen car!" They were referring to the car I had worked and sweated many years to pay for. They each drove one of the two vehicles, with poor Andrew as an unwilling passenger in my Mercedes and Peter and me locked in the trunk. After driving for what seemed to be hours, the car stopped, but the trunk stayed closed. Suddenly it flew open, and instead of seeing the angry faces of our captors, we saw the smiling face of Andrew.

"Please hurry. Don't waste time!" Andrew whispered urgently. Without any further delay we jumped out of the trunk, quickly cast our eyes around, and realized that towering just ahead of us was the Voortrekker Monument, built in honor of the man who came to Africa to take our land. We jumped back into my car, which was already in motion, heading for Soweto and out of the white areas. As Andrew drove, he told us what had happened.

"The policemen discovered the three bottles of whiskey that were to be presented in tribute to Chief Machaka. They started drinking and even gave some to me. I drank very slowly, but because of their greed they were soon getting drunk. I slugged them both and carried them, unconscious and dead drunk, to their car. Then I came to release you." Only an American brought up on cowboy movies would have been so bold!

We were anxious about the possibility that the policemen had taken the license number of my car. We wondered whether we might be followed, whether it might not suit their tormenting nature to hunt us, to imprison and humiliate Andrew and us further, particularly in order to save face; or whether, in fact, the presence of a foreigner would not aggravate the situation and get us all arrested, as had happened to many others before, leaving the foreign guests to be put behind bars and later deported. I could not risk placing my friend Andrew in such a situation, so we drove him to the Carlton Hotel. For the remaining two days of his stay, we dared not visit him. We could not even see him off at the airport. Thus it was that in South Africa simple, everyday human relationships were turned into a nightmare.

The only time we were able to entertain some of our American friends without harassment was when Dr. Herbert Trace and his wife arrived. Dr. Trace was one of the top surgeons at Evanston Hospital. Thabo and I had been his patients and friends. He was also very close to our foster parents.

On the memorable day of their arrival, Thabo and I met the Traces at the airport. We drove them immediately to my office, where we had prepared a surprise welcome party. After a most pleasant afternoon with our guests, and my staff and colleagues, we drove to our house in Dube village, Soweto. On the way we were stopped at Phomolong by the police. They wanted to know who our white passengers were. I told them boldly that they were my treasured American friends, whom we were taking to our home to continue with a welcome celebration.

"Drive on, brother. . . . Let's have a party," the black police sergeant shouted, and I drove on to Dube village with him leading the way. The sergeant escorted our honored guests into

OUR GUESTS

the house and moved back to his police car to watch for trouble. I made sure that sufficient refreshments were given to our honored peace officers, and the party went on undisturbed until the early hours of the morning.

While the Traces were with us, we encountered no confrontation with the system, and we were grateful that our friends were not harassed in our country. Thabo and I only wished it could always be so.

18

Deception

The Bantustans were created by the white minority out of the fear that gripped them when they beheld the collapse of colonialism and imperialism in other parts of Africa, spearheaded by Ghana's independence in 1957. When the Gold Coast won her independence from Britain, Pretoria shivered. Cape Town trembled. The South African government anticipated that the black South African response would be to wage a relentless struggle for power. Realizing that their days were numbered, Verwoerd and Eiselen promoted a fraudulent concept of "self-government" for African native reservations, which were renamed Bantustans.

Two years after the independence of Ghana, the new "homelands" were born of eroded, impoverished desert areas, or rocky mountainous tracts of land set aside as reservoirs of cheap black labor for the comfort of the South African white minority, who claimed for themselves vast, rich, productive stretches of land, abandoning blacks to toil and starve to death. Verwoerd and his regime remained the lords and masters, who sanctioned and controlled what the Bantustans did or did not do in their islands surrounded by a white sea.

The Tomlinson Commission, which suggested the creation of Bantustans, had boldly and unashamedly recommended that blacks should enjoy no equal rights with whites in South Africa. Blacks would be treated as foreigners in their own country, leave urban "white" areas, and return to the Bantustans. Whites would have to learn to work for themselves—do their own housework—but that was a hardship which they refused to inflict upon themselves. They had grown too dependent on us. Hence the Bantustans were established as dumping places for what the South African government called "economically unproductive blacks." Among these were doctors, lawyers, widows, divorced and deserted wives, children, self-employed businessmen, the aged, and the sick. Verwoerd, minister of native affairs, called the Bantustans the "cornerstone of the Afrikaner Nationalist policy." He and his secretary, Dr. W. W. M. Eiselen, pretended they could develop these pockets of poverty into autonomous black governments. Thus the government managed to fragment the black population into ten different ethnic groups—to divide and conquer by establishing these satellite Bantu countries within South Africa. Our only hope would be in active struggle directed at destroying the Bantustan system.

My people, the Batlokwa of Molemole, lost vast amounts of lands to white settlers from Europe. My people now live on shrunken, eroded patches where even goats can find no forage. The grasses and trees no longer grow in the land of Tšhaka-Maimela. The rivers have dried up.

In 1958 I visited Ranhlokana, my father's village, where my widowed mother lived. I arrived at midnight from Johannesburg by car. I looked for the huts and the cattle kraals of my father, but they were gone. Ranhlokana village was gone. I searched until I came to the home of my sister, Mokgadi-a-Matšie Marara, in the nearby village of Mangata. She led me to the new place where my aged mother had been relegated by the South African government.

Early the next morning I went back to Ranhlokana, to see what remained. The huts were flattened. There was nothing but bulldozed walls, roofs, grass, poles, and debris. Lonely graves stood under dry thorn trees. In every direction I saw bare rocks and creeping lizards. My father's village was dead. Tears circled my eyes. I vowed that if the white government ever touched our villages again I would do everything in my power to stop it.

We were able to save a few other villages from destruction, and today they still stand where they have stood for centuries. But the vast majority were destroyed forever.

The Batlokwa of Soekmekaar were not the first or the last Africans whose homes were demolished by the South African government. Other tribes, such as the Batlhaping, suffered the same fate.

George Van Truda Makhura was the ruler of Batlhaping nation at Dithakwaneng, Vryburg, in the northern Cape Province. He and his counselors came to Johannesburg to consult with me on taking action against the government to prevent their being moved.

I asked the chief if he had a deed to the Dithakwaneng land. He and his counselors produced it from their treasured briefcase. He looked at the paper as though it were a live thing. The land had been Batlhaping for generations.

At Dithakwaneng, the Batlhaping produced wheat, peaches, vegetables, maize, and barley. Fruit and grain grew in abundance, and fattened sheep and cattle grazed in grazing camps. The area was also rich in resources like platinum, tin, copper, diamonds, and gold. The government proposed moving the Batlhaping one hundred miles west into the Kalahari, where there were no trees or grass and the only water was too salty to drink. To survive, they would have to drive one hundred miles to Vryburg to buy water in forty-four-gallon drums.

I battled at length to save them from a forcible exodus. While negotiations were afoot to stop the resettlement of the people of Dithakwaneng, an army of police and other government officers descended upon the tribe and pushed down all the houses with bulldozers and tractors, and Dithakwaneng's wealthy community was no more! The people were forcibly conveyed in military trucks to the scorching heat of the Kalahari Desert.

Mampuru was the ruler of the Bapedi of Brakfontein in Sekhukhuneland. He and his people had lived on their land for centuries when they were ordered to move like the people of Dithakwaneng and Molemole. I was asked to act as their attorney to defend their right to remain on their ancestral land. When they entered my office I could see that something was gravely wrong. The king began to speak: "My counselors and I are here in connection with a heavy matter, a matter which is heavier than death. We would like you to help the children of Mashila-a-Gathisa, Mokgonyana-a-Phaahla, the children of Sekhukhune, the blood of Mampuru. My tribe and I have been told to leave. To go away from the land of our fathers to a place far away from our home . . ." His counselors interjected, "The place where they want to take us. . . . It is a place where no one can live. Mampuru's children will die! We cannot move!"

I looked into the faces of the Bapedi delegation and saw the determination and a united will to resist the removal. I assured them that I would work hard for them to keep them from having to leave their land. They pressed me to stop the removal in the Supreme Court.

As with the Batlhapings, I was still communicating with the relevant government officials to stop the removal of the people when Chief Mampuru's emissary came to see me with a heart-rending report. Two days before, at about two o'clock in the morning, while Mampuru's people were still fast asleep in their homes, the army surrounded the villages. They broke down the doors. They threw tear gas into each hut and house while the people slept. The people were choked. Many fainted. They were loaded onto army trucks, together with their personal effects and household goods, and driven to the east behind the Leolo Mountains, where they were dumped in the middle of nowhere—without houses, without water, without streets, without toilets, without health facilities, and without food—left to sleep under a few trees or in a few hastily assembled tin shacks. They were not allowed to bring their livestock with them.

All I could do now was ask the emissary of the Mampuru tribe to convey my sympathy to the chief and his people. The story of Mampuru's removal reminded me of another heartbreaking event that befell Chief Mokata, of Potchefstroom.

Mokata and his people had lived for centuries at Potchefstroom, when the South African government declared their land "white." The chief and his people were ordered to move to Rooigrond, near Mafikeng, an area far to the west. The people of Mokata refused to move. They begged me to defend their right to remain on their land. Again, while negotiations were afoot, the government officials arrived at Mokata's land and bulldozed the villages. Mokata and his people were loaded onto government trucks and dumped in the middle of a deserted area without houses, without water, without food, without schools, without roads, discarded like waste products in the veld. Mokata was no longer young—he was nearly eighty years old when he walked into my office for the last time before he and his tribe were thrown out of their territory.

"The white man says my land is his because it is near Potchefstroom. They say it is theirs because it is surrounded by white farmers' lands. They say the Barolong must move from their own land! I cannot leave the graves of my fathers and mothers; I cannot go from my ancestral home." Subsequently, Mokata and his tribe were relocated to a bare place near Mafikeng, in the Bantustan of Bophusthatswana.

As the white minority regime became more repressive and violent against blacks, it became increasingly clear that the forced removals were radicalizing the black man. In 1959, Chief Luthuli was told to choose between being chief to his people and being president of the ANC. The tactic did not work. Luthuli refused to give up his presidency of the ANC and was promptly deposed by the government. When the South African government under Verwoerd in 1960 banned, outlawed, and proscribed the ANC and the PAC, they thought they could kill the revolutionary spirit of the sons and daughters of our land. The underground successors of our liberation organizations refused to collaborate with domestic colonialism. The government increased its harsh and oppressive measures in order to intimidate us. In black areas a meeting of more than ten people required the permission of a Bantu affairs commissioner or magistrate. In the Transkei, Proclamation

400, authorizing detention without trial, was promulgated. But black people marched on along their path that would lead them to freedom. Under the leadership of Chief Luthuli, our people continued to defy the unjust laws, which included the Bantu Authorities Act of 1951. More chiefs and other tribal leaders followed the example of Luthuli, and the South African government took action against them. Our own Douglas Ramokgopa, a royal counselor at Molemole, was banished to the Transkei.

From the moment I had entered the Jan H. Hofmeyr School of Social Work, I wanted to join my people and demonstrate with them, but I had fears that such a decision would jeopardize the promise I had made to the Everlasting Presences who lay beneath the soil, and to my living guardian angel, that I would do nothing which might threaten the continuance of my schooling. I longed to march with my fellow men and face police batons, dogs, tear gas, guns, imprisonment, and death; but I was tied by my vow to finish school.

Many times I watched from the window of my room at the Bantu Men's Social Center and the Denver Men's Hostel as demonstrators were beaten by batons, their flesh and clothing torn by police dogs. I wept that the white man could be so inhuman. I wept that I could not stop the torture. I wept when my people fell in the streets from bullets, tear gas, and clubs. When I saw the cold bodies of our people lying lifeless like fallen leaves in the streets, I was angry and full of sorrow, but I kept on saying, The sun will rise. Now, in 1973, my time to fight had come.

My children were growing: Selaelo, Sekgweng, and Mothibi were becoming men. I realized the time would soon come when they would ask what I was doing to change things. I had to get moving for the sake of humanity, for the sake of my family, for the sake of my three boys and my people.

"I shall fight with you for our land. I shall struggle for Botlokwa-ha-Machaka Maimela. Our fatherland will never be touched. I am ready to fight!" I said at a meeting of our people. They seemed to say in unison: "Fight, Motlokwa, fight!

Fight, Mmirwa, fight! Fight, Motau, fight! Fight them for us! We are with you! We will fight them with you! Fight them until we are free!"

My king stood up and addressed me. "Murder apartheid! Kill it, Motlokwa! Go there and destroy apartheid! You tell them to go to hell with their apartheid! Kill the Bantustans!"

At this point I could no longer keep tears from my eyes. I could feel the breaking moment coming. The chief and his counselors left me there, thinking. My parents had both already passed into eternity, the village of my father, Ranhlokana, where my umbilical cord was buried, was now demolished; Khaola was gone, and my people had been removed. Botlokwa, Molemole, Mabjanene, the land of my fathers, was now threatened with extinction. I remembered what my parents had gone through, and what my brothers and sisters were going through. Would my children, too?

I decided to tackle the evil system of Bantustans, to destroy it in the spirit of defiance and confrontation. I announced that I had at last decided to stand for election to the Lebowa Legislative Assembly, and that I stood for no apartheid, no separate development, that I was going to demand the immediate release of political detainees and prisoners such as Nelson Mandela, Walter Sisulu, Govan Mbeki, Elias Motswaledi, Andrew Mlangeni, the lifting of all banning orders, the return of political exiles, and the calling of a national convention of all South Africans to sit down and come to an agreement to live as common citizens of one country, Azania–South Africa. I was informed that the minority regime planned to detain me and not allow me to stand for election. I stood despite the threat, and received 100 percent of the votes from my constituency.

In the legislative assembly I became minister of interior and economic affairs in May of 1973. When I arrived at Seshego, the administrative "capital" and seat of the assembly, I found the situation was worse than anything I had ever suspected. My people were living under the tyranny of a Nazi-type administration, in what looked like a concentration camp.

The South African security police, and more particularly the Bureau of State Security's agents, followed me from the first day I announced my candidacy. They were unhappy about my stance against apartheid and racism. The first time I entered my office as minister, one of them rolled in unannounced. He greeted my secretary and me in Afrikaans and attempted to hand me his business card. I asked him who he was and what he wanted. He grinned. *"Staatssekuriteit,"* he said. There was a long pause. "From the Bureau of State Security."

"You are from BOSS? From BOSS?" I exclaimed. He insisted on giving me his card, explaining that my predecessor, Chief A. S. Molepo, kept one of his cards and that he could protect me against anyone who tried to give me trouble. I told him: "BOSS and the Devil are one. I can have nothing to do with BOSS. Leave my office!"

My secretary showed him the door.

Thereafter, I lived under constant BOSS surveillance. They followed me everywhere—to the legislative assembly chamber, to the cabinet meetings, to our political rallies, to social functions, to public and private gatherings—they kept watch like hawks. The day after I became minister of the interior, I asked to see all the bills expected to be placed before the House. I had been informed in our first cabinet meeting that it had been the practice of the South African government to draft bills for all Bantustans and simply forward them to each local legislative body, to be made into laws as they stood. I was shocked to see what we were expected to approve. One of these bills proposed controlling the manufacturing of, handling of, and dealing in liquor in Lebowa. The suggestion was that white people would not be permitted to enter our bottle stores, beer lounges, hotels, and restaurants because of their color. Pretoria was asking "its legislative assemblies" to keep white people off any premises in the Bantustans where liquor was sold. Otherwise, they would be in conflict with apartheid.

In the same bill the South African government tried to impose upon the mothers and housewives of Lebowa the burden and hardship of having to take out a license before they could brew and sell traditional African beer, made in their homes for their husbands and fathers. The House was outraged. Rulers, counselors, and members of the House all angrily shouted, "*No!*" and without a moment's hesitation, the proposal was deleted from the bill.

I, being the only person trained in law not only in the cabinet but in the entire assembly, was asked to look through this bill. I removed all suggestions of racism, and the bill was placed before the assembly. The lawmakers decreed that racism and apartheid should be an offense.

After being passed by the House, the bill was referred to the state president for his signature, and it was passed against the wishes of some white seconded officials from Pretoria who maintained that the Bantustan legislative assemblies could not pass laws that contradicted Pretoria. The Lebowa legislators, however, went ahead and acted as they saw fit for their people. When that bill became law, the secretary of the Department of Justice, who was a white seconded official from the South African government, arrogantly proclaimed, "My government will never allow your Bantustan to legislate against apartheid." I laughed and told him that the people of Lebowa were not suffering from the disease of racism, did not believe in apartheid, and would not be interested in making unjust laws.

We opened the first hotel at Seshego after the liquor law went into effect. The cabinet and the senior seconded officials were invited to the opening party. The same secretary of justice stood next to me, sipping his Black & White scotch in a hotel room full of black and white people. While the liquor was being consumed, I chuckled a little, teasing him, and raising my glass and smiling, gave the slogan of our Lebowa People's party, "Love and Peace." He tried to smile, but the smile would not come.

It was during this 1973 session of the legislative assembly that two commissions were appointed: the Lebowa Civil Service

Investigation Commission, headed by Chief T. J. Mothapo, minister of public works, and the Lebowa Land Commission, headed by the minister of the interior, myself.

When I came into the cabinet, there were serious complaints from our black civil servants. They stated that the white seconded officials from the South African government service were making life impossible for them in their already depressed areas and that black workers were overworked, humiliated, underpaid, and tortured in their jobs. A few days after I became minister of the interior, I called a meeting of all black civil servants so that I could hear their complaints for myself. It became clear from listening to them that a commission would have to be appointed to investigate. A committee was formed, and immediately after the close of the 1973 session it went to serious work.

When the Mothapo Civil Service Investigation Commission began its inquiry, we were told by the secretary of South African Bantu administration and development that the employment, grading, and conditions of service of white staff were a matter over which the Lebowa government had no competence or authority; homeland governments had no power to interview seconded officials from the South African government civil service, and if we wanted to investigate, we would have to interview black Lebowa employees only. We proceeded even though we knew we could not get all the information we needed. The civil servants of Lebowa were also encouraged to organize and make recommendations to the committees. The Lebowa Legislative Assembly made serious charges of mishandling of black civil servants by white seconded officials, and the Mothapo Commission corroborated the reports. No action was taken in spite of the Mothapo Commission recommendations.

Soon after I joined the cabinet of Lebowa Bantustan, I received a letter from Chief Lucas Mangope, chief minister of Bophuthatswana Bantustan, proposing a convention of Bantustan leaders to discuss black solidarity. I was excited by the prospect; it seemed that at last the time had come for the oppressed people of South Africa to unite against domestic colonialism-imperialism with the banned ANC and PAC and all the leaders who were in prison, exiled, or under banning orders in the fight against Bantustanism and apartheid. God was not dead. Our ancestors were with us.

On September 30, 1974, five chief ministers attended the conference. Our own chief minister was in England at the time, so I went on his behalf. But I was shocked by what I saw. Chief Mangope, who had originally called the conference, claimed not to know the reason for the meeting and was reluctant to pursue the path of solidarity. When the other Bantustan leaders expressed confusion as to why they were there, I realized they must have had threatening visits from agents of the white regime. My hopes were high before the conference began, but I left a disappointed man.

In 1973 the South African minority regime decided to consolidate the Bantustans. They amended the Native Land and Trust Act of 1936 to enable themselves to remove millions of Africans from our ancestral homes. They maintained that they were going to create viable, autonomous, self-governing Bantustans.

I researched and found the Bantu Laws Amendment Act of 1973, wherein a list of areas to be excised was given. These areas would be taken away from blacks by whites, their inhabitants removed. Molemole was one of them. Botlokwa, my ancestral home in the Soekmekaar, would be destroyed and the Batlokwa moved almost one hundred miles northwest. My soul wept. The hour had come for me to join our people and fight for justice.

I left my legal practice and returned to my people to teach them how to resist a removal. The government hadn't yet announced when the Batlokwa would be moved; it could be years, and in fact it was not attempted until 1979—six years later, when I was in exile in America. I wanted to take every moment to make my people converts in the battle against the white regime.

DECEPTION

In the Lebowa Legislative Assembly there were five people representing the Soekmekaar district: Chief G. Ramokgopa, a descendant of the legendary Tshaka-Maimela, and great-grandson of King Kgwadu, the grandson of Tabudi-a-Mankwe and son of Masedi-a-Ramokgopa; Chief P. Sekgopo, Sekgopo-a-Bapedi; Chief J. Mamaila; and two members elected by popular vote, H. M. Leshabana and myself. The royal members were elected by other rulers of Soekmekaar to represent them in the assembly.

When I read the announced government consolidation plan in the press, I consulted with the rest of the Soekmekaar delegation. I rushed to Molemole later that day to inform Machaka and Makgato—the Batlokwa rulers. "Fight, Moila-Letsamaka! Fight, Mmirwa, fight! Your fathers' land cannot be killed" was Machaka's response. Makgato listened attentively and said through angry tears, "The war is on, Moila-Letsamaka, the war is on! The time for men to die for their land is now. Mmirwa, fight! The time has come, Motlokwa. The time for us to stand like men is now! Take up your spears and shields and fight! The land of our fathers must never go! Fight, lion of Babirwa, fight! Your fatherland must stay where it has always stood."

In our next cabinet meeting I suggested that Lebowa set up a commission of inquiry. In view of the fact that the South African government had, through its all-white Parliament, declared its lands and the boundaries, the time had come for us to declare where our land stood and draw its boundaries, and lay the government on the other side of them. Time was running out fast—tribes were about to be shifted like goods and whole communities mercilessly uprooted in the name of apartheid and this insane separate development.

I headed the commission to find out where, according to black people—not the white settlers—the real Lebowa boundaries lay.

We visited all the Transvaal areas where our people lived in September of 1973, compiling data to make our claim. At Bushbuckridge, we discovered plans for the removal of Chief

Mathibela Mokwena's people; his territory was earmarked for the Shangaan people of Gazankulu Bantustan. Ill feelings harbored in the hearts of Mathibela Mokwena and his people, ignited by the South African government, turned brother against brother, sister against sister.

"The Shangaans and Mapulana are one people. They are the children of one father and mother. My children," Mathibela Mokwena told the commission. "There is neither Shangaan nor Mokwena in this nation. We are all Mapulana. We are all the children of the sun. We are Malakeng. The South African government wants to see blood flow in the land of the children of the sun." Mathibela Mokwena went down to his grave soon thereafter of a broken heart. At every royal kraal where the commission took evidence from the people affected, the response was the same—fierce opposition to removal, bitterness, and threat of bloodshed by the victims of Bantustanism. They would take the law into their own hands if the South African government insisted they be removed.

In Sekhukhuneland the commission heard Victoria Dinkwanyane, Sekhukhune's daughter, and her counselors testify. "The painful memories of our removal from Boomplaats, Lydenburg, are still fresh in our minds. Now the South African government must leave us alone. How long must we suffer, oh God! How long must we suffer?" Dinkwanyane's and Mohlaba's nations were to be moved to make room for a white military base.

The situation was even grimmer in Groblersdal. Blacks had purchased and held deeds to farms and other properties in the Dennilton area, where there were four rulers and their nations. The government planned to remove these landowners to make room for a brand-new state, the South Ndebele Bantustan. The North Sotho were bitterly opposed, and tempers were high. "Our spears are ready. If the Ndebele want to die, let them try to take our land. The white man is the troublemaker. We were living in peace with Mapogo, the Ndebele ruler, until the white man came and incited the Ndebele to take our land," Chief Mathebe said.

DECEPTION

Prime Minister Vorster and M. C. Botha, minister of the South African Department of Bantu Administration and Development, maintained, in an address to the Lebowa Legislative Assembly, that Bantustan governments had no power to appoint commissions to determine land boundaries. But we refused to be puppets of the white regime. I looked Vorster squarely in the eye and told him that we did not believe in apartheid, that Lebowa was, in fact, the Transvaal Province, and that everyone, whites and himself included, who lived in the territory was equally a citizen. As far as Lebowa was concerned, there were no two South Africas. There were no two Lebowas. There were no two Transvaal Provinces. The territory belonged to all the people who lived in it.

Vorster got angry. "Tell me when your land commission claimed all these white cities, towns, and farms; Pietersburg, Lydenburg, Warmbaths, Nelspruit, Nylstroom, Johannesburg, Pretoria, Benoni, Springs, Groblersdal, Cullinan, the whole Kruger National Park. Did you know that they were situated outside of your Bantustan area? Did you not know that they were all in white South Africa?"

I repeated my statement: "As far as Lebowa is concerned, there are no two South Africas. There are no two Lebowas. There are no two Transvaal Provinces. The territory belongs to all the people who live in it. We do not believe in apartheid."

The discussions ended abruptly, with Vorster promising to discuss the Lebowa land claims at another time. No such time ever came. And Vorster is dead.

The South African minority government tried its independence trick on us in Lebowa as they had done in the Transkei and Bophuthatswana. I told them in our cabinet meetings and in our party meetings that Lebowa would have nothing to do with the sham independence of the Bantustans, which was nothing but a trick to deprive the black man of his land, discarding his own citizenship in the land of his fathers. Bantustan "independence" was the cornerstone of the South African government's divide-and-rule apartheid policy—imperialism at home, their modern form of slavery in the name of independence for blacks. A curse, and an insult to the intelligence of the oppressed.

I was greatly shocked later when Chief K. D. Matanzima betrayed our people and announced that he would accept their independence. Vorster publicly thanked Chief Matanzima for his "statesmanship." He had fallen for a gimmick calculated only to buy more time for this government whose days were numbered.

In September 1973, I spoke at the Progressive Party Congress in Durban. I told the gathering that things were changing fast, the revolution was on the way. I issued a warning to white South Africa that when attacks against them came, the black people would not come to their rescue or defend them in their dark hour of destruction.

I was later told that my statement was debated in the white Parliament in Cape Town. Some members had felt disturbed by my remarks, while others disregarded them. There were those who believed black people would always come to the defense of whites, while others felt what I said to be true. "There is no place to hide," they warned. "Africans will not come to our rescue in the hour of destruction. Let us not be childish. Let us speak to them while there is still time; the Africans are still able and prepared to speak to us. . . . Tomorrow may find us dead."

Some of the members of Parliament accused me of being a terrorist and a Communist because I had said that black people would not fight against the freedom fighters who would enter Azania as part of the liberation forces. I laughed and wondered if white people genuinely could not see the writing on the wall and hear freedom blowing in the wind from all over Africa. The matter was debated until the press conducted a poll in which over 98 percent of black readers indicated that they would not defend white South Africans in the event of an attack. The 2 percent who said that they would fight against freedom fighters from outside South Africa explained that they would only do so because they did not want to die with whites.

From the day I made that speech, I received threatening phone calls almost every morning. Anonymous letters were left on my desk warning me in Afrikaans: "You will be picked up as a corpse. Your home is in the mortuary. Your days are numbered on this earth! We do not need terrorists here in Lebowa. *Paasop!* Be warned!"

Surveillance increased. BOSS agents and the security police watched every move I made, continually harassing me, but I continued to speak out to call for the release of political prisoners, the release of Mandela, Sisulu, and others from Robben Island Prison, and the lifting of all political bans against Sobukwe and others. I warned South Africa and its fascist minority ruling regime that they were moving dangerously close to a collision with black power.

As I traveled and spoke throughout South Africa, I was encouraged by the response of my people, both young and old, but particularly the youth of our land, who were building up and increasing pressure on the government. I organized political rallies all over our fatherland, in the cities and in the Bantustans. In the villages our people began to speak their minds. And everywhere the Lebowa People's party went, we spoke amid ululating chants as if the days of old had returned. Strikes began. Week after week, workers arrived at my office—on foot, in trucks, in cars—to report that a strike was on.

The minister of the Department of Bantu Administration and Development, through his secretary, approached the Lebowa cabinet and other Bantustan governments, requesting them to agree to assume the power to "ban, banish, arrest, and imprison" their own people who were considered troublesome to Bantustan governments. I told the cabinet: "We are not wicked. We are not evil people like the Calvinist from across the seas. We will not torture the oppressed. We do not need those powers. The only powers we prayed the Lord and our ancestors who lie beneath the soil grant us—and the powers we will always want to have—are the powers of good, the power to love and help others, the power to create a society that is to live in love and peace with others. But never, never, shall we ask or wish for the power of evil to ban and banish and detain our people." And that became our official response. When I went back home to Molemole, to Botlokwa, to Mabjanene, my constituency of Soekmekaar were pleased to hear how we had sent the evil powers back from whence they came.

As minister of interior and economic affairs, I had the duty to consider applications for business licenses. The Bantu Investment Corporation had many businesses in Lebowa. They had been granted licenses to trade in competition with blacks in spite of the fact that the Bantu Investment Corporation was an economic wing of the South African government. In fact, it had managed to declare itself a "black person" for purposes of trading in the black areas. I would not under any circumstances grant a license to the Bantu Investment Corporation, because that body had done enough harm to our people. I never accepted that corporation as being black. It was during our struggle against Bantustanism that the Bantu Investment Corporation started grabbing much of our land and many of the economic development projects that had been acquired by the people of Lebowa. After the cabinet had negotiated with the owners of Zebediela Citrus Estate, one of the largest in the country, to acquire it for Lebowa, the Bantu Investment Corporation grabbed it. And it was not only the Zebediela Citrus Estate they took from the starving tribes of the northern Transvaal but farms, stores, gristmills, bakeries, fishing industries, tea and coffee plantations, fertile cattle lands, hotels, and bottle stores. Confrontation was imminent.

During my first year in office, Botha, BOSS agents, and the board of the Bantu Investment Corporation would enter our cabinet meetings uninvited. The first time this happened they sent a "greeting" to the "government" of the "state" of Lebowa of 10,000 rand and entered five minutes later to address us like schoolmasters lecturing their classes. They made it quite clear that they expected the cabinet to allow them to have many privileges in the "state" of Lebowa. White officials would come to us with unbelievable requests—yes, they would ask *us* to permit them to move tribes from their homelands. Botha himself approached the cabinet for consent to the removal of the Bethesda community and the Teacher's Training Institute. In spite of our refusal, they bulldozed Bethesda and dumped the villagers in an open veld.

I went to see for myself. I found our people thrown onto a bare veld where there was not even a single tree for shade. The sun was blazing hot. There was no water, no housing, nothing! On demand from the cabinet, the deputy minister of Bantu administration came with me to see the damage at Moletjie, where the villagers were left in the scorching heat. He wept. It was not the first time I saw an Afrikaner cabinet minister shed tears when face to face with the pain created by his people. I do not know whether they were crocodile tears, but they flowed from his eyes.

As I stood at Moletjie, I looked toward the east, toward Molemole, Botlokwa, Mabjanene, my home. I thought of my people, Botlokwa-ha-Machaka Maimela. I thought that perhaps they would be the next to be attacked by the beastly hands of destruction. The time to say good-bye to the weeping babies came. I was about to leave the discarded people from Bethesda to the scorching sun and howling winds of night when an old and coughing mother of Moletjiela-o-Raphuti, an old, old, grandmother leaning on a walking stick, approached me slowly and said, "The war is on. This is the war in the land of our fathers. War! Revolution! Hard times in the land of our fathers' fathers. Revolution has come!" As I shook her hand, she began to ululate. There was defiance in her voice.

I still remember when the bus drivers for the Bantu Investment Corporation came to my office and declared a strike. They had been insulted one too many times by a certain white man and demanded an apology. Within minutes, I summoned the corporation's officials, the police, the town councillors, and we told them our people had suffered enough and asked for the apology. The demand was met, and the drivers went back to work, leaving the white officials puzzled by their long overdue assertiveness. I was amazed at the helplessness of white arrogance when black people insisted on their dignity. Lebowa workers began to insist more and more on reasonable conditions of work and wages. Where employers did not comply with their reasonable demands and requests, the workers used work stoppages. Every strike thereafter was settled in favor of the workers.

When I first joined the politics of the Bantustans, I was enthusiastic in my opposition to the policies of the minority white governing regime in our land. I was of the opinion that one could organize a revolt against the Bantustan system from within, compelling the minority regime to abandon their criminal designs. I thought that the Bantustan governments had some powers, that every one of those powers could be used against the minority regime, enabling us to take control of our own destiny. I was mistaken and naive in my thoughts. As soon as I got into the system I found that the South African government made the laws and the Bantustans had to follow them. The Bantustans were tied down by these laws. The eye of Pretoria's government was always there, keeping an unceasing watch over their wards.

My naiveté about the power of the Bantustan government to change things didn't last long either. Many of those who saw through the fraud of the legislative system did nothing to change it, especially the chiefs—a bottle of brandy was generally effective enough to maintain their cooperation with whites, and they made up 60 percent of the assembly. To circumvent this problem, we tried to create two houses—one for the chiefs and one for elected members. The House approved the suggestion, but Bantu Administration Minister Botha told the chiefs to remain in the same house with the commoners. He knew they would not go against him because their paychecks came from his department. Pretoria's arm was long.

Bantustans could not make laws to control commercial matters affecting "non-Bantu." They could make no law dealing with ownership of property, industry, workmen's compensation, or insurance. All these were beyond their jurisdiction. Therefore, it was not correct to call the Bantustans self-governing. Bantustans could make no laws affecting multinational corporations in their territories. Pretoria had created tribal homelands that were expected to function according to Bantu law and customs only. Well-known multinational corporations, such as Union Carbide and ITT, which operate in Lebowa could not be regulated by any law made by the Lebowa Legislative Assembly. Therefore the multinational corporations which operated in the Bantustans just did as they liked. The outside world saw through the fraud and stopped inviting Bantustan leaders to visit their countries. No country in the world recognizes the Bantustan governments, which can't even try a nonblack for breaking a law in their towns.

Finally, when I could stand it no longer, I came to blows with the South African government. The Bantu Investment Corporation came in and took over one of the best and largest farms. It was in the Steelpoort area of Sekhukhuneland, and the action created a serious land crisis in Lebowa. I threatened a court action and in 1975 was promptly relieved of my duties as minister of interior and economic affairs.

Such were the politics of the Bantustans, the politics of the fake states and fake governments. We found ourselves dancing strange dances in a den of vipers. We were in a war against men turned into beasts—beasts that fed on the children of our land! My God, what a nightmare! We could make virtually no creative moves and had to step lightly, careful where we tread, dancing as demanded by the vipers. I chose to dance a different dance, a dance of defiance, danger, and dismissal.

19

Viva Frelimo

The independence of Mozambique in 1974 was celebrated by freedom-loving people around the world. I sorely missed my old friend Mondlane and wished he could have lived to see the glorious day. During the week of celebrations, I was asked by a *Daily Mail* reporter, Anthony Holiday (who is now in jail), to write an article on what the actions of Mondlane, the founder of the Frelimo movement, which freed Mozambique, might have meant to South Africa if he were still alive. I felt a statement would be particularly important because the same regime that had deported Mondlane in 1949 was still in power.

A rally in solidarity with Frelimo and the people of Mozambique was organized by the Students' Representative Council at the University of the North, near Pietersburg. My eldest son, Selaelo, was a member of the council. I had heard of an impending attack and harassment of our children at the university by the police and the army from Seshego. I got up at five in the morning and took my official black Mercedes-Benz, provided to me by the Office of Lebowa Bantustan Affairs, without bothering to awaken my official driver. I hoped I could do something to help.

As I neared the university and Mankweng township, I saw the bustling of students and police everywhere. I stopped my car and hoisted the green and gold flag of Lebowa "Territory." As I was given the right-of-way to proceed, I gave the sign of love and peace. Even the archenemies of our people began to give way for the black car to pass. The throng responded by making the sign of love and peace, while the members of the South African police and army frowned at this spectacle. I drove slowly toward the main university gate, which was manned by the police and the army.

As I passed through the gate, I saw what appeared to be one of the laborers of the university carrying a paintbrush and wearing the navy blue university coveralls with paint stains. His face had white and green smudges. On closer look, I realized he was my son, Selaelo. The unsuspecting police allowed him to move out of the university gate, thinking he was a worker.

The campus, its streets, lanes, and terraces were crowded with students, police, and residents of Mankweng township on the morning when the people of Mozambique celebrated their hard-earned independence from the Portuguese after five hundred years of brutal torture. Students and others came from many lands: Bapediland, Vendaland, Gazankulu, Namibia, Swaziland, Lesotho, Holland, France, even America and Britain. The police, hell-bent on breaking up the rally, began their attack and arrests. Everything was chaotic. Police lashed out at random; women ran bleeding and screaming. Police dogs barked and tore at female and male students indiscriminately; youth's tender buttocks were gnashed and torn by the sharp teeth of the snarling dogs and barbed wires, while young children tried to take refuge under their defenseless mothers, brothers, fathers, and older sisters. One boy scaled the high barbed-wire fence and got caught right on top of it. The dogs dragged him by his trousers until he landed at the feet of his merciless attackers.

I drove toward the administrative block on the campus, where the male students were forced to sit on the ground. The female students also were forced to sit on the road near the women's residence, like a flock of sheep. Students and the leaders of the rally were arrested and thrown into the police trucks. The song of freedom, *"Ba hleli bonke etilingweni,"* filled the air as the trucks drove off. The students chanted the names of Mandela, Sobukwe, Sisulu, and many others.

SOWETO, MY LOVE

Now that the crowd had cleared, I could see the slogans painted on the road outside the university gates: AWAY WITH BANTU EDUCATION! VORSTER, ARE YOU MAD? DOWN WITH APARTHEID. DOWN WITH NAZISM AND FASCISM! VOETSEK VORSTER AND YOUR DOGS! AWAY WITH VORSTER'S PIGS! RELEASE OR CHARGE OUR LEADERS! VIVA FRELIMO! LONG LIVE MANDELA! LONG LIVE SOBUKWE! These slogans were on every road, building, wall, tree, and rock. Placards were shown and banners waved throughout the university and township. The police and the army were busy trying to remove the painted slogans which were immediately rewritten as soon as their backs were turned.

I drove to the Mankweng Police Station, where hundreds of students and others were being held. I heard violent groaning and screaming from the cells. When I asked what was happening, I was informed by a sergeant that the "police are maintaining law and order."

Selaelo walked into the house three days later, still wearing the paint-smudged coveralls. We were sitting at the supper table when he appeared, looking tired and grim faced. As a result of the arrest of Mosiuoa General Patrick Lekota, Pandelani Jeremiah Nefolovhodwe, and Gilbert Kaborane Sedibe, students went on strike and closed down the University of the North. Selaelo left school in solidarity with those arrested.

"In school they taught whiteness. I am not white; I am black. From now on I am only going to look into my blackness. To hell with whiteness! Whiteness made me hate myself. I am black! Blackness must teach me to love myself, deeply."

"Are you prepared to fight?" I asked him. I looked at his mother and saw tears in her eyes.

Selaelo spoke slowly and angrily. "I have heard horror stories about how you and millions of our people were humiliated and tortured by the system. As long as I can remember, the story has been the same: murder of the innocent, rape of black women by white men, detentions without trials, our people killed in police cells like animals, our land taken by force, low wages, slavery in our own fatherland, poverty and disease deliberately caused by a system that creates these conditions in the Bantustans. Yes, Dad and Ma, I am prepared to fight; and I am prepared to die! I cannot imagine myself at this age going through the life of suffering the way you and your parents suffered. There is no other alternative for me. If I die, leaving any children behind, they will know the cause for which I died. . . . *Mayibuye* Africa!"

Selaelo and I talked until dawn. He maintained that the only way a black African could exist in dignity was by blowing the white man away with the barrel of his gun. The call from our youth was no longer "one man, one vote" as the call of my generation had been. Now the call was "one man, one gun!" We would never get the ballot through peaceful means. Chief Luthuli, himself the man of peace, had declared that he had "knocked thirty years in vain" at the door of Parliament, asking for "peaceful constructive change," for "the vote and democracy," as others before him had also done. But our leaders and followers were harassed, beaten, banned, jailed, and hanged. Admitting the futility of the nonviolent struggle, Chief Luthuli declared, "We hope for what will never exist in believing that a white government will achieve for us our freedom and peace without having struggled. . . . Our freedom will be purchased with all our possessions and even our blood." Chief Luthuli and thousands upon thousands had died without seeing freedom in their lifetime. Now Selaelo's generation was saying the white man lacked the conscience to strive for democracy and sharing of power on his own—he must therefore be forced. The young people had chosen to follow in the footsteps of Mandela; Chief Luthuli, the last great peaceful leader, was dead; his nonviolent politics were dead too! I was not surprised by Selaelo's words, though Thabo was.

"Ma and Dad, nothing can be more noble than to fight for our own rights, to bleed for our rights, to groan for them on the battlefield, and finally to pay the supreme price for our rights, if it should come to that. It has to be a full-fledged armed struggle if we are to be our own liberators. More men and women, boys and girls are leaving the country, practically every week, for military training in every part of the world."

I was, of course, aware of this from press reports and other information available to me as an attorney. These young blacks would return as freedom fighters, guerrillas, ready to do war to retrieve our land.

Through my son, I now fully realized how blacks had at last decided to follow the advice and counsel of Mandela, to resort to violence, to shoot down this wall that the whites had erected and maintained in spite of the glaring injustices. "Where is the God of these white people who are forcing our children, our people, into war?" I cried out. Our son, who was studying to become a doctor and to save life, was now turning to study war and take life.

The following day Selaelo took the Combi [like the Volkswagen microbus] with him when he left. This did not cause any alarm or concern, because he had our permission to use the Combi whenever he needed it at school. It was a month later when Thabo telephoned me at my office to inform me that Selaelo had returned, agitated. Late that evening he hurried out of our Bantustan government house, which he passionately hated, and disappeared into the darkness, looking over his shoulder to make sure he was not followed. I followed him to see where he was going but soon lost him.

When Selaelo did not return for a long time, I became concerned and began asking around after him. He was reported to have been seen in Soweto, at the University of the North, in Swaziland, Zambia, Botswana, Lesotho, Mozambique, Tanzania, and East Germany. But every lead I followed came to a dead end.

I had just been discharged from the hospital after a bout with heart trouble when Thabo woke me in the middle of the night concerned for Selaelo's safety and angry with me for condoning his involvement with violence. "You don't seem to care about his safety or about what's happening," she said through angry tears. "What puzzles me even more is that you, a member and leader of the system, are so strongly opposed to it. . . . Look what the Bantustan system is doing to you. You cannot stand with your feet astride the fence, one foot in the

VIVA FRELIMO

Bantustan shit which is destroying your health, and the other foot in the freedom fighters' camp. . . . You must make a decision."

She was right. I do not love violence, but there comes a time when men and women must either submit to their torturers or fight back.

Two events came back to me that showed times were changing. In 1942, a black man was driving through Annadale, a suburb of Pietersburg, where I worked as a domestic servant for the poor Afrikaner who tried to make me wash his stinking feet. A car driven by a hefty white man stopped alongside the black man's, and without any provocation, the white man jumped out of his car, went to the driver's side of the black man's car, and began assaulting him. The black man jumped out on the passenger's side and ran for dear life, with the white man close on his heels. Other white men joined the chase. They caught hold of the black man, beat him to the ground, and left him on the pavement, bleeding. The police arrested the black man for public violence.

Now, in 1974, the tide was turning. Recently, I had been driving through Annadale to Seshego. A white man, driving carelessly in a truck, forced a black woman in a brand-new Mercedes off the road. The white man jumped out of the truck, fuming, and said, *"Kaffer, kan jy nie sien waar jy gaan nie?—* Nigger, can't you see where you're going?" The black woman, equally furious, came out of her car and smashed the Afrikaner on the forehead with a lug wrench. Black pedestrians cheered her on as the white man ran for his life.

By now I was convinced that violent response to white violence in South Africa was inevitable and imminent. I feared for my son's life, but I would not stand in the way of his fight for his manhood and the reclamation of our land.

20

Crucial Turning Point

There was no longer peace of mind nor sleep for me. I was under surveillance day and night by security police and BOSS agents. I went to the ruins of Ranhlokana, where my father's village once stood, to communicate with those who lay beneath the soil, the Eternal Presences, the Living Dead, the spirits of my parents, my grandparents, of brave warriors—Moshweu, my great-grandfather, and Moraba-a-Mantedi, my grandfather.

I sat on the mountaintop and looked toward the west, toward the land of Moloto and Poopedi-a-Mothokwa. I watched the sun descending behind Sehlone and Makgabeng mountains, behind Madikoto-a-Mohale, the multicolored mountain where vultures and eagles fly. Ngwana-Rakwasha, my grandmother, and my mother came first to mind. Mothibi, my father, and Malekanyane, his sister, came to mind. Khaola, the ever-trotting elephant buck of Mabjanene, also came to me. Precious memories—I heard myself speaking to them as if they were present in flesh and blood.

My offices were bugged, my home bugged, my car bugged, everywhere I drove I would see someone following me through my rearview mirror. Everywhere I parked my car the security police or BOSS agents would park and keep a close watch over me. In public and in private places they could always be seen—watching, watching.

It was winter—the months of May and June in South Africa—although snow had not fallen but once in seventeen

CRUCIAL TURNING POINT

years. The only snow was on high peaks way in the south, such as the Drakensberg Mountains. Yet I shivered from a cold that penetrated my bones. I could no longer find words to describe life in the degrading, dehumanizing, hideous Bantustans. I had seen too many doors of shacks in the ghettos smashed open in the middle of the night by police who arrested the inhabitants for failing to produce a pass book on demand. I had seen too many natives shipped out to work on white farms, and defended too many such blacks before they were sold like slaves. I had seen millions forcibly removed from their homes and sent to distant places. I had seen thousands starve in devastated Bantustans. I had seen wives and mothers waiting alone eleven months a year, helplessly watching their children starve, their babies die, while their husbands toiled for slave wages in white industries.

The winter sun disappeared behind the Soutpansberg mountain range, the mountains of Malebogo-Moitswene. I said to myself, "Son of Mothibi, you must go!" I looked toward the graves of my mother and grandmother, toward the grave of my grandfather Moraba-a-Mantedi, and pleaded with them to allow me to go. I sipped cold water from the calabash and offered it as a libation to my ancestors. I turned toward Bochum, toward the west, where my father lay beneath the soil, and splashed more water from my mouth. "Mothibi-a-Ramathathe, flesh of your flesh must leave, before it is too late. Blood of your blood has lived under surveillance for too long. I have campaigned for equality between all our people, for majority rule, for harmony and cooperation in this land. The government of Pretoria says my ideas are dangerous, my political thoughts are bad. I speak to you, Mothibi, my father. They say I must be detained without cause. I speak to you, my mother. My health is poor. The heart is weak. I must go."

I left for Britain and the United States while I still had a passport. I wanted to assess the extent to which the oppressed people of South Africa could count on the international community's support in the hour of crisis. I also went for much-needed medical treatment in Chicago.

SOWETO, MY LOVE

On the first day of June 1976, I was warned that my name was on a list of persons to be detained by the South African Security Police as soon as the new Internal Security Act was signed on the sixteenth by the state president. I and others listed would be arrested without cause, without a hearing and without bail. I was in no condition to risk detention. My health was failing seriously. Otherwise I would have stayed and faced the wrath of Pretoria like many of my people, jailed for no reason except the racist fears and bigotry of people unwilling to share in the bountiful land of our fathers.

It was 5:30 P.M., the fifteenth day of June 1976, when I embraced my wife. Tears flooded our eyes. Our children wept. I kissed Thabo good-bye several times, hugged and kissed our children, said farewell, then walked slowly toward the final exit gate to distant lands in search of answers.

As the plane began to roar, preparing for the long journey across the seas, my mind turned to Mandela, Sisulu, and others on Robben Island. My wife and children waved white handkerchiefs from the observation deck. I blew kisses toward them and waved back. I was relieved that I had made it onto the plane without arrest. The bird of the blue skies took to the air. My fatherland lay like a blanket beneath its wings—beautiful South Africa. I looked through the window and saw Thembisa, a black ghetto sprawling like a sickly baobab tree outside the beautiful Jan Smuts International Airport.

I thought of my client Jane Kgare, a dignified, hardworking Christian lady. Four white men had ravaged Jane like wild animals on the side of a road, after brutally assaulting her fiancé, Petrus Mphaha, and leaving him unconscious. Because they were whites, they were not sent to the electric chair. They were not sent to jail. They were not fined. They went free in spite of the fact that they did not deny having committed the atrocity.

Before leaving South Africa I issued a warning. I told a reporter, Richard Gibbs, who interviewed me at the airport: "Our children will not accept injustices any longer. They can see that it got the older generation nowhere. They want their freedom and they want it now!" I looked at my two sons standing next to me and told the white reporter, "I foresee blood, rivers of blood!"

The government had introduced Bantu education in 1954 and closed down the schools built by the missionaries, which had provided blacks with an educational system that would train them to survive in the modern world. When the minister of native affairs, Verwoerd, who was later to become prime minister, introduced the Bantu Education Bill in the South African Parliament, and Prime Minister Malan had to explain why blacks must have separate and inferior education, little did they know what was in store for the structure they were designing.

The Department of Bantu Education decreed that half the subjects offered in secondary schools be taught in Afrikaans; the African Teachers Association of the Transvaal and the Soweto Bantu Urban Council protested the measure. Some members resigned from the council in protest, but the Department of Bantu Education insisted that Afrikaans be used. The government was warned that black people would rise against their racist educational system, but the government chose to ignore the warning. Within a few years after the passage of the education act, there were strikes in every boarding school, college, and university for blacks.

I arrived in London the morning of June 16. It was a beautiful day of bright sunshine. At two o'clock that afternoon I attended the performance of *Ipi Tombi*, a black South African musical that had been running for two years. This theatrical troupe mesmerized audiences back home with their thunderous dance, exotic drumbeats, and music of Africa. I watched the dancers pounding and stomping the stage like Zulu warriors, and they eased the longing I was already feeling for my family and homeland. As the men pounded the floor, sweat dripping down their ebony bodies, and the veins and muscles rising and swelling as if on the verge of bursting, the women ululated and fanned themselves to keep cool. The wizards of African choreography were dancing out their rhythms, and I was thinking of my friends and family at home when I heard the sound of the talking drums. A voice from afar—a voice from those who are forever with us, the Eternal Presences, the Living Dead who lie beneath the soil—telling me of events from home. The dancers on stage were sending out messages to the audience, but only those who knew the beat of the talking drums understood.

I sat up and listened. The drums reported that there had been a massacre at home. The children had taken all they could stand—the blood of the children of Azania was nurturing the tree of freedom in the land of their fathers. The South African police and paramilitary were shooting them. Blood was everywhere. It had finally happened. My prophesy had materialized within hours of my departure.

On the morning of June 16, 1976, the children of Soweto marched in protest against their inferior education. Twenty thousand of them peacefully marched against the decree by the Department of Bantu education that Afrikaans be used as a language of instruction in secondary schools. The children, dressed in their school uniforms, marched and sang on their way to the Orlando Soccer Stadium. They carried placards: DOWN WITH AFRIKAANS! VIVA AZANIA! WE ARE NOT BOERS! IF WE MUST DO AFRIKAANS, VORSTER MUST DO ZULU!

Police vehicles raced to the scene. Many of the eyewitnesses quoted in the newspapers at the time, and many others interviewed later in the United States, said that the violence began when the police tried to seize placards and stop the march. When students taunted the police, they responded with tear gas. The police opened fire before stones were thrown. No order was issued from the police for the marchers to disperse. The senior police officer admitted that no warning shots were fired.

The first child to go down was a thirteen-year-old schoolboy, Hector Petersen. He was felled by a bullet in the back at Orlando West. Several other children were shot dead and fell in the streets of Soweto—defenseless little children, maimed and slaughtered as police opened fire. Then all hell broke loose.

CRUCIAL TURNING POINT

Police vehicles were stoned and set on fire. A black policeman was dragged from his vehicle and beaten, his wrists locked together with his own handcuffs. Police dogs unleashed upon students were knifed and set on fire. Government property was destroyed. Commercial vehicles and delivery vans of white-owned businesses were burned. Beer halls and bottle stores, a white bank, hotel, and several Soweto post offices were set ablaze. Two white officials of the West Rand Board were dragged in the dust and beaten to death.

The government sent an antiriot unit into Soweto in armored cars, known as "hippos." The army was placed on alert and troops mobilized outside Soweto. In little more than twenty-four hours the violence had spread over twenty-eight ghettos, covering more than the thirty-three square miles that constituted Soweto. Within a few days 143 vehicles were destroyed, 139 buildings were destroyed, 172 blacks were killed, and 1,439 blacks were injured.

The rioting stretched over the reef of ghettos by the end of the week, from Daveyton in the east to Mohlakeng in the west, and it wove in and out of the Pretoria ghettos to the north. Outbreaks occurred in Nelspruit of the eastern Transvaal and Jourberton township at Klerksdorp in the southwestern Transvaal. Spreading like wild fire, sporadic violence was seen in the Orange Free State town of Bothaville, Galeshewe in Kimberley, and in the northern Cape area, all the way to the universities of the North and Zululand.

Abroad, I met with exiled leaders of the ANC, president and commander in chief of Umkhonto We Sizwe Oliver Tambo; his wife, Adelaide; Matthews Nkoana, a journalist, friend, and one of the founding members of PAC; and Duma Nokwe, of the famed Marathon treason trial that ran for four years (1956–1960) against 154 leaders, including Chief Luthuli. The path of freedom was strewn with many martyrs, and now the present generation was joining the ranks. The South African regime labeled us terrorists and Communists in an effort to persuade the world that its atrocities were justified. Only Western Europe and the United States appeared to be swallowing the government line—the rest of the world knew the truth, even if the West never came to accept it. We knew this, and wherever we met the message was the same, inside South Africa or outside: "The struggle for Azania continues!"

I prayed for our newly fallen martyrs and flew to New York. I read piles of newspapers, trying to assess the situation back home—the mad hand of destruction and murder, slaughter of the innocent, Soweto, Mamelodi, Seshego, Sibasa, Langa, Sharpeville, Atteridgeville, Kwa Mashu, New Brighton. Soon Duduza in Nigel was on fire. Beer halls, municipal administration offices, buses, post offices, Bantu schools, were ablaze in Soweto and elsewhere as I landed at Kennedy International Airport.

The next morning I visited the United Nations headquarters, where one of the largest demonstrations I ever witnessed was in progress. People from all parts of the world were protesting the massacre of the children of Soweto and the crime against humanity—apartheid. David Sibeko—angry, tough, big, and determined to expose the evils of the apartheid regime—represented the PAC, while Thami Mhlambiso—soft-spoken, diplomatic, determined, and a seasoned Azanian leader—represented the ANC. Duma Nokwe was stopped at Kennedy International Airport. He was, at the time, the general secretary of the ANC and was compelled by U.S. immigration authorities, because of his status, to return to London without having added his voice of protest.

It was dawn when I found my way along the quiet streets of New York to my host's residence. I tried to sleep, but nightmares of blazing flames invaded my mind. I gave up, bid farewell to my host, Rhodes Gxoyiya, and flew to Chicago on June 25, 1976.

Chicago had changed enormously. White flight had struck the city of du Sable. Many had disappeared, their addresses unknown, including some of my friends of the 1960s.

I checked in with my doctors at Evanston Hospital to treat my medical problems. On news reports our black people watched those around them die by the hundreds as military

CRUCIAL TURNING POINT

and paramilitary personnel swept through the black areas. A friend of many years from South Africa, Peter Letsoho, alighted at O'Hare International Airport and found me waiting for him, thirsty for news from the troubled land. Townships, ghettos, and villages were surrounded; streets were blocked and barricaded by hippos; captured children were tortured and girls raped. One child expired when she received the third bullet shot in her stomach; each of her legs were numbed, having been first broken in three places. Another girl was executed by a .45 handgun, the finishing stroke on her breast. As she gave the last gasp, police and army reinforcements were rushing to finish more girls and boys—children killed in merciless slaughter.

"You know, son of my mother," Peter said, "I will never forget what I saw with my own eyes: When the soldiers arrived, I saw a young girl collapsing on the ground. The officers allowed the soldier to finish up the little girl, dressed in her school uniform of black and white. The child was groaning with pain, rolling on the ground, when a second shot was fired at this helpless nine-year-old. In that condition the dying little girl with her broken limbs doubled up and was silenced forever. The merciful angel of death took the child." My friend stood in a trance for a second or two before adding, "But the children of Soweto say they have a nation now to build, roads and bridges to reconstruct. They say whites have to be forced into being a people with human hearts. There is a challenge everywhere in the air. The children complain that there is no law left in Azania." Anger was written all over his face. "But the white man is afraid now—whites had rushed to buy guns to guard themselves against the unarmed children of Azania, whose heroism defied description." Black people were singing a new song:

> *They no longer sleep.*
> *White people no longer sleep.*
> *They sleep on their guns.*
> *They are afraid.*

> *They are afraid of the black nation.*
> *White people no longer sleep.*
> *They sleep on their guns.*
> *They are afraid of the black nation.*

While the unarmed children of Azania sang:

> *Fight for liberation.*
> *Build a new nation.*
> *Join the revolution*
> *Now!*

They crossed the borders into unknown lands to prepare themselves for the onerous task of regaining our land from the invaders from Europe. To Selaelo's generation, the year 1976 was a clean slate on which history was going to be written. The new era had begun, and it brought with it a series of astonishing inventions that reshaped life in South Africa— Molotov gasoline bombs, time bombs, stones, and bare hands as weapons of defense against Pretoria's armors of war. Songs of courage, hope, and faith were heard everywhere.

> *Arise, we have the guns.*
> *The time is ripe,*
> *Grab the bombs.*
> *The time is ripe. . . .*
> *We'll conquer, we'll conquer.*
> *Victory is ours.*

Within two months at least 80 black communities all over the country expressed their fury, and within four months the number had risen to 160. There was upheaval in the Bantustans. Soldiers from a military base in Namibia were called by the South African government to quell the uprisings. Soweto, my love, was at the center of the revolution.

In August the Bophuthatswana legislative assembly building

CRUCIAL TURNING POINT

in Mafikeng was burned. Upheavals reached Port Elizabeth and East London in the eastern Cape, where thirty-three lives were lost. In September there were demonstrations against Henry Kissinger's visit to South Africa to discuss the Zimbabwean question, and on October 17, a large crowd of angry students destroyed thirty vehicles in a municipal depot to which they marched after the funeral of a schoolboy who had died in police custody. On October 24, seven people were killed when police opened fire at a funeral. That night Jabulani Police Station was damaged by explosives, and during the next few days there were more attacks on the homes of black policemen. For the first time, the Boers began to realize what they were up against. Their cannons and machine guns did not stop the rising tide. Police arrested thousands, assaulted and killed the innocent in large numbers. A friend flew into Chicago and told me that the police had arrested my son Sekgweng and my nephew Frans. It was as if someone had poured ice water on my body.

It was only after repeated appeals from me to my wife, who had been quiet about the arrests with the intention of sparing me pain, that I came to know the details. My son and my nephew were awakened in the dead of night by the security police, who, after searching the house and finding no contraband or censored literature, arrested them both. My son Sekgweng was said to have burned down a Bantu education high school, Phiri-Kolobe, where he was a student. At the trial in the Supreme Court of South Africa, he was found not guilty—there was no evidence of any kind. My nephew, on the other hand, was accused of conveying students in his car who had gasoline bombs in their possession. He was tried, convicted, and sentenced to six months in prison.

My American visa, which was only for six months, was nearing its end, but I received warnings from my family and friends in South Africa that I should not return—the system was after my blood. There had been a rumor that I had secretly returned home, and there was a nationwide manhunt for me. I sought and was granted political asylum by the American government, permission to remain in the United States until such time as I felt it safe to return home. But I ran into problems by visiting Toronto while my application for political asylum was being considered by the U.S. immigration authorities. I found myself marooned in Canada, and there was a real danger that I might have to return to South Africa. Thanks to friends such as Ruth S. Turner; Goler Butcher; Congressmen Abner Mikva, Sidney Yates, Ralph Metcalfe, and Charles Diggs; Senators Charles Percy and Adlai Stevenson III, members of the Black Caucus; George Miller; Ann Blair; Rose Hoeckner; Kojo Bennett; Professor Elkin S. Sithole; and many others, I was paroled in the United States, where I was granted asylum in March 1977.

But all was not well. My health was disturbing to me, but my family and homeland were an even deeper concern. My son Selaelo was reported to be somewhere in Africa learning guerrilla warfare. My wife was seriously ill in Baragwanath Hospital in Johannesburg. I felt so helpless. A number of times I thought of going back to South Africa to be at Thabo's bedside, but what would be the purpose of my returning only to be arrested at the airport? What help would I be offering her behind bars? What hurt and frustrated me most was that every time I telephoned my house at Molemole no one answered. I sent messages through reliable sources, which Thabo safely received, telling when I would call next, yet each time it was the same: "Sorry, there is no reply at that number." It became very apparent to me that the South African government was trying to isolate me. The only letters my wife ever received from me were those that were smuggled to her by friends.

Meanwhile, South Africa was in turmoil. A scandal—involving millions of dollars stolen to bribe the world to assist the South African minority regime in pursuing its apartheid fraud—was threatening Prime Minister B. J. Vorster and other cabinet members. The scandal ended the strong-fisted prime minister's career. C. P. Mulder, minister of information and of the interior, Jimmy Kruger, minister of justice and police (who was responsible for the cover-up of Stephen Biko's death), and Vorster were ousted. The tenure of M. C. Botha as minister of Bantu education and Bantu development and administration also ended. But the evil legacy of these men remains. M. C. Botha will always be remembered as the white man who forced our children to rebel against his system—the instigator of the massacre on June 16, 1976.

21

General Whirlwind

One day in 1978, I attended a meeting on South Africa at Loyola University. A young lady from Soweto stood shyly next to me. "Excuse me, sir. I have been looking at you for a long time. Are you Selaelo's father?" I was surprised that I could be recognized by this beautiful young lady so far away from home.

"Oh yes, I am. I am Mr. Ramusi. Where do you know my son from?" I asked, and thought she reminded me of another beautiful woman from South Africa, much older than herself.

"I know him from Soweto. We were at school together, at Hwiti High School and also at the University of the North. In fact I met him in Maputo, last week." For the first time I was getting a positive report on the whereabouts of Selaelo, the blue-eyed Mmirwa, the white-eyed Mmirwa is not him. I found myself chanting the praise name of my Babirwa clan. "You have seen my son? Selaelo? Mmirwa? Where is he? Where is my son? How is he? What is he doing? My son! Motau! Moila Letsamaka! He is still alive and well, is he?" I shouted with joy, throwing questions without waiting for a reply.

"Yes, he is still alive and well. I was with him yesterday at the airport when I was on my way here. He saw me off. He had his bags already packed to go back home today," she managed to tell me after all my questions.

The information she gave me quenched my thirst for knowledge about my son. But what puzzled me was that Thabo had not heard of Selaelo being in South Africa or elsewhere on the continent. I continued to make inquiries, but I never got further than what this girl told me.

"MOLEMOLE REMOVALS! FORCIBLE REMOVALS!" read the 1979 headlines. During my work as chairman of the land commission, as minister of interior and economic affairs, and especially as the official representative of Sekgosese, my constituency, I had prepared my people to fight against the impending removals tooth and nail. The minute the South African government announced its decision to remove my people, opposition arose as if a beehive had been disturbed. Both the aged and the youth joined hands in protest. From newspaper reports and news from friends, it was clear that the government was challenged by my people on an unprecedented scale, to the extent that they were compelled to use force in the Makgato section.

This was not the first time Makgato's people were removed. In 1945 they were moved to Munnik. In 1962 they were moved from Munnik to Molemole, and they were assured that they could consider themselves permanently established at Molemole. But in 1979 they were forced out again.

When Sekole, a migrant worker and father of six children, returned to Makgato village and discovered that his family had been removed, he dismantled the large house in which he had invested years of labor and all his savings and hanged himself in the shell.

My house stood amongst thousands of others to be demolished by the government. I worried about my wife and two younger sons, Sekgweng and Mothibi, who were still there. I wondered even more where Selaelo was, as 150,000 people were threatened with the destruction of their homes. Selaelo had often told me that he would rather fight than see his community destroyed, and I felt the same way.

The Batlokwa of Machaka and Ramokgopa, like those under Solomon Makgato, were to move from Molemole to Bochum. Chiefs Letheba Machaka and George Ramokgopa, together with our tribesmen and women, refused to move. "We will not move from the land of our fathers. The chiefs and the people are agreed. We are more united. Do not worry, Motau, Batlokwa-ba-Tsherane will rather die than move from the soil of Tšhaka-Maimela," my chief, Letheba Edward Machaka, informed me in a letter.

Molemole was a progressive community. We had twenty-one schools built with our own funds; three clinics; gristmills; stores; gas stations; post offices; beautifully constructed homes; gardens; flowing rivers; various breeds of cattle, sheep, and goats; churches belonging to every denomination; electrical plants. Bochum, the new "homeland," was drought stricken, poor, and twice the distance to Pietersburg, the nearest employment center for inhabitants of Molemole. Migrant workers would have even less time for family visits.

The *Johannesburg Sunday Express* reported that my people were waiting to hear whether the government would carry out its threat. "If the move does take place," the *Express* was told, "it could swing thousands of young men and women into violent protest or active support for underground movements such as the ANC."

In his last letter to me, my late cousin Molatelo wrote: "The feelings are running high here at home. People are completely defiant. Our removal from here will cause permanent hatred and mistrust of whites. Our Chiefs Machaka and Ramokgopa are still with us in our opposition to the removal; both of them are united as never before. The war is on!"

Bomb blasts, grenade attacks, and rifle fire sent shock waves through government agencies. I was convinced these attacks were connected with the removals. I was proud and excited for my people and only wished I could be there to fight alongside them.

In the midst of good news, though, tragedy struck. One morning I visited the home of a friend, Mrs. Hazel Gray, on the South Side of Chicago. Soon after my arrival the telephone rang. I picked it up in the living room.

GENERAL WHIRLWIND

"Is that Mr. Ramusi?" the caller asked.

"Yes, who is speaking?" I asked.

"I am sorry, very sorry. Your son is dead," Pule Phoofolo said very bluntly.

"What?" I was dizzy with shock.

"A telephone call has just come through from Alli Twala from Mbabane, Swaziland. He says that I should let you know that your son Selaelo has died." By the time he finished, I was shivering uncontrollably, with the receiver clasped tightly against my ear. I could hardly breathe or say a word in reply. "Are you still there, Mr. Ramusi?"

"Yes," I managed to whisper as Mrs. Gray mercifully walked into the room from the kitchen, grasped the situation, took the telephone, and replaced it on the cradle. My emotions overcame me, and tears ran freely down my face. Mrs. Gray phoned my South African friends, the Reverend Maurice Ngakane and the Reverend Simon Maimela, who were both living on the South Side. They arrived within minutes.

Selaelo's body was flown to Pietersburg Airport, where the casket was met by family members and friends and driven to Molemole, where he was put to rest with his grandmother Motswetla-a-Rasekgothoma, his father's brother, Moraba-a-Mantedi, and Khaola. When the casket was carried shoulder high from our house at Molemole, the telephone rang in my apartment in Chicago.

"Chum, it is me, Thabo. I just wanted you to know that the body of our beloved son Selaelo is leaving the house at this minute. I wanted you to be with me in thought and in spirit at this time."

I said to her, "May his soul rest in peace, flesh of our flesh, blood of our blood. May his blood water the flowers of freedom in our fatherland: Farewell, Motau, farewell Mmirwa. May the son of Mothibi, Moraba, and Moshweu, the warrior who chops to pieces and still returns to the battlefield when other warriors fear to die, rest in peace." In the background I could hear the hymn "Abide with Me."

I was told "officially" by the government that Selaelo died of asthma in detention, but I never believed it and was determined to find out the true cause of his death. In 1980, Oliver Tambo, president of the ANC and head of its military wing, Umkhonto We Sizwe, sent me a plane ticket to come to London to hear yet another official report on Selaelo. For security reasons, I was never told very much, except that Selaelo had been elevated to one of the highest ranks possible in Umkhonto, because he had revolutionized guerrilla warfare tactics. I was never told how. Tambo had warned Selaelo, just before he died in Swaziland, not to return to South Africa—he had become the most wanted man, dead or alive, in the country. Other than an expression of gratitude, it would be years before I would receive more news from a very unexpected source.

Montego Bay, Jamaica, Saturday, July 14, 1983. The Caribbean is as still as the Indian Ocean back home. The summer evening breeze cooled my body and reminded me of the Durban beach at night.

I was walking alone on the beach, dipping my body in the cool Caribbean waters, when I noticed a lanky, young black man leisurely walking toward me. I put down the seashells I had collected as souvenirs for friends in Chicago and noticed that the man was trying to draw my attention. "Mr. Ramusi, please follow me," he said out of the corner of his mouth without making eye contact. I had never seen this man before, but he apparently knew me. I became interested and followed him into the water. "You don't know me, sir, but I know you from Soweto. I have known you for a long time. . . . You are Selaelo's father," he said, smiling. "I have been trying to contact you for the past three days after spotting your arrival in Jamaica. It is very important that we not be seen together." He paused. "What is your hotel room number, sir?" He promised to make further contact and swam away from me before I could ask who he was. To occupy myself, I visited the notorious palace of Rosehall at the famous hill where the feared white witch used to dwell and terrorize the people of land and sea—the children of Marcus Garvey.

GENERAL WHIRLWIND

I had given up hope, when there was a very soft tap on my door at three in the morning. I jumped out of the chair where I was asleep and moved toward the door. *"Thobela*—Dad." He greeted me as if I were his father, as is customary to show respect. I shook his hand and gave him a bear hug. "Good morning, son, good morning, son of the soil."

He beckoned me to sit down on my bed, where he joined me. "Please relax, Dad; I will answer some of your questions. I am sure you will understand if I will not be able to answer all of your questions for security reasons. . . . It is important that I protect you. That's why even our meeting must be in secret." He paused. "You asked me what my name was. Just call me Tokyo. In fact, I am General Tokyo," he said.

General Tokyo had grown up with Selaelo from preschool days in Pietersburg through the University of the North, where they had been introduced to the philosophy and ideology of black consciousness. "To us it was clear that the black man had to become his own liberator. It was inevitable that we should join forces with other freedom fighters to free our people from slavery and bondage." Their chance came when friends were arrested during the Viva Frelimo celebrations, and they abandoned school in solidarity. Selaelo and Tokyo were assigned to organize and transport students who were leaving the country for guerrilla training. That, I discovered, was why Selaelo had taken the Combi. They were given a new one by their white patron, a lady from the Pretoria suburbs who also gave them food, money, and a place to sleep.

They had a system of signals worked out with their patron so that they would know whether the coast was clear when they returned from assignments at night. One night, just before dawn, they saw that the veranda light was on, indicating trouble. Tokyo and Selaelo went to their alternate hiding place, where they were told the security police were looking for them, so they left the country at dawn. I was unnerved by the casual manner in which these kids carried out their assignments.

"You will have to pardon me here, Dad, because there are

secrets of the movement that cannot be divulged, not even to you. We came back and carried out a number of assignments in South Africa. Each time we crossed back to our bases, but on our twelfth assignment we were almost caught. Someone had sold us to the enemy."

After a tough and chaotic battle, Tokyo saw that Selaelo's head was bleeding from shrapnel. Selaelo seemed unaware of his injuries as Tokyo attempted to arrest the hemorrhage. "We had to go underground in South Africa because our retreat was already blocked." He stood up abruptly, and peered through the window. "I have to leave. I will see you again very soon." He opened the door and disappeared. I looked, too, but saw nothing, yet clearly Tokyo had cause for worry.

The following day I looked everywhere for the general, but he was nowhere to be found. After supper I went to my room to rest, because I had not slept the night before. I switched on the light and was moving toward the bed when something struck me as being out of place. When I'd gone to the beach, I had left the bathroom door closed, but now it was slightly ajar. I tiptoed to the bathroom, and there was General Tokyo, in the bathtub with revolver drawn.

"Oh! Is that you, Dad? For some time I thought I'd been followed," he said, as he put the revolver back into his pocket. He went to the medicine cabinet and began checking for concealed recording devices. He checked the telephone and electrical sockets, looked under the furniture, then seemed satisfied. He whispered and indicated that I, too, should lower my voice. He turned on the water, and we continued our talk in the bathroom.

"The last time I ended our conversation by telling you that Selaelo was bleeding. We had to go underground until the search cooled off a bit. We hitchhiked to Witbank, where we stole a car to get to our next contact, a prominent and respectable white minister code-named N. G. Kerk. Selaelo was weaker; his wound continued to bleed and was now infected. To avoid arrest we had only two alternatives: either to continue in the stolen car risking capture or to disappear into

Kerk's church. The latter course would expose our white contact but was the only chance for Selaelo's survival.

"It was eleven at night when we made our choice. Our white pastor friend was already aware of our predicament, because we had telephoned him earlier. He had pushed for the decision that put him at risk. Just before midnight we found him in his vestry. He led us to a trapdoor that opened into a room with a bed and a chair. He quickly closed the trapdoor and went back into the vestry. Then there was a knock at the vestry door. Six uniformed men entered, all carrying guns except the taller one, who directed the dogs.

" 'What on earth is going on? Why, in the name of God Almighty, are you pointing those dangerous weapons at me?' the pastor demanded in Afrikaans. They told him that they had a report that two dangerous guerrillas had been seen entering the church building a short time ago. They had discovered their abandoned car, and the dogs had picked up the scent of blood on it. The police were carrying out a house-to-house search.

" 'I thought perhaps I had been accused of committing a serious crime,' the pastor said. 'By all means, please, search for these criminals, and get them out of this building if you find them here.' He opened the door of the rooms around the vestry, but the dogs kept barking around the pastor's desk, where Selaelo's blood-covered boots were. One police officer remarked, 'Are these dogs crazy? Do they expect two big men to squeeze their bodies into these small drawers?' The pastor feigned relief at the presence of security police in the vestry and requested a thorough search, which was conducted from basement to roof. Two hours later, they returned empty-handed. The dogs again barked at the desk, and the brigadier expressed embarrassment. He again gave the command to track, and the dogs went crazy, racing up and down the stairs to the basement and finally congregating right on top of the trapdoor. There was another door next to the dogs, and the brigadier became agitated.

" 'They must surely be in here,' he shouted. *'Ons het hulle gekry!*—We've found them!' They ransacked the room but only saw boxes of blankets and soup for the needy. The room was otherwise empty. The dogs continued barking, furiously sniffing and scratching on the carpet above the trapdoor. The brigadier noticed another door to the left of the concealed trapdoor. He screamed 'Open it, open this door!' It was a toilet room and it was empty.

"The brigadier apologized. 'I am sorry to have troubled you, Pastor; these dogs must be out of their minds.' He turned to the dog handler and snapped, 'Take these dogs out of here, *Maak gou.*'

"The pastor said, 'You're surely not leaving without your fugitives. What if they come out and kill me?'

"The brigadier assured him that he was perfectly safe. His men had covered every inch of the building. He gave his personal guarantee that they were not there. He apologized for disturbing the pastor and causing unnecessary concern. The pastor went to the window and peered out at the disappearing police. As he saw the taillight of the last vehicle, he chuckled. He removed Selaelo's boots from the drawer, lifted the carpet, and opened the trapdoor to relate the events of the evening. The pastor, however, became very concerned about Selaelo. He had a temperature and was sweating profusely. For two days his condition deteriorated, and they feared the worst. On the third night the pastor went out, promising to bring back a doctor. When they returned at dawn, the Indian doctor immediately put up an IV of antibiotics and gave Selaelo a blood transfusion. By the end of the week Selaelo's condition had greatly improved."

The pastor brought reports of police activities and roadblocks. They remained in their hideout even after Selaelo had gained his strength; their capture, dead or alive, was a top priority.

After a few days, orders came that they should keep themselves busy with new assignments from within the country and forget about trying to leave. They began solo suicide assignments away from Witbank, at places like Durban, Johannesburg, Pretoria, and the northern Transvaal in particular, because of removals in that area. After Selaelo hit Durban, Tokyo would draw attention away by hitting Johannesburg, Pretoria, or the northern Transvaal. Then they would disappear underground while the dust settled. Their targets were always government establishments. Casualties were regrettable but unavoidable.

"We are not brute killers like the white man; we do not torture them just to make their lives miserable as they do us. We only seek to stop oppression and to have our say in the government, and our share in the land and the economy. The white man should not underestimate our ability to fight and to endure. We have endured his tyranny too long. We shall not stop until victory, Dad. If the white man cannot find it in his heart to stop his cruelties, his race hatred, then we will fight until we all die."

There was the same look on his face that I had seen on Selaelo's before he disappeared from home to go underground. And it struck me that I had seen that same resolved look years earlier on the faces of Mandela and Sobukwe, even after Sobukwe was sick and dying under a ban. It was a look that inspired me and gave me strength.

"We caused the South African minority regime a lot of trouble, and both of us were elevated to the rank of general. Selaelo became General Whirlwind. We were called out of the country to organize suicide squads on a large scale. Selaelo was in charge of the northern Transvaal because of the havoc he had already wreaked there.

"Dad, Selaelo and I had made a pact when we started. We promised each other that whatever happened, if one of us got killed, the survivor would move heaven and earth to inform the parents of his mission. As you know, this portion of the story I will not elaborate on, but I would like to tell you this: The facts of his death were distorted by the authorities. Sure, he was arrested in Swaziland, but he did not die of asthma as reported. He was murdered by the dogs that he had once so gallantly and bravely frustrated. Do not worry, Dad, Selaelo shed his blood for the cause, for the liberation of his brothers and sisters, for Azania. His blood is watering the flowers of freedom in our fatherland, his name shall be included in the Song of Freedom, and he will be part of the history of our country and our people as a courageous warrior in our struggle to be free. May his soul rest in peace till we meet again in the land where the Eternal Presences lie forever beneath the soil." He pressed my hand with his.

I stood up and embraced General Tokyo. "Thank you so much, my son! Thank you for this wonderful news, son of the soil! Yes, my Selaelo, my General Whirlwind, now lies with his grandfather, Mothibi-a-Ramathathe, Mothibi the Good. When you go to his home, do not go too early. If you do, you will belch, Mothibi has too much food. He is lying with his great-grandfather, Moraba-a-Mantedi, the warrior who returns to the battlefield when other warriors fear to die."

I would shed no more tears now that I knew that Selaelo did not die in vain. Selaelo had contributed to the struggle for the liberation of South Africa. I was proud to know that the blood of my blood and flesh of my flesh stood high among the heroes and heroines, the martyrs of our times.

"Go well, my son," I said quietly as Tokyo silently departed, promising to see me again before I left Jamaica.

After the third day of waiting for the young general to show up, I decided to look around the beach, hoping to spot him among the vacationers of Montego Bay. I was so anxious to speak to him that I extended my stay another three days. I wondered what could have prevented him from getting in touch with me and began to worry.

It was on the evening of the third day, toward midnight, that the telephone rang, waking me from a troubled sleep. On picking up the receiver, I heard a familiar voice. "Hello, Dad, the clouds are gathering thickly around me, and now I must make my disappearance. Go well!"

I heard a click, and I knew that I would never see him again. "May God bless you and give you strength to overcome!" I said as I replaced the receiver on the cradle.

22

Siya Yinyova

Almost a year later, returning from another trip, I inserted the key into the door of my apartment in Hyde Park, Chicago, as my telephone rang. It was 8:30 A.M. on Monday, the twenty-fifth day of June, 1984. I rushed and picked up the phone.

"Oh! Are you back? We have been looking for you for the whole weekend," said a voice that I knew belonged to Yvone Tiny Mosiea, a student from Soweto living in Detroit.

"Yes, I just arrived from Washington, DC!" I said. "How are you?"

"Well . . . Well . . . I am all right except for this . . . This sad news . . . Very, very sad . . . Have you not yet heard?"

"What is it that I am supposed to have heard?"

"I am very, very sorry . . . It is about Sister Thabo, Mary Jane, your wife . . ." She was reluctant to divulge the message.

"What about my wife, Tiny?" I was apprehensive.

"I am sorry, Boet Rams, sister Thabo is gone. She passed away on Saturday."

I went cold and dry. My earth stood still while I tried to digest this information. I had not even heard that my wife was ill at that time. I was still holding the telephone to my ear when I heard the doorbell ring. I buzzed the caller in with tears flooding my eyes. I thanked Tiny, who tried to console me as well as she could. The Reverend Phillip Moila, a theological student from Molemole, walked into my apartment. Within minutes after my return from Washington, I managed to call South Africa and to inform my family and relatives that I would be returning home for my wife's funeral. I closed my affairs in Chicago and arrived in South Africa on the third day of July, 1984.

When my intention to return became known to the South African public, I began to receive numerous telephone calls from all over the United States expressing concern about my safety if I returned to the land of my fathers. Many American friends made phone calls to their congressmen and senators, asking them to urge the South African authorities not to harm or hinder me from returning home. I informed one reporter that I would indeed return to my fatherland to bury my beloved wife, irrespective of the consequences. If anyone were to detain, molest, arrest, or even murder me, I would still return to bury her. I advised my cousin Manti Ramontja and my nephew Moyahabo Ramusi to wait for me at the Jan Smuts International Airport outside Johannesburg and to watch my plane landing. If I was prevented from entering my country and detained, the funeral of my late wife would have to be delayed or postponed until I was released, and if I was murdered at the port of entry or anywhere within the country, then they were to bury me in the same grave with her. If I was prevented from leaving the airport after I alighted from the plane, the funeral must be stopped until I was found, dead or alive.

I arrived safely, and the long journey to Molemole began. A big crowd of people was assembled at my home when I arrived. They welcomed me heartily. Fortunately for my family and myself, I experienced no difficulties as I prepared to bury Thabo. I peacefully buried her on the seventh day of July, 1984.

I was amazed that some 20,000 people could respond with such generosity and humanity to put my charming wife to rest. Her funeral attracted enough attention that the white press ran articles with headlines such as "HERO'S WELCOME? OR DEATH OF A GREAT LADY?" I was gratified when my ruler, Chief Letheba Machaka, and his counselors and tribe gave my wife a state funeral. I was also gratified when those who spoke at her funeral described her as the black Nightingale of the nursing profession in South Africa, honorary life member of the National Council of African Women of South Africa, a social worker, community organizer, mother, Christian, humanitarian, and adviser. It was said of her that she bore her suffering bravely and alone during my exile, without breaking, to the end of her days.

When I left South Africa in 1976, I had reached the conclusion that Sobukwe, Mandela, and other revolutionaries were correct in their assessment of the situation. Chief Luthuli had tried the peaceful way, but the hard hearts of the regime and their supporters were unyielding. "And now the path must lead inevitably to violence," Chief Luthuli had warned. Selaelo and his generation prepared to meet violence with violence in guerrilla warfare.

I had fought a nonviolent battle for my people in the Bantustans and in the courts, but the laws themselves were unjust. What good did it do to win a court battle against unjust laws, when they remained intact to snag and destroy our people in the cruel, ruthless trap of colonial rule?

The whole South African superstructure was filled with built-in inequalities. The laws were designed to provide and protect white privilege and elitism at the expense of all other racial groups, who were disfranchised so that whites could maintain control. The economic order was likewise established to benefit the European colonial settlers and their descendants, while imposing servitude on blacks. The system of apartheid only further entrenched the racist patterns of government already in place.

Fighting against this wicked system in court was like tilting at windmills. Winning a case was only an illusion of victory, in which the victim received a little relief from pain. The harsh reality—the unending system rolling over victim after victim, crushing them like grain in a gristmill—remained.

SOWETO, MY LOVE

I saw that the only answers to our problem lay in revolutionary change. If change could not be attained by peaceful means, then it must be attained by violence. The system, backed by all the modern military weaponry and trained personnel, opposed peaceful change, relying on their weapons and on their Bibles to protect them while they continued their reign of terror, increasing the repression and silencing the press.

Eight years was a long, long time for me to be away from Molemole. I am back on the soil of my fathers, where my umbilical cord was buried. I am home.

I could hardly believe my eyes when I arrived in my fatherland to see what changes had been wrought by the children. Fear is dead in the minds of our youth. The young and old of our land are now determined to engage the enemy, to train for the short road they have decided to travel before they are free, to educate themselves for the crippling of the economy and eventually the end of tyranny.

When I left South Africa on the fifteenth day of June, 1976, I said, at the airport, that our black youth would not be willing to live under the same conditions under which their parents and grandparents had lived, and that the white regime would resist change. When I arrived in South Africa on the third day of July, 1984, I found our youth making South Africa ungovernable. *"Siya yinyova!"* the youths shouted everywhere, meaning "We shall destroy!" The Department of Bantu Education is unable to run its black schools. Rents are uncollectible in municipal areas. The prisons are full, and yet youths are not intimidated. Urban councillors are resigning their offices everywhere, and those who refuse to resign end up with flaming tires around their black necks. "Siya yinyova," the children and their parents are calling out everywhere in our land.

After my wife's funeral, I traveled around the country, observing things for myself. Many reports were also given to me about what had been happening in my absence.

SIYA YINYOVA

I received more details about the attempted removal of my people—the Batlokwa of Molemole—which I'd heard about during my exile. Our chiefs, Letheba Machaka and George Ramokgopa, their headmen, counselors, and people had united in 1979 and fought against the removals as I'd hoped they would when I lived among them in 1973. "The South African government wanted to cast us out of our ancestral homes to a place almost one hundred miles to the northwest of Molemole, near Vivo in the Bochum area, a desertlike place in the land of Malebogo-Moitswene," said my ruler, Letheba-la-Mabula. "They thought they could manage to remove us because you were gone." The chief told the authorities they would not listen until I came back to explain who they were. "Only Ramusi can tell us," he'd said. The spirit of our ancestors and the warriors of our tribes were on our side. Even our women rose against the dreadful powers of their threatened removals, with hoes concealed under their blankets. "Fifty thousand of my followers refused to move to that barren land! My people would rather die than desert the mountains and rivers, the graves and trees of their fathers. We refused to move an inch, Motau.

"Chief George Ramokgopa joined hands with me and my tribe to fight against the removals. The working men rose up in their thousands and led the way. Even the teachers of our children arose and led the way. I pay tribute to the gallant sons and daughters of Molemole-a-Masehlo-a-mma-tima-o-llale." The ruler was now speaking in the praise manner of our people when they refer to gallant acts of their people.

"We even went to Cape Town to compel the cabinet ministers to come to our ancestral land and homes so that they could see what development had been effected. Two ministers came to see Molemole in a helicopter and became convinced that it would be a disaster to remove us from such a highly developed place." Chief Letheba paused and smiled with deep satisfaction that he had saved our people from certain destruction.

I found many changes in Molemole and in South Africa. The

"whites" and "nonwhites only" signs were gone. Blacks and whites could now enter and use the same facilities: toilets, restaurants, motels and hotels. There were no longer separate beaches for blacks and for whites. Apartheid was greatly modified but by no means dead—the changes were cosmetic; the cruel and inhuman laws were still on the statute books. The Immorality Act was still alive and well according to the minority regime, although there was talk that it was about to die, together with the Mixed Marriages Act, the Pass Laws act, and other apartheid laws. The Group Areas Act of 1950 and the South African Representation Act were still intact, with their provisions for separate land occupation and representation as if South Africans were living in different countries. The white rulers still maintained that one man, one vote in South Africa was a treasonable idea; only over their dead bodies would blacks and whites share power in Parliament. In the Bantustan universities, the rectors were now black, and the residential premises were supposed to be mixed or multiracial, but as soon as blacks moved in, the whites moved out, in many cases twenty miles away, to live with other whites in the neighboring cities or towns. As soon as blacks occupied houses that were previously occupied by whites, a great exodus occurred.

The only place the white man let the black man have any kind of franchise was in the eroded Bantustan reservations, which were still serving as reservoirs of cheap black labor for mines, farms, commerce, and industrial development. Blacks were still living in congested urban or rural areas designed for their destruction, and in those areas the white man was still having final say—even in the so-called Bantustan tribal republics of the Vendaland, Transkei, Ciskei, and Bophuthatswana. In those "republics" the white man still ruled supreme with powers of life and death over the citizens. Although the white man promised the heavens to blacks when offering them the Bantustans, he gave them hell. Bantu "independence" was clearly a farce perpetrated by the South African government to weaken the strength of the black man and to further divide blacks.

When I arrived at Molemole, I found my people rejoicing at the death of the white man's beer halls and bottle stores, the burning of Bantu education schools, the destruction of the urban councils and administration boards. Anyone who stood in their way was necklaced with flaming tires.

White schoolchildren were still receiving free and compulsory education, while black children were still paying for their school fees, uniforms, and books. Although the Bantustan education departments were supposed to be running non-Bantu education schools in their areas, whether urban or rural, the black child was still enslaved by Bantu education. Black youths hit hard against the system. Consumer boycotts were organized. Blacks were not permitting any black person to buy in white shops. The cash intake fell in many businesses. After all, who was supporting white business? The black man. The black businessman in the black areas would finally be at an advantage.

The boycott affected even the banks. When I went to my bank to withdraw funds, I was told, "Sorry, sir, there is no money."

I laughed at the teller for being poor like all of us. I tried my second bank and was told that the money also had run out before lunchtime because few people had banked that day. It was the same story repeated several times by most banks as other people tried to withdraw funds. Shops closed in Pietersburg and Potgietersrus. Big department stores like Bosveldt closed.

The situation became so serious that the South Africa government sent the army into these areas to force consumers to purchase goods to save the white businesses. The army went so far as to distribute pamphlets to the effect that the boycott was over while it was still going on. The youth created roadblocks to prevent blacks from getting into any bus that attempted to pick up passengers to go to town and purchase goods. They did the same to any taxi, truck, wagon, or bicycle that tried to carry goods into black areas. Commercial vehicles were blocked from entering black business areas. Trucks that forced their way in were set afire. Smoke filled the air all over the townships. If anyone was caught bringing consumer goods into the black area, the goods were destroyed.

Foreign investments in South Africa were almost completely dried up. Foreign companies were no longer interested in risking their capital investments in a destabilized country such as South Africa. Profits were off, and many companies were in the process of leaving the country. No one still thinks that dialogue can save the South African economy except the president of the United States, Ronald Reagan, and Prime Minister Margaret Thatcher of Great Britain. Even the queen of England has disagreed with her. They tell us violence will not change the situation. They say peaceful change will be the only thing that can help. Even before the 1976 riots, peaceful attempts to negotiate did not help one thing. There can be no unilateral negotiation, or settlement, and without cooperation from the minority regime there can be only war as an option.

Labor unions have gotten much stronger. Management today cannot do as they wish against the interests of their workers. When the Groovy Company tried to dismiss their striking workers, they landed themselves in severe financial difficulties; their soft drinks, beers, canned products, and other goods were boycotted.

Mandela was still leading his people from behind prison walls. In June 1980 a message, according to Oliver Tambo, president of the ANC, was smuggled out of Robben Island. The statement attributed to Mandela declared:

The guns that serve apartheid cannot render it unconquerable. Those who live by the gun shall perish by the gun. Unite! Mobilize! Fight on! Between the anvil of united mass action and the hammer of armed struggle, we shall crush apartheid and white-minority racist rule!

The gun has played an important part in our history; the resistance of the black man to the white colonial intrusion was crushed by the gun. Our struggle to liberate ourselves from white domination is held in check by force of arms. . . . With the gun successive white regimes have repeatedly massacred unarmed defenceless blacks.

Neither the gun nor the Bible will save the white man from being forced to change his wicked ways. Even in 1976, when he turned his weapons on the schoolchildren of Soweto, he thought the gun would put down legitimate protests. After the Soweto massacre, the black uprisings of 1976 brought fear to the white man, and he realized things were out of hand. Where the gun and the Bible did not keep things in check, he used other tactics.

Mandela described the South African government's response to the black uprisings of 1976 as "vague promises, tinkerings with the machinery of apartheid, and constitution juggling."

The soil of our country is destined to be the scene of the fiercest fight and the sharpest battles to rid our continent of the last vestiges of white-minority rule. The whole world is on our side.

He has cheered his people on. His voice even behind prison walls is more powerful than all the weaponry that the white man can muster. The regime fears him. They tremble when he speaks. During 1982, they transferred Mandela from Robben Island prison to Pollsmoor, maximum security prison. According to Winnie Mandela, her husband with five other political prisoners—including Sisulu, Mbeki, Kathrada, and Motswaledi—all serving life imprisonment, live in conditions at Pollsmoor that threaten their capacity to survive. Mandela and the others are kept isolated, confined together, apparently in one damp cell. They have not been allowed out of doors for a year. All the small "privileges" that made their life bearable have been withdrawn. They are, in effect, entombed together for the rest of their lives. Attempts to make official complaints are ignored. Mandela's message to his wife suggests that the South African authorities are trying to break the mental and physical health of these political leaders. As with Stephen Biko and others who have died in detention, the authorities show a total disregard for the anger ultimately created by the martyrdom of African leaders. The followers of Mandela urge him on: "Persevere, Mandela, hero of heroes. You will hear from us when the right moment comes." The armies of Umkhonto We Sizwe have increased. I had called for Mandela's release for years before I went into exile, but when I returned, I found his name on the lips of each and every man, woman, and child in the black world of South Africa. Mandela is loved and worshiped by children who do not even know him.

A kindergarten teacher told me that one day her children refused to eat their food unless they saw Mandela at their school. The teacher went into the street and found an elegant gentleman, whom she introduced to the children as Nelson Rolihlahla Mandela, and said, "Now that you have seen your father, please eat"; and those little three-, four-, and five-year-olds began to eat because Mandela had come when they wanted to see him.

I returned to my fatherland and found the whites claiming to be involved in reforms that were visible only to themselves and completely invisible to blacks. It was clear that changes were not brought about by the humanity or goodness of the white man's heart, but by his fear of the devastating consequences that his refusal might bring. Unfortunately, whites have tried to get us to settle only for superficial changes. The white man was willing to abolish the pass but quite unwilling to abolish identity documents, which are now the new passes for blacks. Our youths see through the facade. Most of the young people who left the country in the 1970s to undergo military training had returned to South Africa by the time I came back. They brought fear to whites with their guns and bombs. The government was shaking by the time I came home.

The Umkhonto wing of the ANC had made a great impact on the country. Many young people trained in warfare had returned to stage a fierce military struggle in the cities and tribal reservations. Many, like Selaelo, had died as martyrs and heroes of the black struggle.

The people continue to call for the release of Mandela. The white minority regime has molested his family since his arrest and imprisonment. They suggest that he may be released only if he relinquishes violence, forgetting that Mandela resorted to the belief in violence because immense violence was committed against himself and his people. If they free Mandela, the whites say he must agree to leave Soweto, where he lived before his detention, return to his tribal Bantustan of the Transkei, where he was born, and live there quietly in solitude. But black people are insisting that if there should be any settlement negotiations, the negotiating team should be headed by Nelson Mandela, Oliver Tambo, and other senior members of the ANC, the PAC, and the Black Consciousness movement. The white minority government has arrested the black leaders, hoping to discourage the youth movements from forging ahead. But the more leaders they arrest, the more young people emerge to carry on the fight.

I returned to my fatherland to find that my people were now perceiving the American president and the prime minister of Great Britain, as well as the chancellor of West Germany, as the greatest protectors of apartheid on behalf of the Western economy because the Americans, the English, and the Germans have large investments in South Africa. They keep telling the world that there must be peaceful change before serious sanctions can be resorted to. The powerful leaders of America, Britain, and Germany insist that the South African economy should not be weakened for fear that their own economies might be adversely affected. These three leaders maintain that divestment and sanctions would bring hardships to the black workers in South Africa. Even without sanctions, large numbers of blacks are already suffering and out of work. In fact, divestment and economic sanctions will only embarrass, hurt, and make the West recognize the inhumanity of its own policies.

I was amazed to find whites, Asiatics, and people of mixed

race participating by themselves in a tricameral Parliament to the exclusion of blacks. It is doubtful whether the Asiatics and mixed-race people are participating in a meaningful manner.

The whites behave like the pharaohs of old, refusing to let my people go. Like the children of Israel, blacks tried everything possible to get out of bondage. Now Umkhonto We Sizwe has established military bases inside South Africa, while the South African army minds the border. The freedom fighters have come to villages, mountains, and forests to bring the system to its knees.

The fighting is now taking place in the streets of our cities and towns. The freedom fighters hit and run, crossing the borders. The South African army attacked Mozambique, Botswana, Zambia, and Zimbabwe because it suspected these countries of harboring the cadres and freedom fighters, but the army only opened itself to international ridicule and scorn.

I am now back in my fatherland, working among my people as an attorney in the Supreme Court of South Africa. I love my legal work and profession. I struggled hard to find accommodation when I reentered my legal practice in the land of apartheid; in the end I constructed my own offices out of a big hall in an Asiatic bazaar. After a few months I moved into a twelve-room office building, which I share with the Northern Transvaal Council of Churches.

I live in the same house as before exile with my two sons Sekgweng and Mothibi. Sekgweng is a high school teacher, and Mothibi is an electrical engineer studying in London.

The Song of Freedom is sung by the children of the soil. It is sung wherever pain and suffering are felt in the land of our fathers. Slogans are chanted: "Viva Mandela!" "Viva the Spirit of Mozambique!" "Viva UDF!" "Botha are you mad?" the children ask, as they bury the victims of apartheid. At our funerals we no longer cry for our dead and no longer place flowers and wreaths on their graves. We rejoice and sing our songs of freedom, and the martyrs are put to rest amid cheers and chants. In the words of our freedom fighters: *"Aluta continua!"* Our struggle for freedom continues. *Mayibuye Africa! Siya yinyova!* But one day soon we shall rejoice and say:

> *Free at last*
> *Free at last*
> *Thank God Almighty*
> *We are free at last!*

Epilogue

"For I was hungry and you gave me to eat; I was thirsty and you gave me to drink; I was a stranger and you took me in; naked and you covered me; sick and you visited me; I was in prison and you came to me." Then the just will answer him, saying, "Lord, when did we see thee hungry, and feed thee; or thirsty, and give thee drink? And when did we see thee a stranger, and take thee in; or naked, and clothe thee? Or when did we see thee sick, or in prison, and come to thee?" And answering the king will say to them, "Amen, I say to you, as long as you did it for one of these, the least of my brethren, you did it for me."

Matthew 25:35–40

I spent eight years in exile, 1976–1984, in the United States of America, where I received political asylum and medical care, which I desperately needed. The years seemed long and lonely despite the many friends who cheered me up—old friends and new friends, black and white. My thoughts kept returning to South Africa—my family, my people, my homeland, and the turmoil that was consuming that beautiful country turned ugly by racism and apartheid.

In the meantime, I tried to assess the climate of opinion in America, to see whether we would be able to count on America to help us or hurt us in our quest for freedom. Americans were caught up in the celebration of their own freedom and two hundred years of independence from British colonial rule. As a whole they seemed utterly indifferent to the situation in South Africa, except for a few demonstrators and a few newspaper reporters who continued to write about the Soweto massacre and the press blackout.

During the 1980 election, there was no significant stance on apartheid. When President Reagan was elected, his policy of "constructive engagement" was a euphemism for continued support of the oppressive regime. One was hard pressed to find

EPILOGUE

anything in constructive engagement designed to bring about change, our rights, the vote, or freedom for our enslaved and brutalized people.

I felt disillusioned, disappointed that a freedom-loving nation and a caring people could be so indifferent to the blatant oppression practiced in South Africa. I wondered how it was that an America that had fought a war against Hitler's Nazi Germany to help free the Jews, an America that could openly voice opposition to alleged persecution of dissidents in the Soviet Union, could be silent on the persecution of blacks and dissidents in South Africa. I hoped it wasn't that our diamonds and gold were more valuable than our lives.

I tried to understand the policy of the Reagan administration in light of American history. How could a nation celebrate its own violent revolution against colonialism on the basis of "no taxation without representation" and ignore and condemn our South African revolution against taxation, violence, and imprisonment without representation or due process? How could America ignore the oppression of black men by white men with no just cause? Did Americans turn their heads and pretend not to see because the plight of the suffering black man stirred up memories of colonialism, slavery, and injustice in their own history? Was it because they had not yet truly achieved the ideals proclaimed in their great historical documents, the Declaration of Independence, the Constitution of the United States, and especially the Bill of Rights? Was it because they were uncomfortable that their latest documents of freedom for equality of education and equal employment opportunity were still not fully realized and accepted by all of their people? I could not believe that such a people would be silenced by those who oppose freedom for others either at home or abroad. Not the Americans who were my friends, black and white alike. Was this indifference traceable to memories they would rather forget? A history they would like to erase as if it had never been? Perhaps it is something that only the American people themselves can answer and demand from the government that represents them.

SOWETO, MY LOVE

When I look about my country now I see some change, but in many ways we are worse off than ever before. Stripped of our culture, our land, our heritage, our families, our right to live and to feed ourselves by our own labor, we have been given nothing in return. If the white settlers are to ask for something, there must be a trade; they cannot simply take. We demand the right to work, to live where we please, to govern ourselves. The white man will now have to relinquish power in this beautiful land that welcomed him centuries ago and is now turned ugly by racism and oppression.

A few things stand out clearly in my memory about my exile in America, especially the freedom with which I moved about and in which I became immersed, and the kindness of friends who welcomed me back to America and tried to explain to me the changes that had taken place in the country, who tried to explain white flight. I remember my adopted parents, the Grimwades, and others who comforted me; my pastor, the Reverend Dr. David Chevrier, his wife, Eloise, and members of the Wellington Community United Church of Christ, which made representations on my behalf to the House of Representatives and the Senate. They assisted me through the long, lonely years in exile and sickness, nursing me to health and recovery, coming to my aid in my hours of sorrow upon the death of my son Selaelo, and later the death of my beloved wife, Thabo. They also assisted me in making a safe return home. They helped me in every way they could as a loving, caring, sharing people.

I remember Kojo and Maisha Bennett, my principal benefactors; the Reddens (Nathaniel and Connie and their daughter, Crystal), who took me into their home—a stranger; the famous fantastic drummer Max Roach, who composed an ode to the slain children of Soweto.

Foremost in my mind is the visionary experience brought about by Ruth Turner, whom I met in the library at Northwestern University. She had great insight into the South Afri-

EPILOGUE

can situation, uncanny wisdom, and a beautiful intellect. Her bright eyes saw through things that blinded me. She encouraged me to write this book, but more than that, she helped me to see a new vision for a free South Africa and my own role in the struggle. When I left America, I carried with me a great treasured work, which has become my Bible in the revolutionary struggle for change in South Africa—her unpublished dissertation, "Violence and Nonviolence in Confrontation: A Comparative Study of Ideologies—Six Historical Cases (Paine, Lenin, Hitler, Gandhi, Luthuli, King)." It is now widely read and embraced by many black leaders engaged in the freedom struggle.

Together, Ruth and I visited the Mount Vernon plantation where George Washington, America's first president, lived and held slaves kidnapped from Africa in chains, under whips and guns. We saw the big mansion where the president lived and the humble quarters that housed the slaves who served him. We walked the land where they once walked, and relived history, realizing that the histories of Africa and America are merged into a tragic past in which the sins of the fathers of Americans—settlers from Europe—form a significant part of the heritage under which blacks and whites labor today on both continents. It was good to know that in America, slavery was a thing of the past and the slave laws were no longer the law of the land. Even "separate but equal" segregation, America's apartheid system, had been struck down. Racial problems still plague the land, but there is hope for progress in America, where the descendants of slaves now serve as members of Congress, and descendants of slave masters have laid down their whips and their guns and admitted that their forefathers made mistakes which they can no longer embrace. I shall never forget! Long live liberty!

Let it be so in South Africa!

Acknowledgments

I am grateful to all the people who helped me to survive and to write this book. Thanks:

To my ancestors: Moshweu, the dark destroyer of the Babirwa clan who chopped and demolished his enemies at war, my great-grandfather who is the bonus paterfamilias of my family; to my grandparents Moraba-a-Mantedi and Mokgadi-a-Matšie; to my father and mother, Mothibi-a-Ramathathe and Motswetla-a-Rasekgothoma, from whose loins I sprang.

To my God.

To my heavenly wife, Thabo Mary Jane Ma Selaelo—Mopo Sethetele, Letebele-Lekwankwane, Lekgadimana Ntweng ba eja ga ba kgadimane; to my heavenly son Selaelo Charles, General Whirlwind, whose blood is continuing to water the trees and flowers of freedom in our fatherland; to my heavenly sister Tipe Terry Mamahlare Machaka and brothers Moraba-a-Mantedi Piet and Nkwatlapi-a-Marota Mangwadini Johannes Manyefe Squinch, Mofuta wa bothata, who are now part of the Eternal Presences, who are forever with us beneath the soil in the ancestral spirit world from which no traveler ever returns.

To my surviving sisters, brother, and sons: Mokgadi-a-Matšie, Moratwa Maphari-a-Machaka Maimela, my sisters; brother

ACKNOWLEDGMENTS

Matsapola Jack; and my sons Sekgweng Isaiah and Mothibi Glenview Evanston, who are keeping me company and giving me reason for living.

To my guardian angel, Molatelo Manyathe Piet Ramusi, who gave me the rare opportunity of going to school beyond the elementary level when everything appeared lost to me in this world.

To my good teachers in elementary school, high school, the Jan H. Hofmeyr School of Social Work, the University of South Africa, and Northwestern University.

To Khaola Ngwako Matlesshe Scombish Mthimkhuklu Dabula-Masait Mohlopi, Mathumo-a-Masekgala, and other sages of my tribe, who imparted invaluable knowledge of the traditions, customs, values, mores, laws, and culture of our Batlokwa people from the days of my youth.

To my leaders, for the example they set for me and my people to follow, for their inspiring determination and courage to lead our people in the face of harsh and inhuman consequences in the fight for the liberation of our fatherland.

To my American father and mother, the heavenly Eric Grimwade and Pauline Grimwade, who urged me to write this book and to tell the readers what it has been like to grow up in ugly racial apartheid South Africa as a black man; my brother Anthony Grimwade and his lovely wife, Marge, who began typing this book in her home, where I lived as a member of the family when I first arrived in Chicago as a political refugee.

To my American friends who welcomed me back during my exile: my pastor the Reverend Dr. David Chevrier, his wife, Eloise, and members of the Wellington Community United Church of Christ; to Kojo and Maisha Bennett; the Reddens,

ACKNOWLEDGMENTS

Nathaniel, Connie, and their daughter, Crystal; and the drummer Max Roach.

To my dear friend and sister, Dr. Ruth S. Turner, Ph.D., who first listened to my story with tears in her eyes, then urged me to put down the story in writing, and thereafter skillfully, faithfully, and loyally rewrote and collaborated with me in the writing of this book.

To my mentor and friend, Mrs. Theresa de Kerpely, the author of *Arabesque* and numerous other books, who gave a great deal of her time, even when her eyesight was failing, to guide and teach me how to write this book. I owe everything I have come to know about writing to her.

To my literary agent, Ellen Levine, my skillful and loyal friend, who read the manuscript and found a publisher, Henry Holt, for me.

To the editor in chief of Henry Holt, John Macrae III, who acquired and skillfully edited this book, with his assistant editor, Amy Hertz.

To those who sat with me for days, months, and years and gave advice: Professor Elkin S. Sithole, Professor Ben Khoapa, Ann Lorraine Blair, Carol English, the Reverend Attorneys Earl Talbot and Robert Bennett, Professor Bonganjalo Goba, Hazel Gray, Esther Carmichael Adekoya, Maurice Mokgethi Ngakane, Grace Patricia Machaka, Malome Khomo, Moyahabo Frans Ramusi, Mokg adi Machebola Mabitsi, Sewela Mamolatelo Malaka, Nelly Magowa, Mahlare Patrick Machaka, Dr. Phillip Moila, Dr. Simon Maimela, Maroba Matsapola, Dr. Jaqueline Matsapola.

To those who assisted me in the typing of the manuscript from the goodness of their hearts: Marge Grimwade, Virginia Novak, Ann Lorraine Blair, Caroline English, Louise Turner

ACKNOWLEDGMENTS

(daughter-in-law of Dr. Ruth Turner), Violet Mabinad, Mrs. Janice Dandridge, L. Talbot's secretary.

To the library staffs of the Melville Jean Herskovits Africana Library of Northwestern University, the University of Chicago, Illinois University at the Circle Campus, the University of Massachusetts at Amherst, Michigan State University at East Lansing, Roosevelt University, and the University of the North in South Africa.

To the authors whose muscular, rhythmic prose and poetry inspired me most deeply: William Shakespeare, John Keats, William Wordsworth, John Payne, Martin Luther King, Jr., Lerone Bennett, Gerard Manley Hopkins, Andrew Marvell, John Donne, Professor Ezekiel Mphahlele, and Kwame Nkrumah; to writings in the Holy Bible and hymnbooks, as well as the sermons of the Reverend Dr. David Chevrier, my pastor at the Wellington Community United Church of Christ, Chicago.

Finally, to Grace Patricia Machaka, who sat with me in South Africa and revised the entire manuscript, which I had written in the United States and Jamaica. The manuscript was then mailed to Dr. Ruth S. Turner in Virginia, who finally rearranged and retyped it in its present form, which has been published with my personal approval of the final copy. Additionally, Dr. Turner and I thank those who aided with word processing, technical advice, photocopying, proofreading, and moral support: Lt. Col. Roger M. Henry, Maj. C. A. Teubert, M. Sgt. Brad Carter, Sgt. Jeff Corbett, S. Sgt. Napoleon P. Rogers, the Reverend Donnie Gambrel, David A. Turner (Dr. Turner's son), Laura Johnson, Dorothy Dixon, James Booker, Alma Terry, and Marguerite Riley.